POWER, PROTEST AND PARTICIPATION

In contrast to other post-colonial states, India possesses a strong democracy and relative political stability. This book looks at the role of local elites both as the representatives of the state and of the rest of rural Indian society, and explains their importance in the country's development.

This survey deals with the elites' current contribution to the credibility of the state and examines the strategies through which they manipulate the allocation of resources and influence the pace and direction of social change. It contrasts the rural elites in two areas, one more economically advanced than the other. The elites in the first area were shown to be capable of combining institutional participation with radical protest, whilst in the other they tended to rely on state channels to achieve reform.

Mitra concludes that despite the different settings, both groups were informed, active and responsive to political conditions. This contrasts with the conventional view that local elites of the dominant castes oppress the lower ones by obstructing reforms, for reasons of self interest.

This book will be of use to postgraduates, academics and researchers in politics, Asian studies and Third World politics.

Subrata K. Mitra is a senior lecturer in politics and director of the Centre for Indian Studies at The University of Hull.

POWER, PROTEST AND PARTICIPATION:

Local Elites and the Politics of Development in India

Subrata K. Mitra

London and New York

First published 1992
by Routledge
11 New Fetter Lane, London EC4P 4EE

Simultaneously published in the USA and Canada
by Routledge
a division of Routledge, Chapman and Hall, Inc.
29 West 35th Street, New York, NY 10001

Typeset in Baskerville by J&L Composition Ltd, Filey, North Yorkshire
Printed and bound in Great Britain by
Biddles Ltd, Guildford and King's Lynn

British Library Cataloguing in Publication Data
A catalogue record for this book is available from the British Library.

ISBN 0–415–07840–7

Library of Congress Cataloging-in-Publication Data
Mitra, Subrata Kumar, 1949–
Power, protest, and participation: local elites and development
in India/Subrata Kumar Mitra.
p.   cm.
Includes bibliographical references and index.
ISBN 0–415–07840–7: $55.00 (U.S.)
1. Elite (Social sciences)—India. 2. Rural development—India.
3. India—Politics and government—1947– 4. Political
participation—India. I. Title.
HN690.Z9E464 1992
305.5′2′0954—dc20

CONTENTS

v

CONTENTS

CONTENTS

GLOSSARY

adivasi	tribal population
balvadi	kindergarten
bandh	collective cessation of public activities
bauri	a Scheduled Caste from Orissa
bhadralok	upper stata of Bengal and Orissa society
boycott	a form of strike action where all contact is broken off
chowkidar	watchman
dafadar	person in charge of a police station
dalal	commission agent
dalit	literally, oppressed; often refers to Scheduled population
daroga	circle inspector of police
dharma	universal cosmic law
dharna	a form of sit-in strike
garibi hatao	quit poverty; a slogan popularised by Mrs. Gandhi during the 1971 parliamentary election campaign
gaon ka neta	people in a position of leadership in a village
gherao	to surround a decision-maker
gram panchayat	village council, basic unit of rural government
gram sevak	male village-level worker
gram sevika	female village-level worker
hadi	former Untouchable caste from Orissa
halia	agricultural workers attached to landed households in Orissa on one-year contracts

viii

Halpati	former Untouchable, agricultural caste from Gujarat
Harijan	literally, children of God; coined by Mahatma Gandhi to give respectability to the former Untouchables
hartal	strike action
jail bharo	to fill in the jails in a form of radical protest
jajmani	traditional system of patron–client relationship
jamadar	an assistant to the circle inspector, of corporal rank
Jangal Sahkari Mandali	cooperative society for forest products
janata ka neta	people's leader
jati	localised caste
jatra	folk festival
karma	accumulated result of past actions
khandayat	a branch of Oriya Kshatriyas
kharif	monsoon crops
kisan	literally, peasant
kisan mandals	peasants' society
kisan sabha	peasant union
mahajan	a money lender
mai bap	literally, mother-father, an image of the ruler as the source of bounty, protection and indulgence
mamlatdar	a revenue official in charge of taluka administration
matsya nyaya	Law of the Fishes
mahila mandals	women's society
moksha	salvation
morcha	a demonstration intended as a show of force
panchayat samiti	area council, consisting of village panchayats
panchayati raj	local self government at the village, sub-district and the district level
panchas	member of a village panchayat
patidar	middle caste in Gujarat, often landholding
patwari	village revenue and land records agent
prajamandal	State People's Organisation before independence

Pradhan	Chairman of a gram panchayat
Pramukh	Chairman of a zilla parishad
pyraveekar	fixer
rabi	winter crops
raj	literally, rule; hence, British Raj, or panchayati raj
rasta roko	to prevent traffic from passing through in order to exert pressure on the government
sarkar	government
sarpanch	leader of a panchayat, i.e. a village council
satyagraha	literally, truth force; a form of non-violent protest action
sudras	the lowest varna among classical Hindu castes, but still above Untouchables; traditionally farmers and artisans
taluka, tahsil, tehsil, taluk	revenue sub-division of an administrative district, containing around 100,000 people
tehsildar	administrative officer in charge of a taluk or tehsil
touter	a tout
upsarpanch	deputy leader of a village council
varna	four classical social divisions referred to in the Vedas
yuvak mandals	youth groups
Zilla Parishad	District Council, composed of all Pradhans plus others

ILLUSTRATIONS

FIGURES

TABLES

ILLUSTRATIONS

ILLUSTRATIONS

MAPS

PREFACE

The volume explores the attitudes of the *gaon ka neta*s – local elites in the rural setting in India – towards participation in the process of development and protest against policies that they consider iniquitous. The analysis concentrates on the methods through which they seek to intervene in the process of development and on how the process of social and economic change affects their power base. The interest in local elites arises from the fact that they are the crucial hinge group between the state and rural society. Restricted no longer to the ranks of those born to power and privilege, local elites in contemporary India are a socially mixed group, drawing in many cases substantial representation from the lower social strata. Their actions, and in some cases their failure to act, are among the determinants of the course and content of the process of development and, indirectly but crucially, the legitimacy of the state.

Even at the lowest level of the system, development is now an accepted part of the political vocabulary in India. As the ensemble of activities, ranging from collective goods like the upgrading of a mud track to give the village all-weather access to individual welfare in the form of loans and subsidies, development is the staple of rural and district-level politics. A less tangible effect of development is the basic change in attitudes, in social structure and in the relations of power. This change can be seen in the social origin of local elites, no longer confined to the closed circles of the old-style social notables, but increasingly drawn from members of the *panchayat* (village councils which from the 1950s have increasingly become the focus of political life of the village), cooperative societies and community leaders.

Local elites are among the beneficiaries and, in some cases, the victims of social and economic development. While social research cannot proceed without some clearly defined concepts, I have refrained from using a pre-conceived notion of development. Instead, I have attempted to analyse the meanings that local elites themselves attach to it and its implications for society and state in India. A second objective is to understand the variety of stratagems that local elites use in order to manipulate the course of social change and the flow of material benefits. While the multitude of projects and agencies that are engaged in rural development provide the natural backdrop to the study, my aim is not to evaluate their achievements and failures as such. Rather, the goal is the more modest one of analysing the process through which the gaon ka netas conceptualise the basic problems that confront them, the forms of intervention, including radical protest, with which they seek to improve their lot and the overall implications of their action for the institutional structure and the legitimacy of the state in India.

The gaon ka netas occupy a position close to the bottom of the power structure that links India's 500,000 villages with her capital cities. Still, as a group, they are perhaps not among the most deprived members of rural society. As such, the research focus on local elites might at the first glance appear rather incongruous with protest, participation and justice. I make no apologies for choosing these more 'privileged' members of rural society as a critical group that deserves careful study. One of the aims of the study is to question the relatively uncritical bi-polar model of rural society popular among radical students of rural development. The overall picture of development and political mobilisation, as the field data reported in this study indicate, is far more complex than is generally supposed.

The choice of local elites as an appropriate entry point might cause some scepticism for the development planner and the cultural anthropologist. These disciplines, through their own specific forms of reification, leave little scope or necessity for local elites. For the development expert, the local elites are a nuisance, a source of perpetual political interference with the task of rational planning and implementation. Similarly, but from a different angle, the anthropologist seeks to understand the function of the local elites in the allocation of status but not the larger implications of their activities for the state and the pace of development. Hence, while I have learnt much from these classic approaches, the path chosen in this book is different from theirs.

The initial intellectual challenge to write this book came from the very protagonists of the research undertaken here. The hardpressed local leaders, in the course of fieldwork in an Orissa village during the 1977 Parliamentary elections, shared with me their intimate knowledge of the process of development and met my questions with a directness which often took me by surprise. In retrospect, even as minor players in my earlier study, the gaon ka netas had taught me that there is more to development than the simple creation of wealth, or the removal of poverty. In the Indian setting, development has to do essentially with the empowerment of the previously powerless so that they might prevail on social groups who are born to power and privilege. Power, in the creation of which local elites are the key players (and occasional victims), is the principal catalyst of change. It is through the achievement of power that ordinary people can change some elements of the world they live in. That many of them claim to have experienced a degree of real change in their lifetime is indicative of the fact that, after all, there is power behind the rhetoric of development.

The time that has elapsed between 1979 when the project was initiated and 1989 when I made my last field trip to India has affected the study in many ways. The delay has made it imperative to take into account changing trends in empirical research and the increasing sophistication of the nature of questions that are now posed of field data derived from sample surveys. Detailed interviews, on the basis of structured and open-ended questions with over 200 village netas, form the main source of information for this study. However, devoid of its historical context, data generated by a survey are only points suspended in space. Since elite attitudes are a key component of the process of rural development, there is perhaps no substitute to gaining an insight into the working of their minds through interviews. But the roots of continuity and change are far too many and complex to be confined to the limited span of even the most careful survey. As such, in writing this book I have drawn liberally from a variety of other sources as well, notably including historical studies of Orissa and Gujarat and the findings of anthropological village studies. The result, I hope, will show that the trade off between theoretical neatness and empirical eclecticism is eventually to mutual benefit.

The idea of a book first materialised in a meeting with Gordon Smith at a conference in 1986. He maintained a keen interest in its progress during the ensuing period, and, by happy coincidence, took over direct responsibility for its publication. In writing this book I have benefited very much from my introduction to rational choice and quantitative methods at the University of Rochester as a graduate student in Political Science. The support for field research in 1979 was provided by the Indian Council for Social Science Research through a grant to the Center for the Study of Developing Societies, Delhi, of which I was then a member. My research at the Maison des Sciences de l'Homme in Paris during 1979–80 and at the University of Bochum when I was a Research Fellow of the Alexander von Humboldt-Stiftung, Bonn, during 1980–2 have helped me formulate new questions out of the field data. Finally, a personal research grant from the Nuffield Foundation has made it possible to undertake field trips to India in 1986, 1987 and 1989 and to update the data, besides providing for computer and secretarial assistance.

I have benefited very much from the generous advice of Bruce Graham, Satish Saberwal, James Chiriyankandath, Alberto Arce, David Booth, Bhikhu Parekh, S. N. Misra and Pravin Sheth in my interpretation of the field data. Mike Parnwell of the Geography Department and Centre for South-East Asian Studies at Hull University has drawn the maps and diagrams. Friends whose implicit trust has sustained me during the past years will remain anonymous. I do not believe they will wish it any other way.

The book is dedicated to the memory of Het Ram Chaturvedi, Panditji, the name by which he was known to all his friends, introduced me to rural Gujarat, so different from my native Orissa, and helped me appreciate the pan-Indian ethos in which India's regional diversities find a common home. It never occurred to me to tell him during fieldwork in Orissa and Gujarat how much I drew on our friendship and his deep knowledge of rural India for my personal comfort. Now I can only console myself with the thought that he must have known. *Power, Protest and Participation* is the only tribute I can pay him.

xvii

1

LOCAL ELITES AND THE POLITICS OF RURAL DEVELOPMENT

THE PROBLEM DEFINED

Thanks to modest but steady economic growth, mass communication and political competition, Indian society has changed greatly during the four decades since independence. Though per capita income has remained low by the standards of the rapidly industrialising countries of East Asia, the economy has practically doubled its volume during this period in aggregate terms. Economic change has affected traditional social bonds, without, however, irrevocably disrupting either the stability of the state or the democratic character of the political system. India's relative success in securing stability, democracy and economic growth simultaneously has made her an exception to the turbulent history of most post-colonial states. This remarkable achievement has come under increasing strain during the closing years of the 1980s. But, in spite of the unrest in Punjab, Kashmir and Assam, the stability of the democratic political structure remains largely intact. The larger implications of this singular achievement go beyond the narrow domains of the area specialist. The book explores this broad theme, drawing primarily upon the experience of rural *netas* – drawn from the ranks of local leaders and elected representatives – who occupy the key position of intermediaries between the state and rural society.

Rural India to-day has been affected as much by attempts to change its political and economic form in recent decades as by its historical inheritance. Almost every State in India was affected by land reforms in the early 1950s, by the experiments in local self-government through *panchayati raj* in the late

1

1950s, by the institution of highly localised territorial constituencies since 1951 and government policies aimed at the steady expansion of the market of agricultural commodities and labour, particularly since the 1960s. In each such initiative, a significant variation of normative theory was used. The socialist aspirations of Nehru and the myth of the independent peasant producer were intertwined in the policies of land reforms. The neo-Gandhian approach, embodied in panchayati raj, the myth of the nuclear village and community development were juxtaposed with an equally powerful belief in the rational individual as the basis of voting decisions. Much reliance was placed on the ability of such individuals to identify both parties and candidates with reasonable certainty about the relationship of issues to voting choices. The market as the driving force behind production, consumption, credit and communication was promoted with equal vigour as central planning and bureaucratic implementation also aimed at achieving the same objective. These ideas, whether indigenous to India or gleaned from elsewhere, were formulated at the apex of the system and applied in a highly standardised form that took little account of regional and subregional variations in social structure and agrarian economy.[1]

The major objective of field research on which this book is based was not to find out whether any one of these initiatives has been successful or not, but simply to discover whether the process has left the local elites confident of their ability to use the new resources and new conditions of modern India. This concern can be expressed in terms of three distinct but related sets of issues.

The first issue refers to the interaction between the process of externally stimulated change and local elites, strategically placed at the interface of rural society and the institutions of the modern state.[2] Local elites, through a repertoire of political strategies, seek to manipulate the allocation of resources and to influence the pace and direction of social change. This poses a range of questions for field research. What evidence if any do we have of the filtering down of the ideas aimed at rural India from the national and regional centres? What kinds of 'echoes' have they created at the lowest level of the system, measured in terms of the agenda of development formulated by local elites? What conclusions can we draw from the kinds of 'problems'

2

of development the rural netas formulate, the solutions they envisage, the developmental agency they prefer and the political action, both institutional and radical, that they undertake in their efforts to their objectives?

The second issue, introduced in chapter two and used throughout the text as a significant source of variation in the attitudes of local elites, is the remarkable regional diversity of India. To what extent does the regional variation in the material and social conditions and historical legacies lead to different responses to the stimuli of development policies and projects, conceived and in many cases diffused centrally? How does the knowledge of the parts help us to comment on the ability of the whole to cohere and to generate sufficient momentum to ensure future development?

The third set of questions, concerning the legitimacy and resilience of the state, follows from the first two. How successful has the political system been in achieving its goals of political participation, economic development and social change? What is at the origin of social protest and how does this relate to institutional participation? What implications can we draw from the responses of local elites to the issues of participation, mobilisation and mass protest, for democracy and development in India, and what are the limitations of this model?

PUTTING LOCAL DEVELOPMENT IN THE CONTEXT OF SOCIAL AND ECONOMIC CHANGE

The early literature on political protest related radicalism to mostly a sense of relative deprivation.[3] These conjectures have subsequently been modified, taking into consideration the extent of benefit that the individual can expect from the alternative strategies of participation or radical action. These considerations involve other factors like the perception of risk, the cost of failure, and the sense of efficacy on the part of the actor and the state of organisation of the potential beneficiaries.[4] Yet another issue involved in the transition from the sentiment of relative deprivation to political action is the nature of the reward sought. For, if the prize is a public good which will benefit many potential beneficiaries, then it might be irrational for any given individual to take the initiative for radical action. The issue of perception is critical to the action that might or might not follow. Do the leaders of local communities perceive the potential rewards in terms of individual good, welfare of the people of their social class or group, or of the village community as a whole?[5] These issues come within the scope of the book because the overall objective is not merely to describe the empirical reality at the local level but to look for relationships between the political process and the transformation of social and economic relations at the level of the village.

This is more complicated than might appear at first sight because Indian data on development indicate conflicting trends. On the one hand, the record of achievements of the past forty years in key areas such as literacy, life expectancy and the infrastructure of a modern economy, seen against the stagnation of the centuries preceding independence is truly impressive. 'The image of India as a hopelessly poor society no longer reflects reality', says an influential article in *Foreign Policy*. 'Major economic progress, especially in the last ten years, has brought not only economic growth but also increased diversification and reduced vulnerability to bad weather and other shocks.'[6] While the average rate of growth has been rather low in comparison to the newly industrialising countries of East Asia, its result has been 'some truly significant changes in the structure of the Indian economy, attributable partly to the planning mechanism, partly to secular forces'.[7] On the other hand, hidden behind the façade of these impressive indicators of growth at the macro level, there is the other face of development in India. Statistics released by the government itself show about 40 per cent of the population living below a modestly defined poverty line of an annual income of less than $100 per capita.[8] The slow rate of growth and uneven distribution of prosperity have led to a lively debate between the advocates of growth through better technology, management and investment on the one hand and the partisans of radical change on the other. A large group of Indian economists despair of the benefits of development ever reaching the poor and needy. In addition to their structural exclusion from the growing sectors of the economy, even public welfare meant for them hardly reaches the target, for it is alleged that standing between the deprived and the state is a human wall of the locally powerful and socially dominant who have managed to corner most if not all of the fruits of progress.[9]

The fact remains however that whereas Indian development

4

has exacerbated the economic and social vulnerability of some sections of the population and brought greater prosperity to some than others, the growth of democratic institutions has given a voice and the political means to those with a grievance to launch a protest movement of their own. V. S. Naipaul, long critical of the post-independence record of India, has noticed the change:

> the idea of freedom has gone everywhere in India. Independence was worked for by people more or less at the top; the freedom it brought has worked its way down. People everywhere have ideas now of who they are and what they owe themselves.

However, the growing sense of empowerment, enfranchisement and entitlement manifest themselves as much through enthusiastic participation in voting and political campaigns as in radical protest.

> The liberation of spirit that has come to India could not come as release alone. In India, with its layer below layer of distress and cruelty, it had to come as disturbance. It had to come as rage and revolt. India was now a country of a million little mutinies.
>
> (Naipaul (1990), p. 517)

This is the major difference between India and other post-colonial societies with representative institutions on the one hand and the stable, industrial democracies of the west on the other. In the latter, mass participation was introduced after the industrial revolution had pulverised the rights and life-styles of the parochial peasant and integrated them to the urban industrial society and economy. In the former, on the other hand, universal adult franchise was introduced by the post-colonial regimes as a logical culmination to the anti-colonial movement. The post-colonial state was thus caught in a paradox where its democratic credentials required it to turn to the society for political support and legitimacy, whereas its agenda of development and nation-building involved the destruction of the customary rights and parochial ways of parts of the society.[10]

How successful has the state been in reconciling the twin goals of the removal of mass poverty and the diffusion of economic democracy on the one hand and the continuation of democratic liberties and political competition on the other? The large measure of agreement which prevailed among the specialists of Indian politics during the 1950s and 1960s on this issue has given way to a sharp polarisation. Both Kothari and Morris-Jones, whose early works laid the foundations of the theoretical knowledge of the flexibility and strength of India's political institutions, appear less sure of this in their more recent works.[11] With the sole exception of the Rudolphs, a large number of writers on India's institutional structure share this scepticism.[12] Field research on which this book is based poses further implications of these questions at the level of the rural netas. In order to do this, it studies the link between the economic and political aspects of development by first taking into consideration the local elites' perception of both and then by relating their perception to the strategic choices they make in order to achieve their objectives. Our analysis therefore begins with the local leaders' perception of their personal situation relative to that of the others as well as seen against their own past experience.[13] The subsequent steps of research concentrate on the crucial intervening levels between the rural society and the state, the rhetoric through which the leaders seek to add saliency to certain aspects of the agenda of development and even to extend it by adding to it programmes of their own, the different options available to the people at the village level and the historical constraints within which they strive to attain their desired goals.

POWER, PROTEST AND LEGITIMACY

In order to comprehend the nature of local development in India and put it in the context of the larger social and political changes affecting the country, we need to reexamine the political concepts of order and collective protest through which they are normally viewed. Anger at the denial of what one is justly entitled to is a necessary but not sufficient condition of collective protest.[14] Historically, the intensity and frequency of its outbreak has varied with the pace of structural change affecting the society as a whole. India's large-scale mass poverty, coexisting with a democratic political order, ideologically committed to egalitarianism, raises a range of interesting questions on the issue of political protest and its implications. In what forms is protest manifested and how does it relate to a sense of relative deprivation? How does collective protest relate to institutional participation? Under what conditions can protest become a weapon for successful intervention? And finally, does the public articulation of protest, collective or individual, necessarily lower the legitimacy of the state?

Since the publication of Huntington's widely influential *Political Order in Changing Societies*,[15] the relationship between protest behaviour and political legitimacy has been considered generally negative. This is empirically supported by the link between anti-system party strength and cabinet instability, communist party membership and political instability, strength of extremist parties and reduced cabinet durability.[16] There is some empirical evidence which supports the relationship between protest behaviour and instability at the aggregate level. In theoretical terms, however, there is some scope for doubt about the universal validity of this generalisation. In the first place, what are the implications for the relation between protest behaviour and legitimacy, once we introduce the concept of state responsiveness through the policies of economic growth and redistribution as an intervening factor? Is it not plausible to argue that the availability of an extremist party or group, speaking in the name of the deprived, poised Janus-like at the fringe of the system, combining protest behaviour with institutional participation in an effective political repertoire, actually reduces bigger threats to the legitimacy of the system? These speculations are given greater urgency by the findings of Powell who suggests that 'riots and protests are less likely to appear under these conditions, perhaps because of the opportunity for protest leaders to work within the system'.[17] This suggests that extremist parties and groups might surreptitiously transform radical anti-system sentiments into political legitimacy. This is made possible through the instrumental use of radical rhetoric and protest behaviour, an important element of the repertoire of political power in the hands of local elites with which they seek to influence the pace and direction of social and economic change.

In order to situate this process at the level of the village, we need first of all to understand the political nature of the social and economic change in contemporary India. 'Political' signifies an act that affects the local distribution of power, 'provided that there is competition for that power'.[18] The competition for power can take place within the framework of a set of rules. Participation in this process is institutional participation which is to be distinguished from radical protest which takes the competition for power outside the established rules and mobilises resources that are not normally used for the competition of power. Politicisation describes the process through which new resources like the mobilisation of large numbers of people, contacts outside the local arena and symbolic breaking of social taboos, rituals and hierarchy are added to the customary political resources of high social status, wealth and force. Subsequent chapters will explain the gradual politicisation of the local arena on the basis of the rhetoric and political strategies of local elites.

Since political power is a crucial instrument of social and economic change, we need first of all to specify power as a relation rather than a possession such as land which one might enjoy relatively independently of others. The existence of power necessarily requires at least two sets of players, bound together by rules which regulate their relation of power. Power cannot exist unless these rules are accorded sufficient legitimacy by the parties concerned.[19] As such,

> Power is necessarily shared, howsoever unequally, at various levels within the social structure; it is also therefore constantly contested and is constantly changing, even if imperceptibly, even when this contest and change are clouded by arrogance of dominance on the part of the elite and overt submission on the part of . . . the people.
>
> (Mukhia (1989), p. 1338)

Thus, improbable though it may appear at first sight, any act of power requires an implicit complicity by those subject to that power, wherein lies the room for maneouvre by the powerless. The lesson, first given concrete shape in Gandhi's *satyagraha*, has not been lost in the countryside of Gujarat, or indeed in the peace marches of Washington.

Existence of the room for manoeuvre depends on the perception by concerned actors of the nature of the state (authoritarian or accommodative), the collective memory of past struggles (futile or productive of desired change), the individual's sense of efficacy and the existence of social networks among potential

8

beneficiaries of political action. These factors can provide the necessary incentive and organisational back up for collective action. Popular protest is already widely accepted as a part of normal politics in India. It is seen in the strategic use of voting and in contacting politicians and bureaucrats at higher levels. At the other end, violent but localised insurrections provide a more extreme platform for the articulation of political discontent. Situated between the institutional and radical alternatives is a range of methods of uncertain legality such as *gherao, dharna, boycott* and protest movements like satyagraha, *rasta roko, jail bhoro, hartal, bandh* and *morcha* whose ubiquitous presence has made them an integral part of Indian political discourse. Expressed in the vernacular idiom, they make an ideological point of reaching out to the masses outside of the mostly metropolitan Engish-speaking population.[20] Forms of struggle such as satyagraha and hartal involve the cessation of all public activity in an attempt to put pressure on a public or private organisation to concede the demands of the protesters. A dharna is more coercive, involving the refusal to clear an area, where the protestors set up camp in an effort to publicise their cause. Gherao involves the encirclement of managerial staff – to secure 'quick justice'. Jail bharo and rasta roko involve the mass violation of the law by courting arrest in numbers large enough to clog the wheels of the law and order machinery such as jails and courts. The same effect is intended by rasta roko – blocking off traffic on strategic routes. Bandh and morcha, popularised by movements of the left and subsequently appropriated by all sections of the society, are more militant in character, using confrontation with the authorities as an integral part of the struggle.[21]

Though expressed in an Indian 'vernacular' idiom, these forms of struggle are not necessarily unique to India. After all, there are powerful and evocative examples from other cultures such as Martin Luther King's March on Washington at the height of the American Civil Rights Movement, radical protests by French peasants[22] and the anti-Poll Tax agitation in the UK. However, whereas in stable democracies they introduce an occasional burst of colour and fury on the backdrop of grey, institutional politics, in India, in their scope, frequency and reach, they constitute a powerful complement to institutional politics. As strategies of mass struggle, they have a precedent in the Gandhian political repertoire, which blended the tools of liberal politics such as petitions and bargaining with agitational techniques popularised by the extremist current of the anti-colonial movement. The techniques are still very much the same. When an issue is open to negotiation, the available political machinery is used to extract as many concessions as possible. When no further gains are considered obtainable through normal channels, leaders withdraw from the negotiation and resort to protest action. When sufficient pressure is generated by the agitators to coerce the authorities into bargaining once again, the protesters modify their radical rhetoric and come back to the institutional political process. The major differences with the spirit of Gandhian struggle are two-fold. The Gandhian struggle was national in scope and the achievement of independence constituted the overarching objective which subsumed all other considerations. In their contemporary form, protest action and movements are local in scope and the promotion of individual or group material interests are the most common objectives.

The field data on which the book is based are intended to examine the proposition that protest action and movements, constituting a grey area of Indian politics, are an important source of the legitimation of the authority of the state. The state draws strength from protest behaviour by creating new institutions and undertaking new policy initiatives responsive to local demands and continually broadens its political base through the recruitment of protestors into the political arena. The 'efficacy of protest' on the other hand encourages radical movements to use their rhetoric as a source of power but to stop short of outright revolution. The state, for its part, treats protest movements as an alternative form of interest articulation. The fact that protest movements are tolerated by the state facilitates the legitimate repression of revolutionary groups, and the transformation of anti-state movements into instruments of interest articulation and their eventual incorporation into the normal, institutional, political process.

The blending of institutional initiatives such as contacting bureaucratic and political decision-makers at higher levels with radical protest at the level of local politics is an important instrument of the legitimation of the authority of the state in India. The book explores this theme by drawing on the experience of a sample of local elites who pursue a range of tactics from the peaceful and orderly to the militant and coercive, in their pursuit of influence, power and material resources. Drawn from the relatively prosperous State of Gujarat and comparatively backward Orissa, they contain among them a wide range of the variation one is likely to witness among local elites in the rural setting in India.

THE POLITICAL UNIVERSE OF INDIA'S RURAL ELITES

Attempts to understand rural India can easily slide into the stereotype of an eternally passive Indian peasant, complete with a morally self-sufficient worldview of *dharma*, *karma* and *moksha*.[23] To replace it by an opposite 'romantic stereotype of perennial rural rebelliousness' would be an equally untrue representation of contemporary reality.[24] To suggest, however, that the truth lies somewhere in between these two stereotypes might be a happy compromise but one that does not help identify the conditions under which public order and collective protest exist side by side in rural India. It is for this reason that the fascinating political world of rural *netas* provides an appropriate empirical context for the study of institutional participation and radical protest.

Once again, India's rural elites are not alone in occupying a niche within local politics. In Italy, as Sidney Tarrow[25] informs us, local elites, rather than behaving like traditional local notables or acting merely as rubber-stamp administrators of programmes initiated from above, have become important actors in the political adaptation of local communities to social and economic change. The difference with India consists mainly in the range of available political strategies and the frequency and dexterity with which the Indian local elites are able to weave them together in a complex political repertoire. The full extent of the role that local elites play in the process of social and economic change is little understood in cross-cultural studies of development. By a remarkable coincidence, local elites are the *bêtes noires* of both the liberal–modernisation approach[26] and that of the radical–structural critics of that approach.[27] The former 'top-down' theories of development have routinely assumed that knowledge, technology and capital, accumulating

11

at the top of the system in the course of modernisation, will in due course 'trickle down' to the bottom. The fact that, more often than not, the benefits of development do not reach the lowest strata is blamed by specialists on the local elites whose role consists essentially in skimming off the benefits of development for their private gain.[28]

One exception to this generally bleak view of local elites is the remarkably perceptive study of Esman and Uphoff.[29] On the basis of a cross-national analysis of Asian experience, they conclude that effective local organisations, 'accountable to the local people, and involved in rural development functions, generally accomplished rural development objectives more successfully with respect to the available resource base than those with less rural organisation'.[30] While their analysis draws attention to the scope for significant intervention in the process of development at the local level, their focus on formal organisations shifts attention away from local elites who, without necessarily holding elective or administrative positions, give meaning and substance to what would otherwise be merely paper organisations.

An alternative view of local elites, different from the main thrust of the development literature, is to conceptualise them as a bridge between the state and society. They belong, in a way, both to the state as well as the society, interpreting the rational, bureaucratic norms of the state to a society based on social networks and the moral economy.[31] They are, as the model depicted in diagram 1 seeks to convey, a vital interface between the modern state and the traditional society, presented here in the form of ideal types (see figure 1.1; the shaded area represents local elites).

The principal argument of the book is to suggest that India's local elites are a crucial hinge group whose ability to incorporate newly emerging social forces into the political arena and to ease out old style notables is the critical determinant of the stability, legitimacy and expansion of the state. The process of state formation in India is different from the models of the bureaucratic state[32] and the developmental state[33] in the sense that the agenda of social and economic change is not the prerogative of a technocratic elite who are not accountable to the people through the normal political process. Instead, social and economic change are a part of the larger political agenda so that

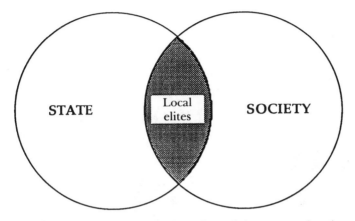

Figure 1.1   Local elites as the interface of the state and society

the statesman committed to development and modernisation is beholden to the local leaders for political support; high politics of the state and local politics, rather than being worlds apart, are closely intertwined. The political role of local elites is thus an integral part of the model of state that has evolved in India after independence.

Local elites perform this role with a complex combination of institutional participation and radical protest. The book seeks to examine this conjecture by comparing the record of development and the role of the gaon ka netas in the Indian States of Gujarat and Orissa. These two regions, one considerably more developed than the other, are quite different from each other in their levels of political awareness, traditions of local self-government, local initiative, and the historical legacy of local protest movements. Of equal importance is the difference in the history of large-scale market transactions. These and other points of difference are discussed at length in chapter two. Despite their differences in these respects, both Gujarat and Orissa, like all the constituent States of the Indian Union, are nevertheless subject to basically the same national policies and political constraints. From this follows both the divergence in

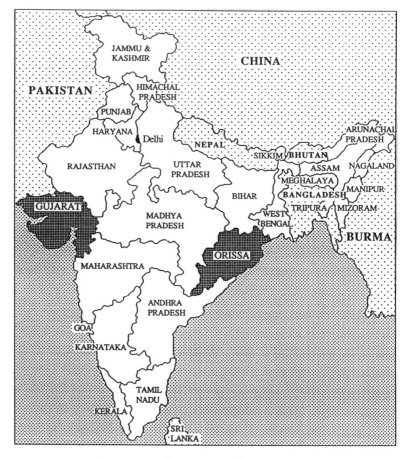

Map 1.1   India: State boundaries, 1987

their responses and the potential rewards of a comparative study of the two States (see map 1.1).

THE REGION AND LOCAL ELITES AS KEY PARAMETERS OF THE MODEL OF DEVELOPMENT

The politics of allocation of material resources provides a connecting thread between local elites, the mobilisation of new social forces and protest behaviour. This takes place in the context of a federal structure where power is generated through

14

a process of accommodation. The critical role of the federal division of powers for the nature and course of regional development is discussed at length in chapter two. This section will briefly introduce the role of social and economic development in the process of state formation in India.

The state in India has sought to gain legitimacy by spreading the benefits of development among its citizens, particularly in the rural areas. The relative emphasis on the key components of this strategy of state formation which was fashioned in the course of the anti-colonial struggle, has shifted from full public ownership of the means of production and distribution to a complex combination of state control and private ownership, thanks largely to the power struggle that characterised the transfer of power in India.[34] However, a broad commitment to economic and social development, with its quasi-constitutional recognition in the form of articles 39–46 of the Constitution, continued to serve as the most important source of legitimation of authority for the competing political forces during the early decades after independence.[35] Development, understood as a generic expression for a series of mostly state-sponsored activities – the construction of roads, bridges, public utilities and other infrastructure, social welfare, rapid economic growth – became the *leitmotif* of political discourse in post-independence India. Political formations of the left, right and centre confronted one another in successive general elections with their specific interpretations of the 'development imperative'. With the important exception of the muted voice of Hindu nationalism,[36] development became the ubiquitous idiom of government policy as well as of the political opposition to those policies.

In their strategy of development, India's planners expected the key elements of growth such as capital, technology of production and management to first accumulate at the apex of the system and then spread out to the lower levels.[37] Why must development, or rather the benefits of development, trickle down, though? The modest equivalent to the forces of gravity is, to use once again the jargon of Indian Planning, the 'felt need' of the people.[38] Radical critics of the incremental, 'trickle down' model vehemently disagree with these premises. The teleological implications implicitly built into the model are considered by radical critics too wishful a foundation on which to base the momentous task of the modernisation of a traditional society. They argue that there are too many hurdles on the way ('bottlenecks' in Indian jargon) for this to be possible. For these critics, radical action from below, by revolutionary 'masses', alone has the necessary political momentum to break through the barriers of class, caste and capital.[39]

While the radical critics of the 'top-down' model successfully bring out the practical difficulties that the model encounters when it is applied to the material and social conditions prevailing in rural India, the two-tier view of Indian society on which they are based is not entirely supported by the political reality.[40] In contrast to this approach, the focus of this book is on the middle level – the interface between the state and society – as an important area of developmental action and change, with local elites, situated in the interface, as the key actors in the interaction between the modern state and traditional society.

It is conceivable that the architects of Indian planning anticipated the 'room for manoeuvre in the middle' without however articulating it in explicit theoretical terms. Local elections at the beginning of the century[41] had already given an early indication of how local participation could function as the cutting edge of national development. Since independence, the process of broadening the social base of the state has been reinforced with successive degrees of devolution of power and new institutional innovations. The broader implications of this process are raised in this book in terms of a few specific questions: How successful has the process been in breaking through the two centuries of social and economic stagnation prior to independence and what role have local elites played in it? What collective problems do local elites face in their everyday experience of development, what solutions do they envisage to these problems and which institutions do they prefer to implement these solutions? The discussion of these questions in chapter four is meant to provide a link to the issues taken up in the subsequent chapters: who gets to share the material benefits of development and why? More pertinently, what do people do when they do not get what they believe is legitimately theirs? What are the forms in which protest against relative deprivation manifests itself and what are the social groups associated with such protest?

The reason for posing these questions to the rural *netas*, seen here as a 'hinge' group between the state and society, is that they are particularly well placed to answer them. Their local standing

16

is closely related to the flow of developmental resources to the village from outside. This also explains why local elites are a fluid and socially diverse category. In the tremendous social ferment of contemporary rural India, relative deprivation – whether of the village as a whole compared to other villages considered more privileged, or by a section of the residents of the village itself – puts pressure on the current set of netas to work towards a solution. The failure to do so is quite likely to result in the more articulate from among the 'non-elites' forcing their way to the ranks of the elites on the strength and urgency of the new demand. In either event, developmental 'discourse' as a source of power ensures the incremental broadening of the agenda and the accommodation of underprivileged social groups.

The field research reported in this book suggests that local elites fulfil a vital role as intermediaries between the state structure, represented respectively by the revenue officials, the police, the development official and the village, with its caste and kinship networks, interwoven within the interstices of a moral economy, based on complementary interests and a collective welfare regime.[42] Metaphorically and often literally, these key elements of the political and cultural interface are located where the all-weather roads end and the mud tracks begin. Collectively, they are the vital hinge groups between the state and society in India. For reasons of the legacy of the freedom movement and the neo-Gandhian concept of the village community, local elites have been thought of as non-political. During the struggle for independence, the imperative of forming a broad anti-colonial coalition encouraged national leaders to give a national rather than explicitly ideological character to the movement. Within this broad rubric, local politics was accorded the comparatively non-partisan task of social reconstruction and rural upliftment. The Congress as the party of government after independence sought to give institutional character to these efforts and initiate new schemes through the Community Development programme. A legal framework for this was provided through non-party village councils under the panchayati raj scheme.

The myth of non-party local elections was subsequently discarded and the increasing role of political parties in *panchayat* elections became an accepted fact of the political reality. This development has come about despite the recommendation of the Ashok Mehta Committee (which introduced the panchayati raj structure in a systematic way in 1957) that local elections be kept above party politics. It is rare, however, with the exception of States like West Bengal and Kerala, to find political parties maintaining a continuous, professional presence at the village level. The usual pattern is for political parties to claim 'active members' at the time of elections. The continuity of political life during the period between elections is maintained by local elites who cash in their accumulated political capital at election time. Every election, in addition to changing the political landscape of the village, inducts some new persons to the local political arena, reflecting both generational change as well as the mobilisation of new social forces.

It is important here to emphasise that compared to elites at the upper echelons of the political system, local elites, generally not being full-time politicians, tend to retain a certain degree of autonomy from political control from above. This is further reinforced by the fact that, unlike the relatively more 'professional' political leaders at higher levels, local elites are full-time residents of the village. As such, they share with the people of the village the consequences of policy decisions and 'non-decisions' originating at the higher levels of the system.[43] The combined effect of these factors gives a certain legitimacy to local elites in their capacity as representatives of local interests.

At the hub of local political life in India, one recognises the gaon ka netas, an ubiquitous presence in rural politics.[44] Though they are easy to recognise, their social origins are far from being static in terms of social class, the turnover in their ranks keeping pace with the process of social change. The social heterogeneity of local elites, discussed at length in chapter three, is accelerated primarily by the nature and pace of economic development and the creation of new political and administrative institutions. The diversity of their social origin is considerable compared to the more rigid categories of local caste and class. Every development programme and every government department in whose jurisdiction the village falls is likely to have its contact neta in the village. The world of local elites is, by its very nature, essentially fluid, with few alliances that are stable over time. The growing social heterogeneity and generational turn-over of rural elites are further augmented through the mobilisation of new social groups and legislative initiatives from the apex of the system. These are important bench marks for the measurement of progress in breaking through the self-reinforcing cycles of a closed and rigidly stratified social system.

The perception of political conflict and need for social cohesion by the local elites, dealt with at length in chapter five, are crucial to the questions posed in this book. Depending on the social composition, ideological structure and access to decision-makers at higher levels, several empirical scenarios are possible for a given situation. Competing local elites, operating within institutions that have at least a modicum of political autonomy, are representative in character and accountable to a larger constituency and can act as the cutting edge of an expanding, democratic state. On the other hand, a socially cohesive local elite, able to accumulate the advantages arising out of their control of land, credit and commerce, and their social status can use local institutions to further reinforce their political dominance.

In view of the diversity and complexity of local elites, their spatial location and their internal and external relations can be represented at best in the form of an ideal type. Thus in figure 1.2, the triangle represents the regional policy environment within which villages, denoted by the bold circle, are placed. Within this environment, a large variety of institutions – bureaucratic, political or voluntary organisations (sometimes referred to as Non-Governmental Organisations) – seek to establish contact with the village. Invariably, the agencies interested in the village establish a bridgehead by designating a contact person, chosen in view of his accessibility, the influence he has on others in the village and his acceptance of the goals of the organisations concerned. The rural netas, situated in the shaded area between the two circles, are a group of intermediaries, who mediate and transform the two-way communication between the village and the world outside. Since the goals of the agencies operating from outside the village are not always compatible, their competition creates in turn a certain animosity and internal competition among the netas. The intra-elite competition opens an avenue for the non-elites to be brought into the play and, perhaps less frequently, for some established *netas* to be discarded by the political process in favour of a more energetic and aggressive leader capable of achieving better results.[45]

19

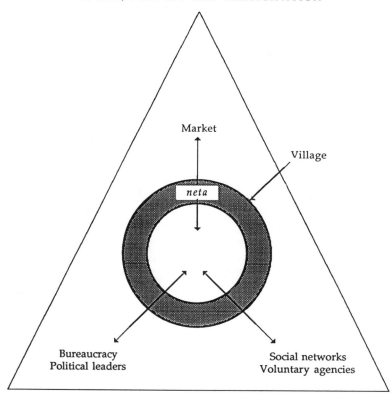

Figure 1.2 Local elites and the regional policy environment

The village, seen from this perspective, is far from an island unto itself. It is part of a grid organised in the form of a pyramid, encompassing at the bottom level a multitude of villages. The political process at the regional level, particularly the territorial constituency, helps establish a transactional link between the village and the world outside. Over the years since independence, most of India's half million villages have thus been steadily drawn into a national development network, constantly reinforced by initiatives taken by the national and regional governments, public and private investment and technological innovations linked to new production systems, and mass communication, revolutionised in the 1980s through the use of the electronic media. The villages are connected with this larger network through the local elites, acting as linkmen. The

20

local elites, located at the bottom of this pyramid of arenas, are sometimes referred to as 'fixers', considered by many as a parasitical presence on the development scene.[46] In contrast to this rather negative image, held by radical scholars, the view offered here is more positive. They are seen as intermediaries between development agencies and ordinary villagers. Their impact on the volume and pace of social and economic change is thus crucial. Their role is vital to the continuous opening up of the village, leading to the empowerment of the previously powerless, and finally, the legitimation of the norms of political and economic democracy at the local level. These propositions are examined at length in chapters five and six.

The model presented in diagram 1.2 seeks to classify the major influences and forces acting on the village into three broad categories: first, the state, the administrative and the political structures; second, the regional and national market forces; and, third, social and voluntary associations and non-governmental organisations. Each of these agencies seeks a bridgehead to the village. In practice, there is considerable diversity within the categories as well as overlaps between them. The broad distinction, however, is important, because the agendas of development they portray, the interests and social groups they appeal to and the attitudes towards authority that they embody, constitute important differences, with far-reaching theoretical and ideological significance. A second point that the model (presented here essentially as an ideal type) does not emphasise is the mutual relationship of the three broad categories. This is significant because there are important variations in the relative political strength and statutory power of the three broad sources of influence from one State of India to another. The market and the voluntary sector are stronger in areas with a longer history of economic growth compared to regions with a more recent history of rapid economic change. Among the less economically advanced States, the bureaucracy, in continuation of the colonial legacy, is more powerful and plays the leading role in the process of development. In more developed States, the elected officials of the panchayati raj structure play a more vigorous role, reflected in their formal statutory power over the local administration, whereas in the less economically advanced Orissa, the District Collector is still very much the most powerful figure.

It is important to emphasise here that more than the high politics of Delhi, regional politics and policy process constitute a critical level for the analysis of development in India. In this sense, the states of India, seen as the regional policy environment, are the appropriate units of analysis. Generally, it is at the level of the regional political process that the competing claims of development agencies are negotiated. Often in practice, a minister of the state government, representing the overarching role of the state, is called upon to arbitrate among the competing claims of the different agencies and to lay down the authoritative norms to act as a guide for their operation. In view of the importance of the state government and regional variations in material conditions of development more fully explained in chapter two, relatively prosperous Gujarat and comparatively backward Orissa have been chosen for detailed empirical investigation.

AN ALTERNATIVE VIEW OF LOCAL ELITES AS SOCIALLY COHESIVE 'DOMINANT' ELITES

The model of state–society relations mediated by local elites presented here provides a contrast to the other view which depicts local elites as obstacles to the democratisation of authority and greater participation in development. This latter view does not recognise their social heterogeneity nor their complex and competing relationship with the bureaucracy, regional political leaders and developmental agencies. Advocates of this view believe that the benefits of development are monopolised by local elites, seen as 'dominant' elites in the sense that they accumulate the advantages arising out of their control of land, capital and high social status. It is further assumed that there is a coalescence, both normative and in terms of material interests, between socially cohesive local elites and the state. From this follows the scepticism about the ability of the state to extend its proclaimed goals of social equality and political participation into the domain of the (traditional) society. In the words of Francine Frankel, one of the most influential writers on this issue:

> Pledges of the prime minister and the Congress party to eliminate mass poverty and accelerate economic progress could not be redeemed *within the existing structure of economic and political power.* On the contrary, the attempt to achieve

both economic development and reduction of disparities in the absence of *basic institutional changes* led, inevitably, to the pursuit of contradictory policies that were bound to result in the worst of both worlds, achieving neither growth nor redistribution.

(Frankel (1978), p. 491; emphasis added)

Observations in this vein about conditions at the local level suggest an irrevocable moral and material bond between the institutions of the state and cohesive, 'dominant' elites at the micro-level. Against the backdrop of this bleak scenario, a marxist revolution in an explicit form, or implicitly in the form of the need for 'structural transformations', is presented as a sort of *deus ex machina* which would simultaneously solve the problems of growth, justice and equality. Frankel concludes after a detailed analysis of economic policy in post-independence India: 'adequate progress toward the multiple economic, social and political goals of development cannot be accomplished in the absence of radical agrarian reform'.[47]

The findings presented here are different from the assertions of the 'dominant elite/structural change' thesis. The latter does not take into consideration the tremendous internal diversity in the social origins of local leaders nor the fragile and variable base of their political support, contingent in most cases on their ability to deliver the goods. Growing politicisation of the Indian electorate has led to the steady broadening of the political arena, considerable turnover of leadership and the entry into the political process of those who were hitherto excluded. Evidence of this mobility is provided by the literature on electoral mobilisation which informs us of the remarkable progress made by the Backward Classes in several Indian States, who, in the politically turbulent 1960s, were successful in dislodging the upper caste leadership from their dominant position.[48] Despite important regional variations, the process is national in scope. And despite occasional setbacks, both nationally and at the regional level, the process contains enough vitality to be able to regenerate itself from these occasional setbacks.

POST-INDEPENDENCE DEVELOPMENT POLICY IN INDIA

The difficulties of giving concrete shape to the agenda of development with its twin commitment to democracy and

23

economic growth can be seen in the fluctuations of economic policy since independence.[49] However, despite the changes in policy, the basic parameters of which were laid down in the Industrial Policy Resolution of 1948, a broad commitment to development, with its quasi-constitutional recognition in the form of articles 39–46 of the Constitution, continued to form part of the political consensus within which all the political parties including the Communists operated during the early years after independence. The emphasis in the 1950s was on the use of the community as a distinct spatial and social unit of development. As such, community development was considered synonymous with rural development, initially for the purposes of financial allocation and, ultimately, as an administrative and political unit through the introduction of panchayati raj which set down the structure of local self government, going down to the level of the village. In the federal division of powers dealt with at length in chapter two, the provision for community development and local self government fell within the exclusive jurisdiction of the State governments. The progress achieved in both, not surprisingly, varied significantly from one region to another. This was one of the reasons behind a radical shift of policy at the national level. A new central initiative in the form of the Intensive Agricultural District Programme (IADP) was launched in 1960. This set the precedent for the introduction of centrally coordinated, sectoral programmes for rural development. The provision for subsidised inputs, distributed by officials keen on spectacular results in agricultural productivity, strongly favoured the better-off sections of the rural population. This approach was strengthened by the introduction of high yielding varieties of seeds, whose effect on agricultural production came to be known as the Green Revolution. Since these strategies were aimed at increasing agricultural output by providing state subsidised inputs to agricultural entrepreneurs, the effect was the growth of agrarian capitalism under the auspices of a state committed to socialism. Eventually, a corrective was provided against the class-bias potential in the 'sectoral' thinking behind agricultural development in the form of the 'target group approach'. Under the slogan of *garibi hatao*, launched as the foundation of the successful electoral campaign of Indira Gandhi's Congress party in 1971, a variety of schemes such as the Small Farmers Development Agency were introduced to orient the flow of development resources towards vulnerable social groups.

Behind the great fluctuation of policy and its attendant institutional innovation, one can see the emphasis on development which greatly affected the nature of state–society relations after independence. Policies leading to social development juxtaposed the values of individual rights, equality and social pluralism against those of a moral community, based on ascriptive authority, communal solidarity and social hierarchy. Institutions of the state – the courts, legislatures and the bureaucracy – became the allies of forces opposed to the more oppressive aspects of the caste system. These measures, particularly the policy of reservation which set aside a quota of positions in the public services, legislatures and in admissions to higher and professional education, further polarised social conflict and led to anti-reservation movements.[50] The cumulative impact of the policy of reservation and the backlash against it has been to create an ideological niche for the concept of positive discrimination and to mobilise their actual and potential beneficiaries into a vocal pressure group.

The requirement of economic development posed problems of a different order. The legacy of the freedom movement was inclined towards a model of development based on import-substitution and a temporary isolation of the economy from the international market. The capital needs of this economy had also to be met from internal sources. The regime could, however, no more expect institutionalised support from the state for the capitalist squeeze than for forced savings through collectivisation. The authority of the state was based on the accommodation of a wide variety of interests. The implications for capital accumulation were bleak: the Indian 'soft' state faced the dire prospects of 'peaceful stagnation'.[51] Other predictions were even more bleak, including a possible disintegration into feuding regional and communal groups or the overthrow of the liberal-democratic state by an authoritarian state of the left or the right.[52]

In the face of these dilemmas, Indian policy makers came up with a 'mixed' model of the state and the policy process that attempted to balance the role of the public sector with that of private enterprise. Within the model of the mixed economy, the public sector was to set the norm of social justice and create the organisational structure for basic industries and develop the infrastructure. Under the shadow of the public sector was the private sector, which opened up for private capital new forms for enterprise, sometimes in collaboration with the public sector and occasionally in competition against governmental agencies, but almost always with some form of public support ranging from subsidised inputs and infrastructural facilities to the protection from internal and international competition. In agriculture, beginning with Zamindari abolition, state action and the market process steadily removed the rentiers from the process of agrarian production. After the brave talk of the late 1950s about cooperative 'joint farming', the state stayed away from direct intervention in the process of agrarian production but government subsidies played an increasingly important role as the pace and quantum of the Green Revolution grew.

THE SOCIAL CONSEQUENCES OF DEVELOPMENT

The economic changes brought about through political reform and market operation have affected rural society considerably. Attempts to conceptualise the social consequences of development range from the functionalist to the structural-marxist. Writing in the 1960s, Bailey noticed the alacrity with which traditional society absorbed the shock of the sudden inflow of developmental funds.[53] Two decades later, Reddy and Hargopal reported in the same vein that social response to development had been to produce the *pyraveekar* – the 'fixer' who specialises as the intermediary between the traditional society and the world outside.[54] Developmental resources, seen from this perspective, only added to the structural complexity of society but achieved little by the way of social and economic transformation.

The main thrust of the radical critics of development has been to show how the impact of rapid economic change has contributed to greater social polarisation. In agriculture, for example, the introduction of new technology and changes in the relations of production have led to a process of proletarianisation of the peasantry of 'depeasantisation'. The process is

> complex but as yet partial in its impact. The new techno-
> logy has produced conditions in which, by a variety of

means, the poor peasantry has lost an increasing share of the operated area to rich peasants. Not only that, but the poor peasantry is in different ways being transformed more and more into a rural proletariat

(Byres (1981), p. 430)

Advocates of the depeasantisation thesis suggest that incentives for the capitalist mode of production have been provided by the extension of state subsidised irrigation, credit facilities, modernisation of agricultural technology, penetration of agrobusiness and the growth of institutions such as sugar cooperatives that have rapidly brought together the previously dispersed activities of production and marketing. To the extent that they pose an obstacle to the new form of production, the creation of capitalist production relations has in many cases led to the severance of precapitalist social relations in some parts of India, including Punjab, parts of Gujarat and Maharashtra.

The polarisation taking place in the countryside can be understood in terms of the growth of specialised, contractual relations in the place of the previous ensemble of social, economic and political relations, described by Indian sociologists as the Jajmani system.[55] The landowning farmers increasingly see themselves as entrepreneurs trying to find the best combination of the factors of production that would produce the maximum profit, part of which would eventually be ploughed back into the process of production. The transformation of relations undoubtedly creates great hardship for those without a viable capital base in land, who must make a living in an increasingly exploitative environment. This form of class differentiation and agrarian capital formation involves a fair degree of ruthlessness on the part of employers, accompanied by private and collective violence. Jan Breman's landmark study of the pauperisation of agricultural workers in Gujarat is illustrative of this form of the capitalist squeeze.[56]

The agricultural workers in Breman's study, belonging to the Halpati community in South Gujarat were previously attached to individual Patidar farmers in a network of social and economic ties. These were in some cases reinforced with outstanding loans passed from generation to generation. Though they were essentially exploitative, they also provided a cushion against the financial strain caused by bad harvests, illness and unforeseen expenses incurred through social rituals such as marriages or funerals. In contrast, the new production relation has pitted an increasing number of landless workers in competition against one another for a decreasing number of jobs in the countryside, leading to an overall collapse of living standards and resultant immiserisation. Whereas the bound labourer of an earlier period could stave off outright pauperisation through a variety of openings available within the precapitalist form of production, the more centralised management and accounting is less sympathetic to such loopholes, considered by modern managers as disguised unemployment and, in any case, made redundant through the new labour-saving technology. 'Present day agricultural labourers are less burdened with debt; they have become free, but in a way that smacks of redundancy.'[57]

PROTEST MOVEMENTS AS AN ALTERNATIVE FORM OF POLITICAL ACTION

Neither the functionalist view nor the adversarial model suggested by the radical approach offer a satisfactory explanation for new forms of political action and local protest movements which are increasingly viewed as variants of 'normal' politics in India. Under the impact of rapid economic change, new forms of rural class differentiation have unleashed great potentials for capital formation as well as the expression of anger and resentment among those who feel relatively deprived. However, in India, interest groups, lobbies and political parties which carry out the task of interest articulation and aggregation in most liberal democracies have been slow to develop. Besides, due to their fragmentation into rival organisations, a phenomenon described by the Rudolphs as 'involuted pluralism', these intervening structures are relatively weak and unorganised.[58] Moreover, they operate in a milieu that is unsympathetic if not hostile to the advocacy of special interests. 'In the name of rationality and public interest, decision-makers have often turned deaf ears to the demands of interest groups.'[59] The refusal to grant them the status of legitimate intermediaries further contributes to the stridency of their style, and acts as an incentive for the articulation of genuine demands in terms of challenges to public order. 'Because the government is unresponsive, groups resort to mass demonstrations, hartals, strikes and civil disobedience to force government action.'[60]

This is expressed in occasional outbursts of popular protest. Paradoxically, the government, by occasionally conceding such demands, contributes to the legitimacy of protest movements as a complementary form of political action geared to development goals.[61]

These acts of collective protest, carried out at the margin of legality, belong to the grey area of Indian democracy. To describe them simply as acts of spontaneous rebellion would be to underestimate the political intelligence behind the strategic use of the instruments of protest. In a different context, Charles Tilly, in his accounts of agrarian conflict in Europe has criticised such theories of 'spontaneous rebellion'. 'The image', as he remarks in a memorable passage, 'is hydraulic: hardship increases, pressure builds up, the vessel bursts. The angry individual acts as a reservoir of resentment, a conduit of tension, a boiler of fury, but not as a thinking, *political* man operating on principle.'[62] As the evidence emerging from such grassroots protest movements reveals, acts of resistance such as gherao, dharnas, demonstrations and others are not always spontaneous nor sporadic but form parts of coordinated, strategic moves which are a far cry from suicidal acts of desperate people.[63]

While the literature on agrarian conflict from early modern Europe is helpful in providing insights into causes of conflict and the motives of the major protagonists, the comparison can be misleading. The overarching role of the state as the neutral arbiter among conflicting groups and the capacity of the bureaucracy to perform this task are both important considerations. The experience of the deprived social groups in India differs sharply from their historical counterparts in early modern Europe. The impoverished European peasantry, caught between the vice-like grip of the capitalist squeeze and the rapid disappearance of their traditional means of living, attempted to roll back the onslaught of capitalism through protest movements, food riots, machine breaking and radical uprisings. However, whereas the state in Europe during these formative years of capitalism behaved very much as the 'executive committee of the bourgeoisie', the state in India, for reasons suggested above, reserves for itself a multiplicity of roles – of accommodation, extraction, production and repression. The state in India steps in when the conflict between social forces poses a threat to public order. But the precise nature of state intervention is context-specific rather than ideological – in a predetermined way. The sources of conflict themselves are multiple, with region, class, community and increasingly, the urban–rural divide adding to the complexity of the political situation.[64]

AN INTERACTIVE MODEL OF PARTICIPATION IN DEVELOPMENT

While the state in India acts as a point of reference in its capacity as institutionalised power (as compared to the personalisation of power which would, in effect, indicate a decay of stateness), we need to acknowledge a plurality of interests that compete for salience within the state structure with the occasional relative dominance of a particular social group or interest in a specific context. Similarly, under the impact of social and economic change, some sections of the rural population have become steadily marginalised. However, the intermediary and regulatory role of the state in India, which seriously questions the two-tier view of Indian society promoted by radical scholars, offers room for manoeuvre to those with a grievance. On the one hand, from the point of view of the destitute and the vulnerable, the possibility of state intervention provides a cushion against the most blatant forms of economic and social exploitation. On the other hand, while facilitating the growth of capital formation through the provision of state subsidy and infrastructure and the maintenance of order, the state, for political reasons, keeps a check on the tendency of agrarian capital to concentrate in a few hands. Subsidised inputs are provided to underprivileged 'target groups' through a whole series of statutory regulations. On the other hand, the marginally better off (for example, those owning 2–5 acres of irrigable land) have shown remarkable resilience and a tendency to fight back the onslaught of agrarian capitalism through methods of intensive cultivation akin to agricultural involution rather than selling up and joining in the urban exodus. The vast rank of 'bullock capitalists' is a powerful indicator of both the vitality of the process of capital formation and the effectiveness of social limits to the growth of predatory capitalism.[65]

The political process in India affects entry into the growing areas of the economy in a variety of ways. To begin with, the benefits of development are available to those with capital, political connections and individual access to the bureaucracy and political decision-makers at higher levels. However, failing all else (and sometimes, in addition), political clout, born out of the horizontal integration and mobilisation of disaffected interests can help achieve the same ends as well. The general picture of conflict and participation in development is, thus, rather complex, varying from one region to another, reflecting the uneven growth of capital formation, state of social mobilisation and political alliances. The process is neither smooth nor irreversible. The attempts by those lower down the scale to assert themselves is resisted by the rich and powerful, sometimes with police connivance and the help of private armies maintained for this purpose. But then, the fact that some of those who were previously excluded from worthwhile and significant participation in the economy do manage to improve their lot, gives hope to others and helps the process to contine.[66]

These conjectures can be conceptualised in terms of alternative 'routes' to participation in development. Rather than defining the objective in terms of a set of narrow, economic benefits, we shall offer a hierarchy of objectives that are material as well as political, ranging between improvement in the standards of living to securing subsidies and obtaining greater influence in the making of policy decisions. The resources that can enhance one's chances of successful participation depend upon the goals one seeks to achieve, the structure of opportunities and the advantages one starts with. On one end of the scale, one might find people with the requisite resources in capital, social standing, information about available opportunities and the skills to put them to their advantage. At the other extreme are people who are resourceless and without contacts at the higher echelons, for whom agitation in one form or other is perhaps the only realistic way of attracting public attention and resources. In between these different categories are people who combine institutional methods (like lobbying, voting and contacts with higher level decision-makers) and agitational techniques. The models presented in figure 1.3 summarise the complexity of this process

Model 1 in figure 1.3 can be seen as a useful baseline against which to understand the complexities of the process of participation in development. It can be noticed at once that there are

Model 1

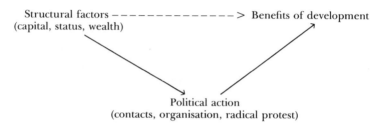

Structural factors – – – – – – – – – – – – – > Benefits of development
(capital, status, wealth)

Model 2

Structural factors – – – – – – – – – – – – – > Benefits of development
(capital, status, wealth)

Political action
(contacts, organisation, radical protest)

Figure 1.3   Routes to participation in development

few 'pure' routes, exclusively available to given social classes. Though people are likely to use the various paths in optimal combinations that maximise their chances of obtaining the desired objectives, for analytical reasons it is useful to maintain a conceptual distinction among them. The first of these routes is the one that requires the least amount of conscious political effort in reaching the desired goal. Provided one possesses the requisite capital, the market itself can deliver the material rewards. The route, of 'participation without politics', is secured through the normal operations of market transactions.[67] *Ceteris paribus*, those with the necessary initial advantages of wealth, social standing and education are likely to be the beneficiaries of this route of participation without politics.[68] The second route to the benefits of development, seen as influence in the making of policy decisions, is secured by contacting the administrative and political decision-makers at higher levels. The second route, which we may call the institutional–political route, should be distinguished from a third route, based on various forms of direct action, where local leaders mobilise their followers to bring pressure to bear upon decision makers. The leaders of the third route could be the recent arrivals on the political arena, more aggressive in style and less familiar with the art of political bargaining. They are also more likely to be members of the most deprived social groups. But, in the politically promiscuous world of India's rural *netas*, it would be unwise to assume that any particular path is foreclosed to any particular social group.

THE CONTEXT OF RESEARCH

A duality of focus, on the one hand on individuals and on the other on social groups of which they are a part, runs through this book. The duality is, in a sense, unavoidable. The changes under way in rural India have in many cases undermined traditional social and economic relations. In the place of the old matrix of social bonds, one finds new structures, created by individuals, who, for a variety of reasons, have formed new groups. Social differentiation is made possible by individuals, responding no doubt to the stimuli of forces not entirely under their control. We have, as such, given sustained attention to individuals, eliciting their opinions and attitudes to a variety of problems that form part of their everyday reality and the forms of intervention they are familiar with, through structured and unstructured questions. Yet, traditional social structures amount to more than the sum of the parts in the sense that they have a residual life of their own that cannot entirely be explained by the attitudes and perceptions of the individuals constituting the group. The continued social relevance of these group identities in a corporate sense makes them a useful level of analysis as well as an index of basic change in the social reality. Accordingly, traditional categories of social status are juxtaposed to the more modern ones of social class as useful tools of analysis. The process of participation in the politics of local development and the factors that influence it are summarised in table 1.1.

Some of the issues raised in this study are also part of the larger debate on the sociology of rural development. One of the better known aspects of this debate to which reference will be made later in the text concerns the characterisation of the process of social transformation in terms of the rational individual, manipulating his or her environment and other individuals in an effort to bring them around to a position

Table 1.1 Local politics and participation in development

Routes	Hierarchy of goals	Resources	Principal mechanism	Decision-makers	Modes of operation	Social base
Market	Economic gain	Wealth, status, labour	Market	Individual producers, consumers, investors, civil servants	Market transactions	Most likely but not exclusively upper and middle social strata
Institutional	Influence in policy decisions	Political power	Parties, interest groups	Groups, individuals, civil servants	Voting, contact-lobbying, Agitation	Likely but not exclusively middle social strata
Radical	Status, influence, material gain	Radicalisation, potential violence	Protest movement	Groups	Agitation	Most likely but not exclusively lower strata

preferable to him or her[69] in contrast to the moral economists[70] who situate their universe in the context of groups based on complementary interests whose major objective is the achievement of a collective welfare regime. The debate has now been joined by cultural anthropologists[71] who have questioned the uncritical extension of the cultural basis of value from one context to another. Above all, despite trenchant criticism from all sides, students of development continue to be inspired by the earlier breakthrough of social history in demonstrating the impact of structural change on the everyday life of the individual, regardless of whether he or she is seen as a rational, moral or cultural being. The impact of these recent theoretical innovations can be seen in the evolution of new directions of research in the major writers who defined the field during the 1960s and 1970s.[72] One of the net contributions of the larger debate on development has been to inject a degree of healthy scepticism against exclusive attention to any particular source of data. Despite the obvious importance of individuals and groups, the student of social analysis can no longer afford to devote themselves to attitudinal data alone. Individual perceptions and behaviour are but reactions to the specific social context in which they are placed. Macro parameters such as the structure of opportunities, larger historical changes such as the introduction of new technologies of production, changes in land tenure and holdings, population movements and organisation deeply affect attitudes and behaviour. Our understanding of the social reality will remain incomplete if we were to confine our attention to survey data alone, if we fail to consider the social, economic and political context in which they are placed. Through natural evolution, and deliberate political design, India's constituent States present relatively homogeneous policy environments within which one can conduct a comparative study of the role of local elites in the development process. The choice of relatively more advanced Gujarat and the comparatively more backward Orissa (explained in more detail in chapter two) for detailed empirical investigation is intended to give the study a comparative perspective and historical depth.

The book reflects the merging of two major traditions of research in social and economic change. The first of these is the anthropological tradition which focuses on the village and social groups as the unit of analysis. Some of the key questions posed in this study have emerged out of the earlier study of an Orissa village.[73] Second, the methods of survey research and comparative politics have, in this sense, been added to a pre-existing stock of knowledge. The substantive questions concerning change, first raised by village studies, can be applied to a larger empirical domain through the application of the method of comparative politics. The added advantage in this case is the ability to incorporate the role of the regional government and the regional policy process for a comprehensive study of micro-level change. The intimate knowledge of the empirical universe typical to the village study makes it possible for the investigator to look for all possible relations between the key variables. On the other hand, the design makes it difficult to abstract from the study a general image of the larger universe of which the village is only a part. While trying to retain some of the richness of village studies, the book seeks to go beyond their narrow empirical confines by drawing samples from two different regions of India, separated by levels of development and historical context.

Spatial and temporal limitations are among the inevitable prices of empirical research. The most important body of evidence on which this book is based is drawn from detailed face-to-face interviews with local elites in Gujarat and Orissa during 1979–80. In contrast to the authoritarian interlude of 1975–7 or the large-scale drought and famine of the 1960s, this was a 'normal' year in both Gujarat and Orissa, where elected governments were busy restoring some of the damage done to Indian democracy during the period of authoritarian rule. Care has been taken to protect the study from these possible temporal limitations by stipulating a large time-span on the key questions where I have relied on the respondents' memories to speak in terms of the general situation 'as they have experienced it over the past ten or fifteen years'. (See the questionnaire and the discussion of field methodology in the appendix.) Also, where possible, I have relied on the respondents to place themselves in the context of regional history and secular trends of development leading to the present condition. Where feasible, the findings have been supplemented with evidence drawn from other regional studies for the sake of greater generality.

PLAN OF THE BOOK

The book takes its shape in the style and substance of the attitudes and political discourse of local leaders in Indian villages. These rural netas, in their role as the intermediaries between the society and the state, are the catalysts of social and economic change. The process of distribution of material resources and challenges to and modification of the norms of allocation are the substance of local politics in India. These themes are among the enduring concerns of this book.

Since the regional policy environment is of great importance to the politics of development at the local level, chapter two spells out the major factors influencing the pace and history of development in Gujarat and Orissa, and their location within the research design of the study. This is followed by the specification of the elements of design and the socio-demographic characteristics of the sample. Three substantive chapters then discuss the image of development from below, the perception of the role that local elites play in it, the strategies they adopt to involve the non-elites or to prevent them from playing a more prominent role and the complex political repertoire they have evolved in order to influence decision-makers at higher levels. The discussion sets the stage for some concluding observations on the state, democracy and development in India.

2

THE REGIONAL CONTEXT: THE SOCIAL AND ECONOMIC BACKGROUND OF RURAL DEVELOPMENT

THE OBJECTIVES

The chapter presents the social and institutional context of the process of development in Gujarat and Orissa. Its objective is to provide the background for the link between the central issue of the 'room for manoeuvre in the middle' and the field data on attitudes and behaviour of the gaon ka netas. This is done by first identifying the significant levels of developmental decision-making in India, particularly the regional government and the district administration. Next, the developmental organisations available within each district chosen for detailed study in Gujarat and Orissa are discussed in detail. The political process and the history of collective protest movements in each region is introduced in an effort to link the specific situations obtaining in Surat and Dhenkanal districts with the general framework of the book.[1]

The geographic location of a village, its natural resource base and its institutional linkage to the regional and national political arenas are important factors that affect the pace of social and economic change. The historical legacies of movements for political representation, collective protest and social mobilisation are of great importance as well. Without the knowledge of these essential facts, information about attitudes and behaviour of individuals at a given point of time can only provide suggestive but partial glimpses into the politics of development. To get the complete picture, therefore, we need to specify the institutional constraints and social networks in which individuals are ensconced. In a second and perhaps more important sense, the context is more than merely a backdrop against which individuals play out the drama of development.[2] Through their impact on public policy and the creation of new structures of opportunities, institutions play an active role in the unfolding of the central theme of development. As a crucial link between the locality and the nation, the regional government provides a useful vantage point for the observation of regional diversity in rural development. The chapter studies some of these issues through a comparative study of the institutional and historical process in Surat district in Gujarat and Dhenkanal in Orissa.

Since this chapter examines the linkages between the geographic context of development and the attitudes and behaviour of individuals placed within a specific context, it is useful at the outset to explain why such a relationship exists in the first place. One of the key aspects of development that interests us in this book is the element of choice that is realistically available to individuals and groups in order for them to define their own agendas of social and economic change and to give them concrete shape. The baseline which defines the point of departure here is the closed, rigid, stratified social system where most individuals lived out basically pre-determined roles and life-styles. Typically, the choices open to people in a village are affected as much by forces active within it as by factors present in higher-level arenas like the *taluka*, district, region and the national government. There is considerable variation across India's regions in these and other factors such as the scope for local initiative, financial allocation and the accountability of local administration to popular representatives.

The process of administrative implementation of central development plans opens up the possibility of wider participation and local initiative lower down the system.[3] Implementation involves the connected activities of communication, interpretation and transformation, all of which create room for manoeuvre for the social actors located in the interface between the development planner and the people at large.[4] The greater the emphasis on small-scale units of production, cooperatives and voluntary agencies in the development process, the more there is room for manoeuvre at lower levels of the system. Local autonomy and authority invested in the local arena are a cumulative and historically recursive process because, in most cases, the leverage gained by one generation is institutionalised into local norms, which are then handed down to the subsequent generations as a historical legacy.

The adoption of this perspective for the analysis of development in India is based on the assumption that local elites behave as 'rational actors', aware of the range of choices available to them and choosing from among them those that maximise their expected gain.[5] A second assumption made here refers to the influence of social class, a shorthand expression for social groups that are affected by a particular set of material conditions and life-style in roughly the same way, on the behaviour of the individual.[6] Understanding the process of social change brought about by the specific nature of historical development of the area is therefore crucial to our study. The structure of opportunities which at a given time tends to be socially discriminatory, favouring those who have a head-start in terms of their initial advantage, is yet another factor with serious implications for the attitudes and behaviour of individual netas.

Thus, there are a range of factors – spatial and temporal as well as those specific to individual leaders such as social status, the positions they occupy (or aspire to) in the local economy and politics, the supra-village political network of which they are a part or from which they are excluded – that affect the pace and direction of rural development. These assumptions question the moral economy view of Indian society which conceptualises the individual as an element of a largely undifferentiated tradition-bound milieu where every departure from conventional behaviour is met with disapproval.[7] Of these two rather different perspectives, the rational choice perspective is the less familiar view among the students of development in India. The more widely shared view is one where traditional social hierarchy plays a preponderant role in the determination of economic and political behaviour. The approach adopted in this book is closer to the rational choice paradigm, though a caveat should be added here. In its classic form, the rational choice model reduces society to a historically absurd sum of the revealed preferences of its individual members. In my view, the historical context within which the individual is placed and the social network of which they are a part, condition the structure of opportunities and the individual choice of alternatives. In a recursive process, both are, in turn, affected by the outcome of the aggregation of those individual preferences.[8] More than being merely a passive background, the political geography of

40

development thus emerges as an active player in the process of development.

THE REGIONAL GOVERNMENT AND POLICY ENVIRONMENT AS ELEMENTS OF THE NATIONAL DEVELOPMENT GRID

Despite their importance as an empirical reference point for local elites, it is not always easy to identify the historical and social contexts at the ground level in a form that is amenable to comparative analysis. Unfortunately for the social researcher, neither nature nor the process of national development arrange the data in neat, comparable categories. However, despite the difficulties it entails, a comparative format is indispensable for our enterprise, because the different regions of India (and the administrative districts within these regions) represent varying levels of resource endowment, administrative traditions, different historical time-scales of development, and widely different experiences of social mobility, political organisation and the growth of large-scale markets. These factors are important in influencing the pace and direction of rural development. Collectively, as indicators of state formation and the growth of markets, they are part of the larger theory of the structure and process of rural development.

In many important respects, the process of social and economic change had preceded the actual achievement of independence in 1947. The post-independence state, committed to economic growth, democracy and equality, exacerbated the pace of change and constituted an important reference point for the future course of rural development. Following independence, the central government, under the leadership of Jawaharlal Nehru, attempted to coordinate developmental policy through the central Planning Commission. However, the process of economic and social policy making was rendered extraordinarily complex and fragmented by India's federal structure which divided the power of decision making between the central government placed in Delhi and State governments responsible for regional administration. The adoption of a mixed economy instituted a public sector at the commanding heights of the economy but left enough scope for the operation of capitalist enterprises operating within the private sector.[9]

The responsibility for creating administrative harmony and coherent policy was left to extra-constitutional factors. During the formative years of the post-independence state lasting up to the mid 1960s, coordination of this process was facilitated by the fact that the Indian National Congress ruled not only at the centre but in practically all the regions.[10]

The Seventh Schedule of the Constitution of India specifies in the State List a number of subjects, including such important areas as agriculture, rural development and administration, health and education, for which State legislatures have the power to make laws. After independence, as the regional social forces gradually found their way into a position of authority within the regional government, this provision endowed them with the formal authority in determining the quantum and pace of rural development. Putatively, regional governments functioned under the authority of an omnipotent central government, constitutionally endowed with extraordinary powers of lawmaking that could, in principle, drastically

Table 2.1 Indicators of development: Gujarat and Orissa (the availability of infrastructural facilities in per cent of villages)

Indicator	National average %	Gujarat %	Orissa %
Railway station within 5 km	18.34	27.46	8.65
Metalled roads within 2 km	45.76	58.10	29.14
Bus stop within 2 km	40.26	71.18	26.45
Post office within 2 km	53.24	63.41	50.73
Primary school within 2 km	90.12	95.72	88.29
Dispensary within 2 km	24.59	26.96	13.92
Seeds store within 5 km	40.33	35.63	30.94
Agricultural pump repair within 5 km	18.76	21.34	5.86
Storage/warehouse within 5 km	20.72	25.70	8.09
Credit cooperative within 5 km	60.75	74.71	58.08
Bank within 5 km	39.88	50.87	24.24
Daily market within 2 km	14.81	20.76	10.72
*Hat** within 2 km	26.84	13.45	19.84
Fair Price grocery shop within 2 km	35.05	51.67	16.88
Electricity	33.36	37.42	18.48
Drinking water within village	92.61	93.09	86.26

Note * Large inter-village market which meets once or twice a week.
Source First economic census, as reported in Government of India (1985). The field operations of this census were carried out in the last quarter of 1977 in all the States except Nagaland and Sikkim where the census was conducted in 1978 and 1979 respectively.

compromise the federal character of the polity. However, in practice, the national government became dependent on the States for much of the substantive decision-making. The administrative machinery responsible for implementation was itself a part of the regional government. And most important of all, as the hegemonic position of the Congress party declined and regional parties started wielding the levers of government, the political initiatives for rural development shifted their location largely to the State capital.

Despite the vast potential for initiative in development policy making, in actual practice India's regional governments present great diversity in the extent to which they have succeeded in transforming the potential reality in the form of an administrative infrastructure (see table 2.1).

Additionally, in terms of their investment in development and the political machinery directly concerned with development, the record is uneven. The level of economic development itself, of which per capita income is a summary indicator, is indicative of this underlying diversity (see table 2.2).

Gujarat and Orissa belong, respectively, to categories of States

Table 2.2 Inter-State income differentials (per capita income as a percentage of the national average)

States	1960–1 %	1980–1 %
Punjab	110	176
Haryana	107	149
Maharashtra	134	145
Gujarat	**118**	**119***
West Bengal	127	98
Karnataka	97	86
Andhra Pradesh	90	84
Kerala	85	84
Rajasthan	76	81
Uttar Pradesh	82	81
Tamil Nadu	109	81
Assam	103	78
Orissa	**71**	**73***
Madhya Pradesh	85	72
Bihar	70	55

Note * Chosen for comparative study.
Source Calculated from CMIE estimates in 'Basic Statistics Relating to the Indian Economy, 1983' reported in Economist Intelligence Unit (1986), p 25.

which are placed on opposite sides of the national average of per capita income. They have been chosen here as representative of two different types of regional contexts of rural development. As policy environments for the process of development, they provide a striking contrast. Situated in the south eastern part of the country (see map 1.1, p 14), Orissa is in many respects one of the most backward regions of India. Some of the indicators of the 'quality of life' for Orissa are among the lowest in India as evidenced by the high infant mortality and low literacy rates. Two thirds of the population of Orissa live below the poverty level. Gujarat, the longstanding gateway for European and foreign capital to the western Indian hinterland, on the other hand, scores highly on each of these indicators of growth and development.

Important as it is, per capita income is only a gross indicator of average well being. It does not indicate the extent to which inequality persists. Therefore, while we may use these quantitative indicators of development as a gross measurement of the levels of development of the regions, we have to look at other factors to understand the full extent of welfare and the response of social policy to issues of justice and new political demands. In that respect, the most significant aspect where the two States present sharply contrasting experiences is that of social mobilisation and collective protest. A brief examination of this aspect of State politics is called for before we move on to the district level – the next stratum in the sampling process.

The dislocation caused in the social life of the village brought about by the process of development and the political protest that has accompanied the replacement of moral bonds by the cash nexus of a market economy have been studied on a comparative basis across India's regions by Frankel and Rao.[11] The political upheavals that the mobilisation of the lower strata have caused critically affect the policy environment and the pace of popular participation in development in the region. In this respect, Gujarat provides a richer base of secondary information than Orissa because the subject has been examined at length in that region.[12] Rather ironically, it was the 'anti-reservation' movement of the early 1980s in Gujarat which attracted national attention to the extensive provisions that the Janata government had already made in 1978 for the improvement of the material conditions of the lower social strata.[13] The agitation in 1981 was

44

by nature an upper-caste backlash against the attempts by the government to extend the scope of the policy of reservation by implementing the recommendations of the Second Backward Classes Commission, appointed by the Government of India. The Commission had recommended the reservation of jobs, places in institutions of higher education, particularly in medical and engineering schools, already implemented in the case of the Scheduled Castes and Scheduled Tribes, to the 'backward classes'. As the protagonists of the anti-reservation movement saw it, the attempts to further extend the scope of reservations, covering practically half of the total places available, would drastically reduce the traditional avenues of upward mobility for the upper strata. The anti-reservation movement, which raged intermittently for several years, leaving a trail of collective violence and caste and communal tension, reflected changes within the political system of Gujarat at a deeper level. As a matter of fact, the initiative by the government in 1980 to further extend the scope of redressive political action itself reflected this change in political support. Far from being a gratuitous act of political generosity, it was rather a politically expedient move, aimed at reinforcing its support among a coalition of social groups who could expect to benefit from this policy.

Paradoxical as it may sound, the radical challenge to the social base of power in Gujarat politics has come about as a result of peaceful political competition between sections of the upper social classes.[14] The phenomenon of intra-elite competition leading to the politicisation of previously underprivileged groups and, eventually, to the widening of the circle of participation, is by no means unique to Gujarat. The generality of the model can be appreciated from similar trends with regard to the mobilisation of the Nadars in Madras, Marathas in Maharashtra or the Jats in Uttar Pradesh.[15] The mobilisation of the Kshatriyas in Gujarat is illustrative of some of the basic changes that have come about in the distribution of power in Gujarat society. Unlike Kshatriyas in North India, the subcastes that came together under the broader classification of the Kshatriyas in Gujarat were considered socially backward and of low ritual status. Though one of the commentators attributes the phenomenon to the leadership of 'higher caste groups',[16] the organisational efforts of their own leadership should also be taken to account. The Gujarat Kshatriya Sabha (as a federation of various groups introduced as the 'Kshatriyas') emerged as an important support-structure of Congress in 1962 and 1967. In 1962 it shifted its support to boost the strength of the Swatantra party, a right-wing challenger of the Congress which eventually faded away from the political scene. The Congress, which was largely responsible for the demise of the Swatantra party, succeeded in achieving this objective by encouraging a rival Kshatriya organisation, the Kshatriya Seva Samaj of the backward and poor Bariyas. It further neutralised the political damage that the Swatantra party intended to inflect on it by forging an alliance between the Patel and Kshatriya communities. In 1972 the Kshatriya onslaught withered away before it could gather momentum and it has since then considerably weakened as a pressure group, only to resurface in a major political role in the 1980s, as a part of a broader alliance of backward social groups.

The impact of social mobility in Gujarat can be seen in a variety of ways, including, most prominently, changes in the social composition of the regional government. In the first cabinet of the newly formed State of Gujarat in 1960, there was hardly any presence of the lowest social stratum. By contrast, the Congress (I) government formed in June 1980 under the Chief Ministership of Madhav Singh Solanki had as many as thirteen ministers out of a total of twenty-two belonging to the Kshatriya, Harijan, Adivasi and Muslim communities. The political coalition of these communities, celebrated under the acronym of KHAM, signified a shift in the social location of power, from the upper reaches of the society which had long dominated the Congress movement in the State to the lower social strata. Data on caste distribution among members of the Gujarat Legislative Assembly are even more significant. The percentage of Members of the Legislative Assembly belonging to the Adivasi, Harijan and the Other Backward Classes groups went up from 22.6 per cent to 31.8 per cent between 1967 and 1980. The change is even more dramatic if we look at the Congress party (Congress (I) in 1980) alone. In this case, the corresponding figures go up from about 24 per cent to 37 per cent.[17] The pattern of ascendance of the lower social strata was also reflected at the panchayat level since December 1975. During the third, fourth and fifth panchayati raj elections held in 1975, 1980 and 1987 in Gujarat, the Kshatriyas and other backward castes displaced the Patidars, the traditional dominant elites, from positions of power in rural Gujarat.

By 1980 the mixed group of Scheduled Castes, Scheduled Tribes and the Backward Classes had started organising themselves politically, creating a sense of alarm among the groups which had long enjoyed political power. They were particularly concerned about the extension of the reservation of government posts to still more categories of people, thereby further restricting the number of places open for general competition. The mobilisation and counter mobilisation on the issue of affirmative action further exacerbated the tendency by social forces to reinforce their vertical and horizontal links. Evidence of this form of differential mobilisation, whereby specific social groups attach themselves to political organisations of their own or sympathetic to them, can be seen in the Khedut Samaj which united agrarian producers for better conditions.[18]

In contrast to the polarisation of Gujarat society on political lines, where relatively new organisations have transformed political discourse through the introduction of new concepts of sectional welfare, politics in Orissa have largely retained their traditional ways. With about 90 per cent of her population classified as rural and about three quarters of the workforce engaged in agriculture, the population of the State, compared to Gujarat, is predominantly rural. They live within an essentially agrarian economy where subsistence rather than capital-intensive, market-oriented agriculture is the norm. Also, in contrast to Gujarat and indeed to the dominant trend of politics in North and West India, differential mobilisation of the rural population on the lines of the *kisan* or *dalit* movements is not a major factor in Oriya politics. Politics at State level continues to be dominated by the rivalry among the upper social strata – mainly Brahmans and Karanas – for the relatively limited opportunities for upward mobility. This is seen from the preponderance of Brahmans in Nandini Satpathy's council of ministers and that of Karanas in J. B. Patnaik's first cabinet.[19] Once again, compared to Gujarat, the agricultural castes of Khandayats and Chasas, more visible at the district level, continue to play a minor role at the State level.[20] Orissa has had only one Khandayat Chief Minister, Nilamoni Routroy, during the Janata rule, and he could attain that office only through the blessings of his party leader, Biju Patnaik. Unlike North India, this did not herald the rise to political prominence of the intermediate castes (also known as Backward Classes) in the struggle for leadership in Orissa. Explanations for the relative absence of caste associations, particularly in view of similar developments in other parts of India, are many and complicated. One of the hypotheses which is of considerable interest to the main argument of this book is the continued presence in Orissa of an aspiration for upward social mobility through assimilation to the upper strata through the process of sanskritisation rather than striking out an independent path to status, power and wealth through horizontal mobilisation on the basis of ethnicity and communal solidarity.

In Gujarat the upward mobility of the lower strata has taken place in two historic stages. Many lower status groups first came together within the broad framework of a convenient label of Kshatriyas within which they shared ritual proximity. The Kshatriyas, a neo-caste, subsequently became an important political group in regional politics. This distinguishes the situation in Orissa from that in North and Western India where kisan movements, with the support of the intermediate cultivating castes, have emerged as an independent political force. Similar political formations are conspicuous by their absence in Orissa. The Khandayats of Orissa with their militia background and larger landholdings seek the status and influence of the Karanas or the Kshatriyas. Without the cementing force of a powerful kisan ideology, cutting across different peasant castes and landowning groups, the cultivating castes remain socially and politically fragmented. The potential political strength of the lower strata is further dissipated through social fragmentation within their own ranks. The Chasas and the dalit agricultural labourers are divided on caste lines, since the former put themselves above the latter in the social hierarchy. Artisan castes, such as weavers and blacksmiths, whose trades became less and less remunerative because of the steady intrusion of cheaper machine-made goods in the course of the colonial period, have suffered the most. The migrant labourers from Orissa who travel great distances searching for work in areas as far away as Assam or Punjab are usually of the Chasa, the artisan or the scheduled castes and the scheduled tribes.

48

Compared to Gujarat, Orissa lacks larger networks linking social and economic interests to political organisations. Instead, the consciousness of thwarted mobility attempts remain at a potential level, occasionally manifesting themselves as widespread, amorphous discontent, leading to sporadic outbreaks of lawlessness. The development of organisations and networks is a slow historic process. The contrasting experience of Gujarat and Orissa in this respect can be partly accounted for with reference to the history of the national movement. Generations of national leaders have used Gujarat as the testing ground of new concepts of justice and weapons of mass struggle. The national movement has acted as a major catalyst for raising consciousness and then cementing that consciousness into purposeful organisation. The Patidars were first drawn into politics during the Kheda Satyagraha (1917), the Ras Satyagraha (1923) and the Bardoli Satyagraha (1928) under Gandhi and Vallabhbhai Patel.[21] After independence, they gained in influence through links with the Congress party and the Swatantra and reinforced their position during the second panchayati raj elections of 1969.

Orissa, which has seen periodic outbreaks of protest against colonial rule and other forms of oppression induced by it, has for a variety of reasons stayed outside the ambit of the national movement.[22] Though the freedom movement in the coastal districts of Orissa had on occasions parted company with the national movement as a whole, they were more active than the hill districts which, during the colonial rule, were ruled by native Indian princes under the overall paramountcy of the British government. However, people living in these areas were not completely cut off from the freedom struggle. The State People's movement was in most cases both anti-colonial and anti-feudal, and as such drew repression from both the colonial state and the princely rulers. One of the puzzling facts of Oriya politics after independence is the rapidity with which the State People's movement disappeared, without leaving any enduring historical residue. Former princes of the Garhjat princely states appeared on the scene and took over the leadership of the new political arena with alacrity. After trying unsuccessfully for a while to create a central province with rulers from the princely states in the Madhya Bharat region, the Ganatantra Parishad, set up by the former princely rulers, became a major player in

Orissa politics, sharing power on several occasions. This party accounts for the different path taken by the Orissa Khandayats as compared to the Gujarat Kshatriyas. The Orissa Khandayats, who, compared to Gujarat Kshatriyas, have higher ritual status, sought political power, social mobility and material affluence within a relatively conservative social order. As the former Rajas have 'stooped to conquer', so the former subjects have looked upwards for bonds of solidarity rather than spreading horizontally like the Gujarat Kshatriyas. They have not tried, like the middle cultivating castes in North and West India, to seek political solidarity with the chasas whom they consider their social inferiors. Nor have they tried to go it alone and seek power on their own like the Gujarat Kshatriya Sabha.[23]

Rather than class differentiation or political mobilisation from below, occasional collaboration, alternating with confrontation, between the leaders of the Western Hill districts and the Eastern Coastal districts is the most decisive factor of Orissa politics. Following Mohanty and Mishra,

> In a peculiar way, the Congress has helped the Swatantra to maintain its dominance in Western Orissa. One or the other faction of Congress has always formed coalition governments with the Swatantra and its predecessor the Ganatantra Parishad from 1959 till June 1972 except during the 1961–1966 period. By sharing power with the Swatantra, the Congress has allowed that party to strengthen its power base.
>
> (Mohanty and Mishra (1976), p 240)

The Congress party in Orissa has not developed cohesive or mass organisations on the same scale as in Gujarat. Internal factional rivalry has prevented the party from developing a strong tradition of organisation and partisanship at the local level. As such, compared to Gujarat, both at the level of political discourse and organisation, Orissa has remained comparatively backward. The only major political campaigns which took place in Orissa in recent years are the student agitations and the campaign for a second steel plant in the State in July 1970. In organising the poor and the landless peasantry to change land relations, the rich-peasant dominated political parties of Orissa have not shown any interest. On the trade union front the organisational work by the parties has not gone beyond an elementary stage.[24] Lacking institutional avenues of articulation, popular protest and the consciousness of injustice remain dormant, occasionally bursting out in the form of sporadic violence.[25]

THE INSTITUTIONS CONNECTED WITH DEVELOPMENT AT THE DISTRICT LEVEL

While the regional governments constitute a major source of initiative in the making of policies relating to rural development, for historical and administrative reasons the district continues to be the ultimate territorial unit for the implementation of development policy. As a unit of administration, districts have deep historical roots and specific traditions. As more resources have been made available for development projects, the district has steadily gained in importance as a unit of development, planning and administration. Most important of all, this is the ultimate territorial unit where the officials of the state and representatives of the people meet as members of the *zilla parishad*, the highest decision-making body for the district.

The identification of a district in each of our two States was therefore the next logical step in our sampling strategy. However, the volume of development activity and infrastructural facilities vary from one district to another. Surat in Gujarat and Dhenkanal in Orissa were chosen as a 'modal' district in each region on the basis of district-level development in each region. Being at neither extreme, the study districts contained the essential characteristics of the policy environment of each State while at the same time retaining their specificity as administrative units.

It has already been suggested that the nature and extent of participation in development is greatly influenced by the institutional framework through which most development policy formulation and implementation take place. The institutional framework can promote as well as thwart individual motivation for participation in the development process. It operates through the rigidity or flexibility of the given set of rules and procedures, the opportunity structure it makes available to individuals and groups to intervene in the process of policy formulation and implementation, and the volume and quality of material resources they are able to generate for the purpose of development. However, both the institutional structure and the developmental infrastructure are products of historical forces. They evolve and take their specific shapes within a particular matrix of social, economic and political forces. The process of participation in development can be best understood against this larger socio-cultural, economic and political setting of the district.

SURAT DISTRICT: HISTORICAL BACKGROUND AND INSTITUTIONAL FACILITIES

Situated in South Gujarat, Surat district covers an area of 7745 km^2 and accounts for 3.95 per cent of the State's total geographic area. On its north and south lie, respectively, the districts of Bharuch and Valsad. Its eastern end is surrounded by Dhulia district of Maharashtra and the west by the Arabian sea (see map 2.1). The district can be divided into two parts: the eastern hilly tract is bounded on the north by the Satpura ranges and on the south by the Satmala Hills and the fertile alluvial plain of the Tapti river. The eastern hilly tract is also covered by thick forests in some places and is relatively backward. The eastern part of the district is predominantly tribal. Though it is rather poor in mineral resources, it has plenty of water resources with an average rainfall of about 1000 mm. Further contributing to its water resources are four major rivers, the Tapti, Kim, Mindhola and Purna, which flow through it. An

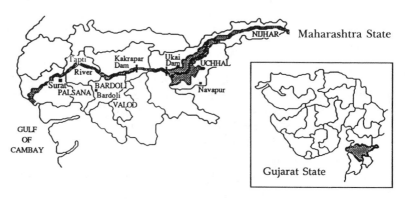

Map 2.1   Surat District

effective scheme of irrigation has harnessed some of the water resources for agricultural and industrial production.

The historical context

Surat has figured prominently in the political and commercial life of western India practically from the beginning of recorded history. Reference to the city of Surat has been made by Greek geographers as early as the first century after the birth of Christ, Surat. one of the greatest maritime cities of the Southern Peninsula, was one of the oldest entry points of seaborne commerce. The port of Surat enjoyed the place of pride during the sixteenth, seventeenth and the eighteenth centuries. Its decline came in the wake of the emergence of Bombay.

The Portuguese attacked Surat twice in a brief span of about two decades (between 1512 and 1531) in a vain effort to capture it. In 1573 Emperor Akbar captured the town and for nearly 160 years it remained under the administration of the officers appointed by the Mughal court. Surat enjoyed unbroken peace and became one of the first mercantile cities of India during the reign of Akbar, Jehangir and Shah Jahan. But the Portuguese remained the undisputed masters of the sea adjoining Surat. The arrival of the British early in the seventeenth century created great rivalry between several European contenders for the control of the ports of Gujarat, for, by this time, the Dutch and the French had also joined the competition for maritime trade, political influence and control over territory. Finally, with the capture of Surat by the British in 1759, the area passed under the rule of the East India Company. A collector, a judge and a magistrate duly appeared as visible symbols of the new authority. It should however be noted that Company rule did not extend to the entire area falling under the jurisdiction of the present district of Surat. For instance, Mandavi was under a Hindu Chief, Rander was under a Muslim Nawab and parts of Vyara taluka were under the Gaekwads who were erstwhile rulers of Baroda. Thus, administratively speaking, the present district of Surat has inherited a fairly diverse set of political traditions including Indian princely rule as well as colonial administration.

Under the impact of British rule, the city of Surat and its surrounding areas witnessed a substantial change in the economy. A variety of factors contributed to this change. One of the major factors was the growth of means of transport and communication. The construction of a railway line in 1860 and the building of a bridge (the Hope Bridge) on the Tapti in 1877 contributed greatly to trade and commerce. Closer links with the world outside also provided incentives for greater mobility and started the famous stream of Gujarati migration to British colonies in Africa. However, possibly thanks to close caste and communal ties, the migrants were not completely lost to the world that they left behind. Some of those who had migrated overseas eventually came back with fresh capital and experience and contributed to the development of their native villages. The presence of foreign contacts stimulated native talent and industry and continued to serve as an important catalyst for the growth of an enterprise culture.

Evidence of the rapid strides that the society and economy have taken in Gujarat, and particularly in Surat, can be seen in the demographic trends, literacy, agriculture as well as in the excellence and relative abundance of infrastructural facilities. The population of the district has almost doubled since independence. With an annual growth rate of 3.6 per cent, compared to 2.9 for the State and 2.5 for the country as a whole, the district has experienced something akin to a 'population explosion'. Population growth has been accompanied by migration, primarily from rural areas to the fast-growing urban centres.

Despite rapid urbanisation and industrial growth, agriculture continues to be the main occupation in the district. The agricultural sector gives an overall impression of polarisation between cultivators who own their land and agricultural workers. The mainstay of agriculture are the group of middle-level owner-cultivators, employing wage workers as well as family labour. Interestingly, Surat is the second district in the State and one of the few in the country where agricultural workers outnumber owner-cultivators. Among the owner-cultivators, there is a further stratification, with a large cluster of small farmers living cheek-by-jowl with the large- and middle-level cultivators. About 74 per cent of the farmers own less than 4 hectares of land and, even from among these, 52.4 per cent have less than 2 acres.

The major crops of the district are paddy, jowar, sheat, pulses, cotton, groundnut and sugarcane. The cultivation of sugarcane has received a boost in recent years due to the availability of irrigation facilities and the establishment of a few sugar factories. Agriculture has shown considerable improvement in the district, surpassing the other districts in the level of productivity in most of the major crops. Among the factors that have contributed to this are the development of infrastructural facilities like irrigation, credit, growth of large-scale markets, supply of imported seeds, fertilisers, availability of new farm and industrial tools, spare parts and repair shops. Concerted efforts are made for this purpose by various organisations under successive Five Year Plans. The Intensive Agriculture District Programme was launched in Surat during the Third Five Year Plan. It was meant to demonstrate the potential for increasing food production through a coordinated approach to agricultural development. This was followed by the launching of the High Yielding Varieties Programme in 1966–7. Subsequent innovations saw the emergence of the Small Farmers Development Agency (SFDA), aimed at ameliorating the condition of small and marginal farmers.

Agricultural development has been accompanied by a number of problems which need to be noted here. First, there is growing pressure on land. There is not much scope for further extension of the area under cultivation as 60 per cent of the geographic area is already under cultivation as compared to 42 per cent for the country as a whole. Ironically, though the introduction of cash crops and the availability of irrigation and credit facilities have rendered agriculture into a potentially lucrative occupation, a very large segment of the population engaged in agriculture, including agricultural workers as well as small and marginal farmers, are not in a position to take advantage of these possibilities. The introduction of the new technology has thus exacerbated the traditional conflict and tension.[26] At a different level, though the facilities of irrigation have grown significantly, the effective planning for optimum utilisation of the water potential with the help of water channels, land levelling and draining has not kept pace with the extension of irrigation facilities. This has brought about the problems of water-logging and degradation of cultivable land through increasing salinity. Some of the pressures on employment are taken off by further developments in the economy including the tertiary and the industrial sectors. Besides agriculture, dairy, poultry and fishery have also shown considerable growth in the district. This has helped by generating additional income and employment, besides providing new sources of nutritive food to the poorer sections of the society. There has been an equally significant industrial development in the district, and Surat ranks second in the State in this respect. But it has to be recognised that, as elsewhere in the country, industrial development has been rather lop-sided. As per the 1971 census, 83.5 per cent of the 6402 industrial units were based in Surat city alone, accounting for 71 per cent of all industrial workers.[27] However, the imbalance in the distribution of industrial units notwithstanding, a significant feature of industrialisation in Gujarat has been the growth of the small-scale sector, which has been an important source of employment generation. Spinning, weaving and textile processing alone account for about 43 per cent of registered factory employment. The other important industries in the district are diamond cutting, wood polishing, wood products and food products. Of particular interest are diamond cutting and carpet weaving, because they are making inroads into the rural areas.[28]

The cooperative movement

Economic development in Gujarat in general, and in Surat, Kheda and Mahesana districts in particular, has been accelerated by the cooperatives. The cooperatives have contributed a great deal to the economic development of the district in various ways. The development of cooperatives in the district could be traced as far back as 1908. The cooperatives, which were initially established for giving credit facilities, slowly extended to other spheres of production including marketing and transportation. The cooperatives have made notable contributions in sugar production, paper, dairy, poultry, cotton ginning, oil crushing, fisheries and housing. A host of cooperatives, in diverse branches of the economy such as housing cooperatives, services, cooperatives, consumer cooperatives, forest cooperatives and labour cooperatives, are growing evidence of their effectiveness as an important mode of economic organisation. The success of *Jungle Sahkari Mandalis*, cooperatives which specialise in the

56

collection and marketing of forest products run by tribal functionaries, is matched by few of its kind in the whole country. Although cooperatives have a long history of development in this region, their growth during the post-independence period has been phenomenal. The figures are revealing enough. The Surat District Cooperative Bank had a membership of 2503 institutions by 1976–7, with a number of branches spread throughout the district. There were 331 agriculture credit societies with 90,000 members, covering about 97 per cent of villages in the district. In the area of cotton alone, by 1976–7 there were ninety-nine primary cotton cooperatives and one cotton sellers' organisation. The rural cooperatives have been manned mainly by well-off farmers, mainly Patidars and Desais (Anabil Brahmins), while the forest cooperatives have contributed to the economic well-being of the educated tribals. Again, they have thrown up new elites and leadership among the tribals.[29]

Social services and infrastructural facilities

The impact of economic development can be directly felt by people through the expansion of social services like education, health, drinking water, housing and transport facilities. Reciprocally, economic development can be sustained and accelerated only if it is backed and supported by infrastructural facilities. Compared to the national average, Surat, partly for historical reasons, measures quite favourably from this point of view.

Educational development in the district has a long history of over 150 years. The initial impetus for the spread of education came from the efforts of Christian missionaries, the former princely rulers, voluntary organisations and Gandhian workers. The schools, both for boys and girls, were started in the district as early as 1842 and 1874 respectively. Even technical education was started quite early in the district. For instance, the Parekh Technical Institute was set up as early as 1878. In this predominantly tribal area of Gujarat, the Christian missionaries and voluntary agencies took a leading part in the spread of education during the pre-independence period. These efforts were further stepped up by them as well as by the government in the post-independence period. Consequently, educational facilities grew fast and the literacy rate was as high as 39 per cent in the district in the census of 1981. Unlike elsewhere in the country, Scheduled Castes and Tribes in Surat have not lagged behind in this respect. At a more basic level, education has not remained confined to the socially privileged or the urban population.

It should be noted that even the idea of compulsory free primary education was already known in the district as early as 1920. The Surat municipality had decided to give free education to children in the age group of six to eleven years. The scheme worked well over the years, and the 1951 census revealed that in the city 98.4 per cent of the children in the prescribed age group attended school. The rural areas did not lag behind. The district local board had introduced compulsory free primary education in 1946. Estimates based on the 1951 census indicated that about 63 per cent of the children in the age group of six to eleven years attended school in rural areas.

The record of educational development is quite impressive with 90 per cent of the villages in the district having a school. There was an increase in the number of primary schools from 1239 in 1965–6 to 1297 in 1969–70. An important feature of this development is that women did not lag behind. Of the total enrolment in 1969–70, 43.52 per cent were female. Further, the change seems to be more marked in the case of secondary education where the increase in the number of schools is of the order of 26.82 per cent and of enrolment 20.76 per cent during the same period.

Health services also have a long history. Modern medical facilities were introduced in the pre-independence period. For instance, a civil hospital was set up in Surat city as early as 1864. The Dayakar Malvi Hospital for Women and Children, the first of its kind in Gujarat, was started in 1895. A lepers' home and a T.B. hospital date back to 1927 and 1939 respectively. But most of these facilities were developed in urban areas and more particularly in the city of Surat. Patients from rural areas had to travel long distances to use these facilities. Developments since independence have sought to correct this imbalance to some extent. By 1975 there were nineteen primary health centres, to which were linked 111 health sub-centres. Besides, there were eighty dispensaries and twelve hospitals. But then, as the resources and the means to provide health care have increased, the sources of health hazard appear to have increased as well. A case in point is irrigation, which, besides spreading waterborne diseases, appears to have created a spurt in water-logging and malarial fever.

POLITICS AND SOCIAL MOBILITY

Surat has a sizeable Scheduled Caste and Scheduled Tribe population. The population of tribals is as high as 46.32 per cent of the total population of the district, and over one-fourth of the total tribal population of the State. The concentration of the tribal population is higher in the rural areas, where their percentage goes as high as 65. The Scheduled Castes are smaller in proportion, with the district average at 3.56 per cent. It is important to note, however, that together the Scheduled Tribes and Castes constitute close to a majority of the population.

The tribal population had more or less lived a fairly autonomous and self-contained existence before the establishment of the colonial rule. With the establishment of feudal rule, they were brought under the subjugation of people from the plains. Research into the social history of the Adivasi protest movements has shown how, over the years, they have been able to integrate themselves into the larger society and, starting from a position that was peripheral to the local political arena, have risen to a position of sharing power, under their own leadership.[30] The Scheduled Castes, particularly those like the Halpatis who depend upon agricultural wage labour as their principal occupation, appear to have done less well.[31] However, even in their destitution, the dalit population are not devoid of political means of resistance, or of political intervention for improving material conditions. The relatively high rate of literacy among the Scheduled population of the district, respectively at 45.23 per cent and 17.1 per cent for Scheduled Castes and Scheduled Tribes as against 27.74 per cent and 14.72 per cent for the State as a whole (according to the 1971 census), is one indicator of their upward mobility.

Gujarat in general and Surat in particular have a long tradition both in participation in institutional politics and direct political action through mass movements going back to pre-independence days. Surat municipality, founded in 1853, was one of the first in the country to bring civic responsibilities directly into the hands of those immediately affected by it. The Prajahit Vardhak Sabha, founded in 1882, took upon itself the task of promoting the interests of the people. This was one of the first organisations which provided a channel for political activities by Indians. The historic twenty-third session of the Indian National Congress, held at Surat in 1907, infused a spirit of nationalism and mass awakening among the people. The national movement had a particularly significant spill-over in terms of a tradition of social work among the underprivileged, for, in the wake of the national movement, many urban, educated outsiders took up residence among tribals in order to engage in the task of material and 'moral' upliftment of the downtrodden.

Even before the national movement gave an overarching framework for local protest movements, the people of Surat had perfected the art of taking to the streets to express a collective grievance and to demand redress. In 1844, the people had organised agitations against the introduction of Salt Tax. A similar protest was organised, in 1848, when an attempt was made to introduce the Bengal standard weights and meaures in Surat. So effective was the mobilisation that shops remained closed for seven days in protest, and a sum of Rs. 50,000 was collected to contest the case right up to the highest court in the United Kingdom. The government was compelled to change its decision.[32]

The national movement has further reinforced the tradition of popular agitation and mass involvement in politics. The Bardoli Satyagraha and Dandi March which took place in 1928 and 1930 respectively had contributed substantially to the mass awakening and politicisation of the people. This enthusiastic response of the people and the leaders of the area created conditions for the hosting in 1938 of the fifty-first session of the Congress at Vithal Nagar, Haripura in Bardoli Taluka. This event of national significance had a deep impact on the people of the area.

The social changes that took place in the region expressed themselves in the development of voluntary activities which created a network of institutions and induced a number of public-spirited workers to dedicate themselves to social service. It is probably to this sentiment for common and collective good that we can trace the growth and success of cooperative and panchayati raj in Gujarat. Some examples would indicate the variety and number of such voluntary organisations. Thus, a number of voluntary organisations like the Bardoli Ashram, Vedchhi Ashram, Halpati Seva Sangh, Valod Intensive Area Development Scheme, Manav Seva Sangh and a host of Ashram Shalas in remote villages grew and developed in different parts of the district. These institutions have not only taken up the task of initiating and organising developmental activities, particularly for the deprived and poorer sections of the populations, they also serve as an important link between the people and the government. This has enabled these institutions to make effective use of various programmes meant to benefit the people. In addition, these institutions have provided a social base for organising cooperatives, youth clubs, *mahila mandals* and *kisan sabhas*. Compared to Orissa, this impressive institutional network has given and added impetus to popular involvement with development policy formulation and implementation.

Behind the local political and administrative practices, one gets the impression of a certain communitarian ethos that persistently seeks to cut across the relatively narrow confines of caste and class. To some extent, this is an enduring legacy of the Freedom Movement in Gujarat which provided an overarching and integrative framework for local conflicts and movements over a long period. Following independence, the Congress party was able to build its electoral fortunes on this legacy. Indeed, so well entrenched were the foundations of the party in the social fabric, that, despite fluctuations of its electoral fortunes elsewhere in the country, Surat (table 2.3) continued to be an area of solid Congress support through the post-independence years.

Considering the number of seats it consistently managed to gain, it would appear from table 2.3 that the electoral base of the Congress remained unshaken up to 1972. Interestingly, the split of the Congress in 1969, which saw the crumbling of the Congress bastion in several Indian States, does not appear to have affected its electoral fortunes in any significant way in Surat in the Assembly elections of 1972, the first to take place after the split. In the Assembly elections of 1975, the Congress (R), which, under the leadership of Mrs Gandhi, presented a radical alternative to the rest of the Congress party led in Gujarat by the older leadership of Morarji Desai, made a concerted bid for the allegiance of lower social strata. The electoral results for the State as a whole, however, saw the opposition in a majority, leading to an opposition-led Janata Front government. However, the new Congress, which split again in 1978, had succeeded in organising around itself a new political coalition, whose social base under the acronym KHAM, had a distinctly lower-caste character. It swung back to power in 1980 and pushed the older Congress and its electoral allies, now firmly fixed in their public image to the upper social strata, to the opposition.

Table 2.3 Party performance in Assembly elections: Surat District

| Parties | Numbers of seats secured | | | |
	1962	*1967*	*1972*	*1975*
Congress	10	10	11	4
Swatantra	0	1	0	–
Congress (R)	–	–	0	7
Janata	–	–	–	–
Total	10	11	11	11

DHENKANAL DISTRICT

In comparison to the early growth of participatory institutions and mobilisation of social forces in Surat, Dhenkanal offers a study in contrast.[33] There is a marked difference in the level of development of the economy and infrastructure. Unlike in Surat where agriculture and the rural economy as a whole have experienced a revolution in the technology of production and management, the general norm of land relation and production in Dhenkanal continue to be geared to the subsistence economy, with the conspicuous exception of a few islands of 'progressive' farms using the new agricultural technology. Political life, keeping in line with the social fabric, is fragmented, with no mass organisations to provide a coordinating mechanism to the disparate social forces within the district nor to provide them with a voice at the State level by joining together with similar forces from other districts.

The difference in the historical paths of evolution that society and politics have followed in Dhenkanal provide an explanation for the general fragmentation of its social and political life as compared to the growth of a rich institutional and associational life in Surat. The larger part of the district, consisting of five erstwhile princely states, have not experienced the impact of the integrative effect of colonial rule. As such, minor differences in the administrative procedures persist to this day between the Angul sub-division which was ruled directly by the British and the rest of the district. Angul was a princely state prior to 1848 when its last ruler, Somnath Singh Jagdev, was deposed for alleged insubordination. The territory was then annexed by the East India Company. In 1936, when the separate province of Orissa was created, Angul was carved out as one of the districts. In 1948, after the integration of the princely states, the present district of Dhenkanal came into existence comprising the former states of Dhenkanal, Hindol, Talcher, Athmallik, Pal Lahara and Rairakhol. But in 1949, Rairakhol was taken out and merged with Sambalpur district (see map 2.2 of Dhenkanal).

Dhenkanal in a sense occupies the geographic centre of Orissa, being situated at the meeting point of the fertile coastal districts and the relatively backward western hill region. Its topography presents a balance of hills and plains. The district covers a vast area extending to 10,826 km^2, which, at the time

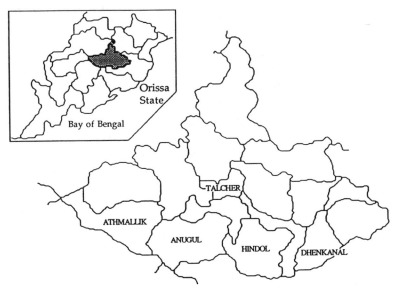

Map 2.2 Dhenkanal District

of fieldwork, occupied the seventh position among the thirteen districts of Orissa. The district is for the most part covered with forests, extending to over 53 per cent of its total area. The vast forest wealth has not, however, given rise to a complex of forest industries, exploitation of forest resources being limited to the primitive form of supplying timber, bamboo and other raw material to industries in the coastal districts of Orissa or beyond. Deforestation has already reached serious proportions but the land released in the process has not been put to alternative use. As one drives through the district along the national highway connecting the fertile coastal districts to the main urban centres of the sparsely populated and hilly districts of western Orissa, the view that greets the eye is of miles of uncultivated wastes that were once rich forests, but have been reduced to wasteland through the indiscriminate felling of trees.

The demographic characteristics

Unlike Surat, Dhenkanal, perhaps on account of its arrested economic growth, has not experienced a precipitous demographic growth. Compared to Surat, as well as the average of Orissa as a whole, the density of population of Dhenkanal is rather sparse. The district is predominantly rural, with 96 per cent of the population living in 3140 villages. The population of the district consists mainly of Hindus, with a small minority of Muslims and Christians. It is a multi-caste district, most communities being spread out through the district rather than being concentrated in specific areas. The Scheduled Caste and Tribal population is quite sizeable with, respectively, 16.76 per cent and 12.91 per cent belonging to the two communities. The predominant Scheduled Castes in the district are the Panas, who account for nearly 60 per cent of the Scheduled Caste population of the district. Literacy, at 27.8 per cent, is lower than Surat, but more than the average for Orissa. Though Oriya is the main language of the district, as many as thirty dialects remain the principal means of communication for the population. Combined with low literacy, the separate dialects contribute to the fragmentation of the political and social life of the district.

The economy

Agriculture is the main source of livelihood for the bulk of the population of the district, with cultivators and agricultural workers constituting up to 78 per cent of the working population. However, agriculture, being underdeveloped, offers limited opportunities for upward mobility. Though the Mahanadi and the Brahmani, the two main rivers of Orissa, flow through the district, their water resources have not been harnessed for irrigation. By the year 1973–4, only 7.23 per cent of the cultivated area of the district was under irrigation. As a result, most of the area has only *kharif* crops. The kharif crops include paddy, maize, jowar, millets and jute. *Rabi* crops, raised on a small area of the cultivated land with irrigation facilities, are composed mainly of wheat, kulthi, gram, mung, peas, til, mustard, tobacco and potatoes. The most important of all crops is rice which covers about 80 per cent of all cultivated area. Absent from the list are cash crops which, in Surat, have acted as an important catalyst of agricultural change.

The supplementary sources of occupation and income, like dairy, poultry and fishery, do not present an encouraging picture either. The district is poor in milk supply as Dhenkanal is yet to experience the kind of 'white revolution' that has brought a major source of income to dairy farmers in Gujarat. Unlike in Surat, the cooperatives, which organise credit, the collection of milk, the supply of fodder, and provide veterinary services, are almost nonexistent in Dhenkanal.

The situation as regards other specialised forms of agriculture such as poultry or fishery is comparable to dairy farming. We have the same scenario of 'model' units, set up under government auspices, operating over a considerable stretch of time without being able to spread out, thanks largely to the absence of the fortuitous combination of entrepreneurship, private capital and local markets that have resulted in the large-scale adaptation of these specialised and supplementary forms of agriculture in Gujarat. Thus, a State poultry farm, the only one of its kind, was started at Angul during 1951–2. Besides supplying breeding birds, hatching eggs and table birds, this farm acts as a demonstration centre for the rearing of improved breeds. A small poultry demonstration centre has been established at Talcher. The centre supplies poultry feed in the area.

The rearing of chickens in the district as a whole, however, is largely done for personal consumption and very little of it is commercially developed. There is a general preference for country breeds as they are easily available throughout the district and their rearing is not difficult. There are growing attempts by the government and the nationalised banks to develop poultry farming, but so far only a tiny fraction of the full potential has been tapped.[34]

The experience of dairy farming where government initiative and investment have not been matched by a significant response from the society is repeated in the area of fisheries. Efforts to develop fisheries were started as early as 1947. After three decades the record is far from impressive, the causes of poor growth being attributed to the lack of storing and transport facilities in the area. In addition to the district fisheries office at Dhenkanal and a centre at Angul, twelve fish centres were opened in different parts of the district. Besides, two research centres, one in Angul and another in Dhenkanal, were set up for developing suitable fish breeding centres in different parts of the district. With the efforts of the fisheries department and the research units, some innovations have been made in fishing methods and the quality of fish. By and large, however, the present techniques continue to be traditional. The main stumbling blocks have been the lack of storage and marketing facilities.[35]

While the growth of agriculture and agro-industries is undoubtedly important, the historical experience of development suggests that a dent can be made on the hardcore of the problems of the economy and employment through industrialisation. However, the handful of large-scale factories set up in the public sector remain in spendid isolation from the economy and the general production in the district where technology, credit, marketing and management facilities, compared to Gujarat, remain at a fairly basic level. The only industrial units one comes across are traditional small-scale and cottage industries such as carpentry, handloom, pottery, bamboo basket and mat making, oil crushing, smithies and molasses making. As a whole, instead of growing and expanding, these are on the decline. The reasons cited to account for this are quite revealing. The cause most often cited is the general decline in the demand of these goods as their substitutes are available at much cheaper

rates.[36] Apparently, the goods produced by small-scale industries cannot withstand the competition with the large-scale
industrial sector and large-scale production. Economic viability
poses a serious threat to the survival of the small-scale industries.
Also, capital and raw material have become scarce for the small-
scale and cottage industries.

The interview material suggests some interesting insights
into the arrested industrialisation of the area. It should be
remembered that the small-scale industrial units of Dhenkanal
originated in response to local markets, and had largely had
to cope with a limited supply of raw material and limited
local demand. The intricate system of tariff barriers and administrative obstacles that princely India offered to the outsider
had provided a protection to local industry from outside
competition. Organised mostly as traditional crafts, they had felt
neither the need for nor the impact of modernisation. So, when
the integration of princely states removed at one stroke the
protective barriers, they experienced a collective crash, as the
market was suddenly flooded with more competitive goods from
outside the district.

The organisational problems involved with modernisation
and balanced industrial growth were solved to a large extent
by the cooperative movement in Surat.[37] These cooperative
societies not only brought the producers together, but organised
them to operate at a level and scale whereby they could
safeguard their economic interests. However, despite official
encouragements, the cooperative sector has not experienced
anything similar to Surat. The ultimate beneficiaries themselves
express deep scepticism and cynicism towards the possible
utility of cooperatives. The opinion of a Dhenkanal farmer is
quite revealing: 'Cooperatives,' he lamented, 'are merely paper
organisations and have been floated by vested interests to service
their own ends. This is the easiest way for them to collect money
both from the people and the government and to use it for
personal gain.'[38] Thus, cooperatives which have given a boost
to rural economy and created conditions for widespread
participation in Surat did not grow in Dhenkanal in a similar
way. Cooperatives not only helped in pooling material resources
for economic gains but also provided a social base for developmental efforts in Surat. The pooling of human and material
resources, which could have promoted popular participation

and accelerated the pace of development in Dhenkanal through cooperatives, was arrested by unimaginative and poor leadership which contributed to a negative image of the movement as a whole.

Social services and infrastructural facilities

There was a certain degree of rivalry in princely India about the setting up of showpiece model schools. As early as 1868, Maharaja Bhagirathi Mahindra Bahadur of Dhenkanal established a Middle English School in Dhenkanal town. The school was upgraded to a high school in 1896. The rulers of other princely states, not to be outdone, soon followed suit, with similar projects of their own. But the royal initiative did not go much further beyond the setting up of the token schools. No major initiative was taken for the removal of primary illiteracy. So, at independence, the district could boast four high schools and a low rate of literacy, with abysmally low figures when it came to female literacy (2.5 per cent in 1951) and low literacy among the scheduled population (1.1 and 10.1 per cent respectively for the Scheduled Castes and Scheduled Tribes according to the census of 1961).

Compared to education, health and medical facilities were in a worse situation. In fact, the modern medical system did not enter the territories of the princely rulers in any significant way before independence; and no vital statistics relating to birth rate, death rate and patients suffering from various diseases were recorded until 1952. One gets the impression from district gazetteers though that diseases like malaria, dysentery, typhoid, T.B. and filaria were quite rampant in various parts of the district. Perhaps, as a result, preventive measures introduced after independence have had some spectacular results. For example, following measures for malaria eradication, there occurred a definite decline in the incidence of the disease in the district. From over 21,000 cases in 1962 it came down to only 5000 cases in 1969. But health care remains a priority area for the district. Certain statistics of illness are quite suggestive. For instance, cases of typhoid increased from 675 in 1962 to over 1600 in 1969, filaria from 1160 in 1962 to 2686 in 1969 and T.B. from 335 in 1962 to 1855 in 1969.

The uncertain legacy of the State People's Movement

Though sporadic uprisings against excessive oppression and highhandedness are known to have occurred in different parts of Dhenkanal during the period following the establishment of British suzerainty, the freedom movement which swept through the country during the 1920s did not make much headway in the area until late in the 1930s. The Dhenkanal *District Gazetteer* reports two separate incidents which marked the commencement of the movement. Though not consciously coordinated, the agitations in Dhenkanal and Talcher appear to have influenced one another. In Dhenkanal, the *Gazetteer* reports that the authorities of the princely state arrested a number of agitators on the 11th September, 1938 and, when large groups of people protested against this arrest, fire was opened to disperse them, as a result of which many people were seriously wounded. The situation after that became very tense and 'for sometime it went out of control'.[39] The Talcher movement took a leaf out of Gandhi's book in its choice of techniques of agitation.

The Talcher *prajamandal* demanded recognition of their fundamental rights, such as, right to form associations and hold meetings, abolition of forced labour and forced gifts and modifications of Tenancy rights and Forest Laws. The Raja of Talcher tried to suppress the political ferment by following repressive measures and the people launched a new type of non-violent challenge against his maladministration. Large numbers of people left Talcher and took shelter in the neighbouring British territory of Angul. It has been estimated that about 65,000 people out of a total of 85,000 left the state.[40]

The agitation in Dhenkanal and Talchar appears to have spread gradually to the other States in the form of a general no-rent campaign. The height of the movement was marked by the celebration of the All-Orissa Garhjat day on the 29th October, 1938. The emotionally charged period saw fresh skirmishes between the agitators, reinforced by batches of volunteers from Cuttack and the forces of law and order of the native rulers. The arrest of the ring leaders, including many Satyagrahis from Cuttack, failed to reduce the tempo of the movement which saw further groups of refugees from the native states heading for British-administered Angul. The administrative problem caused by the unprecedented exodus into British territory caused concern at higher levels. A conference was called in Angul on the 21st March, 1939, attended by the Revenue Commissioner of Orissa, the Assistant Political Agent and representatives of the Congress as well as of the refugees.[41] No immediate results came out of the conference in the face of the intransigence of the Raja of Talcher. But, as a spin-off, the distant leaders pulled off their troops, with Mahatma Gandhi instructing the agitators to withhold satyagraha and to concentrate on 'constitutional agitation for the redress of their grievances', and the Political Department 'advising the rulers to adopt conciliatory attitudes'.[42] The consequence of all this was the proclamation of constitutional reforms by Dhenkanal and Talcher in June, 1939 which considerably improved the political atmosphere. Ultimately, the lingering residue of the agitation subsided as the last of the refugees headed home at the approach of the paddy season.

The conciliatory gestures of the princely rulers appear only to have given a further boost to agitation. By then, the late-awakening freedom movement in the Garhjat had linked up with the national movement and Congressmen from Cuttack were now available to keep the momentum going. The State People's Movement had received the official blessing of the Indian National Congress in the Haripura session of 1938. The following year, the All-India State People's Conference met at Ludhiana and elected Pandit Jawaharlal Nehru as its president and Dr. Pattabhi Sitaramayya, then President of the Indian National Congress, as its Vice-President. This conference declared that the struggle of the States' peoples should be carried on under the guidance of the Congress. The merger of the two separate movements were consummated at the height of the Quit India Movement of 1942. With senior Congress leaders under arrest, prajamandal movements in several princely states rose in a final encounter with the forces of the native rulers. On this occasion, the war-weary British government, not disposed to tolerating any distractions from the war effort, was not prepared as on previous occasions to prevail upon the native rulers to live up to their constitutional responsibility. British forces now reinforced the overstretched native police in ruthlessly suppressing the agitation, in the process making no distinction between Congressmen from outside the State and local agitators.

In this atmosphere of splendid harmony of interest, the emotional distinction between Garhjat and Mogulbandi parts of Orissa were momentarily obliterated. Local heroes like the twelve year old Baji Raut, killed in an earlier encounter with the police, were elevated to the regional pantheon of Freedom Fighters and would continue to be part of folk heroes of the national struggle for independence in Orissa. But in retrospect, independence and the merger of the native states with the State of Orissa appear to have come too soon for the native movement to be institutionalised into a political network. The veneer of unity that had dominated the period of struggle fell apart when the elections were announced. The nomination of Congressmen from the Mogulbandi, who were perceived to have parachuted themselves onto the local struggle, was resented by the leaders of local origin who, eventually, moved out of the Congress party.[43] The fragmentation was repeated in successive elections as former agitators made common cause with former rulers against the Congress party under the banner of the Ganatantra Parishad, a new right-wing, regional party that attracted wide support in the former principalities of western Orissa (see table 2.4). As an ultimate irony, in the parliamentary elections of 1977 where Mrs Gandhi's Congress party paid the price for the imposition of the Emergency, the former King of Dhenkanal

Table 2.4 Party performance in Assembly elections: Dhenkanal District

Parties	1952	1957	1961	1967	1971	1974	1977
SSP	0	0	0	1	0	0	–
Swatantra	–	0	0	3	0	0	–
Communist	2	1	0	0	0	0	0
Jan Congress	–	–	0	4	1	1	–
Congress	5	1	4	0	0	0	0
Ganatantra Parishad	–	5	4	–	–	–	–
Utkal Congress	–	–	–	–	3	1	–
Congress (R)	–	–	–	–	4	6	0
Janata	–	–	–	–	–	–	8
Independent	1	1	0	0	0	0	0
Total	8	8	8	8	8	8	8

was nominated by the Congress party to fight a former Freedom Fighter who stood as the Janata candidate.

In the folk memory, the freedom movement in Dhenkanal survives as a rather heady period when ordinary men and women rose in a body against the might of the oppressive King and the colonial state. Beyond that, there are not any concrete achievements that one can point to. The princely order came to an end as a result of negotiations in Delhi and Cuttack between Sardar Patel and the representatives of the princely rulers, events over which the local population had little control. The political mobilisation during the uprising did not leave any enduring legacy in terms of party building, except for contributing to the radicalisation of a fragmented political culture.

CONCLUSION

The main objective of the chapter was to provide an introduction to the social and historical context in which the local elites operate. The various strands of the foregoing discussion would help us compare Surat and Dhenkanal, mainly highlighting the aspects of the society and economy that act as constraints on the alternatives available to local leaders and the strategic choices they make within the specific model of development. It would be useful briefly to recapitulate the points of comparison.

In the first place, the struggle launched in Surat to fight the repression of the colonial rule was linked to the reform movement and subsequently with the national struggle for independence. In the process, the movement acquired an enduring mass base. Bardoli Satyagraha and the Dandi March, the two prominent movements held in the area, created political awakening among the people and inculcated a tradition of local leadership and organisation for a common cause. The concrete achievements credited to the movement bred a feeling of self-confidence in the participants in the fight against repression and exploitation. The sense of efficacy, the aspirations for upward mobility and an instrumental view of authority provided a psychological base for active mass involvement in the developmental process set in motion after independence. In Dhenkanal, on the other hand, unrelieved feudal repression practically up to independence did not in any significant way alter the traditional image of authority as distant and necessarily exploitative. The outbreak of periodic uprisings belie the general image of a passive and diffident population. But the sporadic nature of the anti-state movement and their short span compared to Surat did not create a mass base or enduring political network. General attitudes towards authority continued to be deferential and manipulative rather than instrumental, combined with a sense of individual efficacy.

In the second place, the geographic location of Surat, which accounts for its much greater integration with a vast commercial hinterland and much greater volume of commercial trans-actions, has deeply affected both the quantum and pace of development and the process of participation. The location of Surat on the coast and its importance as a seaport are of crucial importance. Surat was the first city where the British East India Company established its headquarters. It was exposed to the west, its ideas and liberalism much before the rest of the country. It emerged in the country as the second 'renaissant' city, next only to Calcutta, during the nineteenth century. The western railway line between Bombay and Delhi, passing through the central plain, and the Tapti valley railway, passing through the eastern forest belt from Surat to Bhusabal, con-nected Surat with the central railway to Calcutta in the east and up to Delhi and further in the north. The early link was of considerable commercial and cultural value. The regular movement of goods and people introduced many new ideas. It also established social and commercial networks, stretching to India's capital cities and beyond. Moreover, Gujarati talent and capital did not always leave the homeland with a one-way ticket; it was not uncommon to find people who have returned from a comfortable life abroad to settle down in their native village and enrich its cultural and material life with new innovations. Dhenkanal, which remained in relative cultural and geographic isolation practically up to independence, started with a compara-tively more parochial worldview and without the advantage of far-flung commercial and cultural networks.

In the third place, a wide institutional network had developed in Surat to sustain and strengthen the reform movements and the freedom struggle, initiated by several public-spirited persons and organisations like the Swaraj Ashram at Bardoli and the Vedchi Ashram, with sub-centres connecting them to remote villages like Valod, Varad and Sarbhon. In addition to their direct contributions to the development of the areas, they provided a tradition and experience for voluntary action and trained many workers to initiate and promote such efforts. Consequently, one finds a considerable number of voluntary initiatives reflected in developmental activities like the management of schools and the setting up and running of *balvadis*, *yuvak mandals*, kisan mandals, mahila mandals and a variety of cooperative societies in Surat. There is ample evidence in village studies to suggest that these institutions were started and sustained by voluntary initiative. In the absence of any strong base for voluntary work in Dhenkanal, voluntary organisations of the kind that are found in Surat either do not exist in Dhenkanal or are seen merely as paper organisations, floated by vested interests to serve their own ends.

The widely different experience as regards the cooperative movement deserves special mention in view of its importance as a key vehicle for the activities of local elites. The experience in the initiation and management of voluntary organisations in Surat has been extremely useful for the rapid proliferation of the cooperative movement. Surat offers many kinds of cooperatives, including credit cooperatives, labour cooperatives, milk cooperatives, forest cooperatives (*jangal mandalis*), weavers' cooperatives (*vankar mandalis*), leather workers' cooperatives and so on. These cooperatives provide a strong non-governmental institutional base for implementing developmental programmes initiated since independence. But in Dhenkanal there was at best a very limited experience of managing voluntary organisations. Both the organisational skills and the social base required to build a viable cooperative movement were missing. The cooperatives set up with government help covered a limited field and were mainly service cooperatives. These were not managed effectively.

Finally, Surat, which has historically attracted major national and regional leaders, represents a different leadership tradition from that of Dhenkanal. The institutional network and instrumental attitude towards authority in Surat are to a certain extent the products of innovative and enterprising leadership. Local reform movements and political activities attracted the attention of some of the national leaders like Mahatma Gandhi and Sardar Vallabhbhai Patel, under whose influence many people became actively involved with the national movement and settled down in different parts of Surat. In fact, so strong and assertive did the local leadership become at times that it could oblige even a national leader of Gandhi's stature to submit to its wishes. These workers not only provided the required local leadership to the movement; they were readily available for managing the developmental programmes initiated in the post-independence period. This is particularly significant in the case of many tribal leaders occupying positions of responsibility in the panchayati raj structure who began their political career in voluntary organisations or in Ashramshalas.[44]

In comparison, the institutional and political base from which leaders are drawn was historically weak in Dhenkanal. Even from this limited group of leaders, thanks to intense political fragmentation, only a few were available to mobilise new social forces and integrate them to the state-sponsored developmental initiatives. In the process, the places in these institutions were filled by people who neither had the requisite skills in political management nor could count on a mass following. As a result, the performance of these institutions in Dhenkanal was well below expectation, which further lowered their legitimacy. In striking contrast to Surat, panchayati raj in Dhenkanal remained moribund and faction-ridden, rather than generating energy and enthusiasm through developmental action and creating a convenient base from which to launch political careers at higher levels. The subsequent chapters will examine the legacy of the contrasting historical experience of development and social mobilisation which provide an important insight into the nature, pace and direction of social and economic change in Gujarat and Orissa.

3

THE ELEMENTS OF DESIGN

THE OBJECTIVES

The main objective of this chapter is to move in the direction of empirical arguments in order to substantiate the abstract and analytical model presented in the introduction. Detailed, face-to-face interviews with over 200 rural netas from Gujarat and Orissa constitute the main body of evidence on which these substantive arguments are based. The research design elaborated in this chapter has the specific function of identifying these local elites in the rural setting for the purpose of detailed study. In addition to the constitution of this sample, the second objective of this chapter is to analyse the social origin of local netas, and to examine the paths they take to reach their social, economic and political objectives, and to infer from their social composition the impact of rural development on the local power structure. Since the theoretical edifice proposed in the introductory chapter is national in scope, the objective is to identify a sample of local elites which reflects the diversity of the field situation prevailing in rural India. In order to select this sample, we need first of all to discuss how to recognise the individual netas in the field situation.

The gaon ka netas, as indicated earlier, are not mere political operators. They are men (and infrequently, though increasingly, women) of a certain standing and influence in the village. They are essentially people in a leadership position within the village, but the fact that they act as the interface of the village and the world beyond it gives them public visibility outside the village as well. However, not all public persons present in the village qualify for the status of gaon ka neta. It is important to distinguish them from other public persons

76

present on the scene, notably, the *dalal, mamlatdar* or the *touter* – political operators of low social esteem and dubious legitimacy – and the agitator, who is a respected figure on the local scene but does not form part of an enduring social category.[1] They are known under a variety of appelations in the literature on rural development in India. They are 'men on the spot who act as interpreters of the higher level leaders and their links with the people'.[2] They are equivalent in some respects to 'brokers'[3] and 'fixers'[4] with whom they share some essential characteristics.

As suggested earlier, the crucial feature that distinguishes local elites from bureaucratic decision-makers and political leaders at higher level and other villagers is their role as intermediaries between the two. The epithet of gaon ka neta can of course be a misnomer, for one is likely to come across people whom the whole village respects but who are past their prime as netas. Despite the high esteem and exaggerated respect in which they are held, particularly by those with ambitions of their own, potential clients – people looking for contacts outside the village or outsiders seeking an entry to the village arena – no longer come to them. It is possible to take a judicious decision to exclude such *eminences grises* from the sample, for, with some field experience one acquires the skill to recognise honorific titles with a hollow ring to them. It is, however, harder to come to a clear conclusion in the case of leaders of specific groups or communities whose motives and status are contested by others in the village. An aggressive, up-and-coming leader of former untouchables may be derided as a touter and a charlatan by members of upper castes, whose leadership qualities are nevertheless much appreciated by people from his social strata. Such a person will qualify as one of our rural netas, though some further questioning, particularly of who comes to him and whom he contacts, is necessary before a firm decision can be taken in this case.

The social origin of local elites has changed significantly since the introduction of universal adult franchise. The decentralisation of power to the regional and local level and the creation of new administrative and political institutions like the panchayati raj structure with locally elected officials, have given teeth to the concept of local accountability of power. They have also provided the incentive for greater political participation and mass involvement with the process of development. As a result of these changes, the local netas in rural India to-day, compared to the old-style social notables, are not necessarily highly born. Nor is their position the necessary outcome of social origin, education, great wealth, or ancient lineage. Their power derives from their ability to present themselves as indispensable for transactions by the villagers with outside authorities and representatives of the state, the market and voluntary and non-governmental organisations. The transactions can range between those that are essentially for the personal benefit of the 'client' or for collective welfare, involving the implementation of development projects. In a more covert way, part of their standing derives from the potential threat they pose to public order through non-compliance with the wishes of the state and, more seriously, through incitement to open rebellion. However, the recognition granted to them by the state, society and the market as well as members of the village dependent on their transactional skills is not unmixed with an element of envy and resentment.

> For the peasants these are the men who know where to get a licence for a shotgun, how to get a real injection in the hospital instead of distilled water, how to get the file of a court case moved from the bottom of the list to the top or how to keep the file out of the court's hands until one of the litigants gives up in despair or runs out of money, and a variety of other ways of 'fixing', virtually all of which are normatively forbidden in the rule of the bureaucracy, being considered corrupt.
>
> (Bailey (1963) p 41)

But each of these services is provided for a consideration: the material exchange that must precede or follow the act robs the power of the neta of the mystique that is the essence of the moral authority of a superior. Through its own act of demystification, the slightly shop-soiled authority of the gaon ka neta also brings power within the grasp of ordinary people.

Though the gaon ka neta is a recognisable social category, being a local elite is not a customary 'occupation' and, as such, there is not a particular *jati* that corresponds to it. However, though they are bereft of a traditional ritual category, they are not devoid of a social identity altogether. Their role and function provide plenty of indications of their place in the social matrix. Bailey's vivid prose describing an Oriya broker conveys the sense of one of the profiles of the neta:

> He has no degree, no matriculation even; he cannot speak English; he is not in Government service. It is true that he has been successful in the world outside the village, and relatively he is very rich, but at the same time he is, so to speak, promoted out of the ranks.
>
> (Bailey (1963), p 62)

Because of the many functions and attributes that local elites share with the 'broker', it is important to emphasise their differences so as not to lose their distinctiveness as a category of political actors. Broker is a generic name: one expects to find him under one appelation or another, securely settled as a 'facilitator',[5] at the junction of two arenas or the meeting point of two different political idioms. But the gaon ka neta is specific to the local arena. Though their horizons stretch beyond the physical limits of the village, the local elite ordinarily reside in the village. As such, the term is specific to the local level of Indian politics. It is quite possible that they might use their position as a spring board for a similar role in the taluka or even the district arena. In that case, however, they can no longer be considered a local elite. Bailey describes the predicament of a broker who seemed to be heading in that direction:

> although he still has a house and lands in the village, most of his time is spent in Phulbani [the district headquarters]. Indeed, he could not be a successful broker for Bisipara people if he did not live in Phulbani. But his absence means that he is cut off from the day-to-day affairs of the village, and, little by little, the villagers are beginning to think of him as a Phulbani man, rather than a man of Bisipara.
>
> (Bailey (1963), p 62)

The second, critical difference consists in the self-perception of the neta and his or her public profile as a norm interpreter, one who might accord legitimacy to political norms coming from higher levels of the system by adapting them to the local situation, or question the authority of existing norms and replace them with alternative norms in whose making them and others like them have a voice. The gaon ka neta is above all a leader of the village, kin or community, a representative of the people in a local institution, somebody to whom others look up to not only for the delivery of tangible goods, but for help and advice in coming to terms with the new world of modern technology, legislation, norms of egalitarianism, citizenship and entitlement. Finally, local elites also create new norms, often at considerable risk to their power and social standing. They set precedents and, building on past precedents, they contribute to the creation of new political traditions of protest and participation. Their authority derives from their ability to represent collective interests, though the motives behind setting themselves up in this capacity may derive as much out of a desire to do good to the community as to improve their own material situation. In the ruthlessly competitive world of local politics, there are few sentiments or permanent loyalties, independent of the ability to deliver the goods. These considerations go into the making and unmaking of a neta. Underneath the placid and apparently immobile façade of the Indian village, the gaon ka netas are thus more than merely the chorus line in the drama of a fast-changing political landscape.

THE PERSONAL AND SOCIAL ATTRIBUTES OF LOCAL ELITES

The research design elaborated in this chapter has the difficult task of capturing a still picture of a dynamic political reality on the basis of a representative sample of rural netas. Towards this end, the preceding discussion offers some indications of the social profile of the local elites we need to identify. For the purpose of sampling, three important factors have to be taken into consideration. These include the element of 'rootedness' of the gaon ka netas, their role and function as a window of the village to the world and the world to the village, and, above all, their transactional relations within and beyond the village. These attributes are rendered rather difficult to pin down in practice because of the fact that our quarry consists of 'born men of the village [who] have chosen to become partial outsiders'.[6] Both metaphorically and literally, they are Janus-faced; they continue a long tradition of 'facing in both directions at the same time' in their function as the intermediaries for the modern state and the traditional society. They derive their political power through a combination of two distinct yet related attributes.

80

With regard to the village, they draw their legitimacy and power by virtue of their singularity as individual actors. And yet, *vis à vis* the state with its commitment to social, economic and political justice, and 'rural upliftment',[7] local elites are *par excellence* the advocates of group interest and sectional welfare. For local elites, both these elements – their local roots and their character as the representatives of local and sectional interests – are important in their self-definition as an integral part of village life.[8]

The research design, in its attempts to pin down a group local elites representative of rural India, retains this duality of focus that was already alluded to in the introduction. Our sample of rural netas consists of people who are first and foremost members of the intimate, face-to-face world of the village, bound by ties of caste and kin to people of the village. But they are also spokesmen for the village and of sectional and class interests, having been invested with the role of representatives for transactional purposes by their actual and potential clients. As such, in the elaboration of the empirical instruments, particularly in the identification of the sample, close attention is paid to the element of 'rootedness' of the local elites as well as to their role as 'social actors'.[9] Both objectives are achieved through the use of the reputational approach.[10]

The gaon ka netas are the visible tip of the iceberg of a complex series of exchanges and interactions which form part of the process of development (see figure 1.2, p. 20). The focus of the sample is to extrapolate our understanding of the larger process from a detailed study of their attitudes and behaviour, and to identify the variations across the cleavages of social class and region. As such, the sampling process has to take into consideration the appropriate comparative dimension and tap some of the diversity of India. The nature and course of rural development is deeply influenced by the policies of the regional government and the district administration, the latter in some cases with a long history of administrative continuity going back to the colonial period. In order to take these factors into account, we have chosen the regional government and the administrative district as two intervening levels in the process of sampling.

In view of the geographic immensity and social complexity of India, the construction of a representative sample of local elites is a daunting task. However, the selection of a sample is less formidable than it might appear at the first glance. The process of sampling is made easier by the dual focus of the study, which helps us incorporate both geographic diversity as well as levels of development as criteria of sampling. While, statistically, the total diversity encompassed in the universe of local elites in India is impossibly large if not infinite, only a part of the total diversity, defined by 'experimental variables' arising out of the parameters of the model, need concern us here.[11]

Uppermost among the considerations that are desirable in the sample are the inclusion of the broad range of issues that local elites have to deal with, the diverse social groups from which local elites are drawn, and the access and linkage they enjoy with decision-makers at the higher levels of the system. Naturally, these aspects of local politics are deeply influenced by the district and regional political arenas of which they are a part.[12] In order to be representative of India's regional political systems and the range of issues that constitute their political agendas, the sample will need to reflect India's geographic diversity as well.

The nature and structure of local politics are greatly influenced by the State-level leadership and political process. While India's federal structure has allocated several important aspects of rural development to regional governments, the extent to which they are able to give concrete shape to these constitutional provisions varies from State to State. The historical process and different levels of economic development that account for this have been examined in chapter two. These considerations point towards the constituent States of India as the first level of stratification for our sampling process. By selecting Gujarat and Orissa, we have the possibility of comparing two sets of local elites who, while subject to the same constitution, operate in contrasting ways. Thus, Gujarat and Orissa are the first level of stratification of the sample. Within each State, we have next selected a district which is situated at the modal level in some common indicators of economic and infrastructural development. Thus, within our contrasting regions, we have an administrative unit which, while providing the advantages of a cohesive and manageable administrative unit, nevertheless retains the essential social, cultural and developmental character of the regions.

STRATIFICATION BELOW THE DISTRICT LEVEL

While the district has been able to retain its importance as an administrative and a developmental unit through the years of restructuring following independence, the divisions below the district level, originally created for the collection of revenue and the maintenance of law and order, have done less well.[13] Emphasis on the allocation of resources and deployment of talented and well-trained personnel has increasingly been placed on the developmental block as the quintessential unit of development. The development block (like the single-member electoral constituency, another post-independence innovation), has not yet acquired the status of a natural cultural and administrative division. But, thanks to the very considerable effort undertaken to popularise the new terms of administrative usage, the development block has increasingly appeared as the ubiquitous point of reference in planning, allocation of resources and local politics. However, for reasons suggested in chapter two, the developmental block as a term of reference has gained wider currency in Surat as compared to Dhenkanal where the village neta, at the time of the field work, continued to use the old police circle as the unit of administrative demarcation.

In terms of the intervening strata, the sampling strategy aims at identifying geographic units that are in some sense 'natural' units, besides being representative of the diversity of the underlying universe. As such, in Surat and Dhenkanal, we have chosen the development blocks and police circles, respectively, as the next level of stratification. From among these intermediate sampling units, working on the basis of six indicators of development – literacy, medical facilities, power, the supply of drinking water, communication and transport facilities available per capita – three sampling units in Surat and Dhenkanal were chosen. These units, chosen from the high, medium and low strata, represent the diversity in levels of development in the district as a whole.

Identification of the study villages is the penultimate step in the sampling process. Towards that end, the next logical step is the formulation of theoretical and empirical criteria according to which we could stratify the villages in the sample blocks and police circles. The village, besides being a natural and historical unit, is simultaneously an administrative and a developmental unit. Significantly, the Indian village is both a place of habitation and work, unlike the European village which can serve either function. It is at the level of the village that we have a chance to observe the local elites in action. Some further empirical assumptions are necessary in order to select study villages from among the hundreds of villages situated within the intermediate sampling units of development blocks and police circles. Village size, as we shall see subsequently, is one of these crucial assumptions that needs to be made operational as a sampling criterion.

In a comparative study of two regions, one should ideally have a balance in the size of the samples which provide the basis of comparison. However, while local elites are a ubiquitous presence in the Indian village, the available pool of gaon ka netas from whom the sample is chosen is affected by the total volume of developmental activity within the village and the institutional context within which it is placed. The volume of developmental activity itself is determined to some extent by the size of the village and its accessibility. In a very small village, with little outside interest or internal turmoil, the local elites do not have the same scope to exploit the full potentials of their role as in a large village. A large village is likely to generate greater socio-economic activities and lead to complex problems of both human organisation and material management. There is also a possibility that a large village may have greater infrastructural facilities like roads, schools, health centres and electricity, and these in turn may qualitatively influence the life of the people and their involvement with development. The results are cumulative. The more conspicuous the village, the more it is likely to draw the attention of officials of various developmental organisations. The chances of this occurring are greater in larger and well-connected villages compared to small and remote ones.

Thus, *ceteris paribus*, size alone is likely to account for higher developmental activity per capita and, hence, more activity on the part of local elites. However, the basic objective of the study is to measure the relationship between the values, norms and attitudes of the local elites and their developmental transactions with political and administrative decision-makers at higher levels. The contribution of village size to the variation in the activities of rural netas is itself a significant factor but does not form a part of our theoretical edifice. As such, it needs to be excluded at the outset for a proper verification of our basic conjectures.

The practice usually followed in experimental designs is to eliminate the impact of factors such as village size which are important to the process of development but exogenous to the model of developmental interaction by comparing units of equal size so that size ceases to be a source of variation.[14] In a fully experimental research design, an attempt is made to match the experimental and control groups in all the known causal variables except the effects of those that are being studied. In our comparison of Gujarat and Orissa, we do not have the same freedom of choice to incorporate the variation in other factors like soil and climatic conditions, patterns of historical evolution, percentage of Scheduled Castes and Tribes, to name only a few of the many factors that affect the level of developmental activity in a village. Thus, village size is the only realistic control variable in our 'quasi-experimental' research design.

In order that we could control the contribution of village population size (which has so far remained only a supposition but for which no evidence has yet been provided), we need first of all to ascertain the nature and significance of its impact. In order to do this, we have measured the relationship of the size of the village population to four indicators of development – educational facilities, medical facilities, power supply, and availability of drinking water – on the basis of data from the 1971 census for the respective districts. These hypothetical relations were tested on 562 villages spread over one taluka in Surat district and two police circles in Dhenkanal. The results are presented in table 3.1.

The results reported in table 3.1 generally support the conjecture regarding the relationship between village size and the level of development as measured by the four selected indicators. Interestingly, in Gujarat, the relationship between size and the respective infrastructures regarding health and power supply are statistically non-significant, perhaps because practically all villages in Gujarat have some form of medical facility and all were electrified regardless of population size. However, the number of schools and wells did vary with the number of inhabitants. Similarly, Angul in Dhenkanal, perhaps thanks to a comparatively longer spell of close administrative

Table 3.1 Relation of village population size and indicators of
development (correlation coefficients)

Village	Number of schools	Number of hospitals	Power supply	Number of wells
Bardoli (n=85)	0.54	NS	NS	0.13
Angul (n=193)	0.75	0.67	0.72	NS
Dhenkanal (n=284)	0.59	0.69	0.36	0.20

Note: All coefficients except those marked NS are significant at 0.01 level.

attention to infrastructural facilities under direct British rule,
had at least one well in each village. However, the number of
wells did not vary with population size, which accounts for a
statistically non-significant relationship.

Thus, with the odd exception, the results obtained from
the correlation of village size with indicators of development
confirmed the anticipated relationship between village population size and the level of infrastructural development. As such,
to control for this source of variation in the attitudes and
behaviour of local elites, we decided to include in our sample
only villages of between 3000 and 5000 people. This restricted
group of villages in the selected blocks and police circles in
Gujarat and Orissa was further stratified into three groups in
terms of their level of development on the basis of consultation
with local development and administrative officials. One
village was then selected from each of the three developmental
categories in each of the three blocks in Gujarat and police
circles in Orissa. In this process, we ended up with a total of
eighteen sample villages, roughly in the same population range
in Gujarat and Orissa.

USE OF THE REPUTATIONAL METHOD FOR THE IDENTIFICATION OF THE INTERVIEW SAMPLE

The last step in the sampling process was to identify the
actual individuals to be interviewed. This was far from straightforward because of the ambiguities surrounding the operational
specification of *neta*s, seen so far in the study as a functional

category. A positional approach, which would mechanically list the holders of formal positions in the local arena, is unlikely to yield a comprehensive list of rural *netas* because, as Singh points out in his criticism of Sirsikar, Carter and Narain et al., 'holders of position do not necessarily correspond to the holders of power'.[15] Those who wield real power might prefer to do so from behind the camouflage of front men, placed in elective office as decoys to ward off enemies as well as the possible loss of status through involvement in 'dirty' politics. As Singh suggests,

> It is an accepted fact that in Rajasthan ex-rajas and ranis did not seek elections to the relatively inferior positions of the panchayat samiti and zilla parishad. And, when one makes a study of only the members of these bodies by first according them an elite status, one is liable to give the impression that those who do not occupy such an office are not elite.
>
> (Singh (1988), p 31)

The reputational approach attempts to overcome the possible discrepancy between formal and real positions of power. The application of the approach consists in first identifying several 'nominators' and asking them to prepare independent lists of local leaders, ranked in order of their importance. These lists are then used to generate a group of elites on whom there is most agreement.

Use of the reputational method involves a certain degree of subjective judgement on the part of the investigator. To some extent, this reflects the underlying imprecision about the social location of local elites and the fluidity of the local political arena. In practice, it is made even more complicated by the fact that there are no clear cut-off points to distinguish local elites from non-elites. An element of dynamism and movement characterises the achievement and loss of elite status. Some decline from their relatively exalted position to the situation of non-elites from natural causes like old age or sickness, and some from less natural ones like a spate of erroneous political judgements in terms of alliances, changes in the topography of power in the higher-level arenas or the rise to power and status of previously powerless groups who have no use for leaders from upper social classes. There are yet others who are in the process of moving away from the village arena to higher levels and are not perceived any longer as gaon ka netas properly speaking. On the other hand, some non-elites move up in course of time, so that, while they are in transition, some ambiguity is likely to be voiced about their situation. Thus, though 'local elite' is a distinct analytical category, a certain amount of fuzziness is unavoidable in its empirical specification because there is no definite cut-off point which separates local elites from the non-elites in the village.[16] On the other hand, without definite boundaries, it is not possible to incorporate a phenomenon into an analytical structure to be eventually subjected to empirical verification.

The solution we adopted was to fix an operational lower threshold of 'eliteness' at a point below which one had no regular dealings with the world outside nor was one sought out by people from outside to act as contact points for the transactions they wished to undertake in the village. Within these relatively fixed boundaries, the number of people perceived as local elites within a village tends to vary with the size of the village and the importance of its market. One of the factors that influences the number and extent of activity of the gaon ka netas in a village is geographic location of the village at important cross-roads or rail junctions, which might cause it to serve as an entry point to a cluster of villages in the area. These factors create an environment conducive to the attainment of neta status in the village and thus increase the pool of netas in the village.

No a priori upper or lower limits could therefore be set to the number of leaders to be interviewed in each village, which created a certain imbalance between the number of local elites interviewed in Gujarat and Orissa. In all, in Gujarat we were able to interview 131 leaders whereas the Orissa sample did not exceed 102. The explanation for the higher figures for Gujarat despite the equality in the number of villages is signficant. The Gujarat villages have a larger institutional base, and, as such, a larger number of leaders to choose from, who in turn represent a larger number of categories. The extent of developmental activity and number of institutions are both at a lower level in Orissa. Besides, the Orissa netas often manage to have a finger in every pie, which for our purposes further reduces the leadership base from which the sample was to be recruited.

The group of netas which was thus identified for closer study included the *sarpanch, upsarpanch*, the members of the *gram panchayat*, chairman of the village cooperative, prominent social workers, leaders of political parties and voluntary associations like yuvak mandals and kisan mandals. Important caste and community leaders who wield a certain influence in the village though they do not occupy formal positions also found a place in the sample. Also included were other local leaders who do not formally or informally represent any groups but are influential in their own right. Examples of this category are some resident school teachers, freedom fighters and some 'village elders', who even in their declining years still command some authority which can be cashed in for transactional value in the new market of political influence and economic resources.

INHERITED STATUS AND ACQUIRED POWER: THE SOCIO-DEMOGRAPHIC PROFILE OF THE SAMPLE

The social profile of the rural netas in Gujarat and Orissa suggests several paths one might traverse to reach elite status. One point is abundantly clear from the outset: not all elites are 'born' into their relatively exalted situations, nor are all of them 'highly born' either. Being a neta is no guarantee that one could remain an elite through one's lifetime. The son of a neta might get a head start, but political succession is not guaranteed.[17] The potential impermanence of elite status in the local arena is best understood in the context of the political process that operates within the village and which links the village to the world outside. Since this assertion is at variance with what is often believed to be the case, we need a brief review of the literature on the subject to bring the difference into sharper focus before moving on to an empirical examination of the evidence from Gujarat and Orissa.

A Latin American reading of the local political scene sometimes leads to the description of rural India in terms of clientelism.[18] Defined as 'a special form of exchange relationship between individuals, one relatively more powerful than the other, which serves as the basis of networks of alliances',[19] clientelism does manifest features that are familiar to the Indian rural scene. The most prominent among these are patrimonialism, which combines traditional authority with personal power,[20] and fictive kinship, which camouflages a relationship of unequal power between patron and client and reinforces it with mutual pseudo-obligations.[21] The major difference between the Indian situation and Latin American clientelism lies in the fact that the former does not share the closed, static character of the latter. An alternative and more appropriate formulation is the faction, seen as conflict groups recruited by competing leaders on diverse principles.[22] Under the leadership of one or more local elites, competing factions manifest an unstable political alliance structure. Essentially opportunistic and episodic in nature, factions represent coalitions of interests and social networks. Working largely on the same principles, competing and unstable alignments develop at the macropolitical level of which the village factional structure becomes part and parcel.[23] In view of the static political order of the clientelist literature which provides a sharp contrast to the changing power structure of rural India, it is difficult to sustain the equivalence that Scott suggests between factionalism in India and 'loose structures of patron–client networks'.[24]

The other major distinguishing characteristic of the Indian situation is its 'creeping revolution'[25] – a recognition of an incrementally expanding political arena which periodically inducts new social forces that were hitherto mere onlookers. Factionalism is more than a permutation and combination of a limited number of enduring clientelist units: the reformulation of factional alignments causes further differentiation *within* micro-level factions, leading to the greater visibility of new interests and new local elites promoting those interests. A more appropriate formulation is the 'parapolitical system', which suggests that the rise in factions can be seen as evidence of the weakening of traditional forms of social control.[26]

Social heterogeneity among local elites is one of the consequences of political competition and pervasive factionalism. Though the higher social strata are present in large numbers among local elites in both Gujarat and Orissa, and manage to control the more important organisations in the village, the lower strata are also present, not as supplicants, but as challengers. The major difference in the profile between the two samples consists of the difference of their social compositions. The proportion of the Adivasi/Harijan is higher in Gujarat compared to Orissa. Since protest movements around the issue of statutory rights and safeguards for the lower strata have played a key role in the politics of Gujarat, it is important to understand the soci-economic attributes of this crucial segment of the sample in the two States.

THE SOCIAL HETEROGENEITY OF LOCAL ELITES

The main thrust of the literature on social change which makes an implicit or explicit reference to local elites has been to present them as socially undifferentiated middlemen who skim off resources meant for developmental work in the village. The empirical basis of this supposition can be examined through the analysis of the internal stratification of local elites in Surat and Dhenkanal according to age, caste, education, occupation and land based on information presented in table 3.2. The second objective of this section is to examine the interrelationship of these criteria of differentiation in order to examine the status of social class as a summary indicator of the internal differentiation of local elites in Gujarat and Orissa.

Stratification according to caste status provides a contrast to the relative similarity between Surat and Dhenkanal of the distribution in terms of age. For the purpose of stratification according to social class, caste status is used as a cleavage that is a political and a social category with incidental economic features. In Indian society to-day, there are three big cleavages, along the lines of the upper social strata, the middle strata composed of agricultural castes and the lowest social group consisting of former Untouchables and the Tribal population. Corresponding to these cleavages, the local elites have been grouped into clusters with jatis ranked high, middle and Adivasi/Harijan according to the regional *varna* scheme.[27] Thus, Baniyas and Brahmins are considered 'high' castes in Surat and Dhenkanal. However, whereas in Orissa, Karanas and Kshatriyas and Khandayats, an Oriya variation of the generic category of the warrior caste, are locally considered as upper caste, the same is not true in Gujarat. The addition of these landowning cultivator castes to the high category swell the ranks of high castes among the local elites in Orissa, bringing them to an impressive 31.4 per cent compared to Gujarat's 16 per cent. It also indicates the absence of horizontal alliances of

Table 3.2 Socio-demographic profile of the sample: Gujarat and Orissa

	Gujarat %	Orissa %
Age		
Less than 34 years	16	18
35 to 49	41	44
50 and above	43	38
Caste		
Upper	16	31
Middle	37	46
Adivasi/Harijan	42	22
Other/non-Hindu	5	1
Education		
Illiterate or barely literate	19	15
Primary or middle level	41	55
Matriculate or above	40	30
Occupation		
Owner-cultivator	65	69
Agricultural worker	9	4
Small trader/professional	22	20
Other	4	7
Land holding		
Less than 5 acres	18	45
6 to 20 acres	49	43
More than 20 acres	33	12
Organisational involvement		
None	5	7
1 to 2 organisations	41	47
3 to 5 organisations	31	36
More than 5 organisations	23	10

landowning castes in Orissa as already indicated in the previous chapter. The middle ground is occupied in Gujarat mainly by Patidars (27.7 per cent of the total) along with small groups of Darjis, Naikas, Ahirs, Sonis, Rathods and Parmars, bringing the group as a whole to 32.8 per cent. In Orissa, it is a relatively more heterogeneous group with a sizeable representation of Chasas (23.5 per cent), who are the ritual equivalents of Patidars in Gujarat but who possess neither their horizontal solidarity nor their economic and political influence. As a group, the middle strata among local elites in Dhenkanal, at 46.1 per cent of the total, is larger than that in Surat, containing representatives of other intermediate jatis including Sundhis, Telis, Gopalas, Gudias, Kumbharas, Tantis, Hansis and Dhobas. Among

the Adivasi/Harijan category in Surat, the numerically preponderant groups are the Gamits (19.1 per cent), Chaudhris
(16.8 per cent) and Halpatis (4.6 per cent), with some representation of Kokanis, Bhagats and Dhodias, bringing the group
as a whole to 46.7 per cent of the total. The Adivasi/Harijan
category in Dhenkanal, at 21.6 per cent of the total, are
relatively less numerous among local elites and internally more
fragmented, with representatives of Panas, Sabaras, Sudhas,
Domalas, Khairas, Gandas and Nehuras. The Panas, though
numerically not the most preponderant, are nevertheless the
most vocal and aggressive within the lowest strata.

The cross-tabulation of caste status and age (see table 3.3)
reveals an interesting insight into the factors leading to the
attainment of elite status. The overall relationship in Dhenkanal
is weak and statistically non-significant. One interpretation of
this finding is that life-cycle exerts its influence independently
of caste-status: regardless of one's social standing, one has to
pass a certain critical threshold of age to be recognised as a
proper neta. This is even more true of the Adivasi/Harijan
category from among whom only 13 per cent are thirty-four or
less whereas among the upper strata one is likely to find twice
the number from the youngest cohort of below thirty-five. The
pattern is reversed in Surat where a statistically significant
negative relationship is observed between age and social status,

Table 3.3 Cross-tabulation of caste status and age of local elites

Caste	Age in years			
	34 or less %	35 to 49 %	50 or more %	Total %
Gujarat[1]				
High	9	48	43	100
Medium	12	35	53	100
Adivasi/Harijan	23	43	34	100
Total	16	41	43	100
Orissa[2]				
High	25	38	37	100
Medium	15	49	36	100
Adivasi/Harijan	13	41	46	100
Total	18	44	38	100

Notes: [1] Kendall's tau B −0.14; significant at 5 per cent.
[2] Not significant at 5 per cent.

with far more younger people from among the Adivasi/Harijan leaders reaching elite status than is the case either among the high or the middle strata.

On education, compared to the Orissa sample, Gujarat has a higher number of the highly educated as well as a higher percentage of those who are barely literate (see table 3.4). Apparently, as shown in the table, some Gujarat leaders have reached the status of local elites in spite of low educational attainments. The Gujarat elites from the Adivasi and Harijan categories have a much higher percentage of highly educated (23 per cent matriculates and above) compared to Orissa's 9 per cent. The cross-tabulation shows a significantly negative relationship between social status and level of education, even stronger in the case of Dhenkanal than in Surat.

Table 3.4 Cross-tabulation of caste and educational attainment

Caste	Education			
	Just literate %	Primary/Middle %	Matriculate and above %	Total %
Gujarat[1]				
High	9	9	82	100
Medium	23	37	40	100
Adivasi/Harijan	25	52	23	100
Total	19	41	40	100
Orissa[2]				
High	6	28	66	100
Medium	19	66	15	100
Adivasi/Harijan	23	68	9	100
Total	15	55	30	100

Notes: [1] Kendall's tau B −0.29; significant at 0.000 level.
[2] Kendall's tau B −0.41; significant at 0.000 level.

The occupational structure of local elites also presents a similar profile, with a clear domination by owner-cultivators in both (see table 3.5). Though as a status category, there is a certain degree of comparability between being an owner-cultivator in Gujarat and in Orissa, as an economic category, there are major differences between the two. The Gujarati local elites from the owner-cultivator category operate very much as market-oriented agrarian entrepreneurs, alert and watchful of the fluctuation of prices and of demand in the regional and national markets, subsidies, infrastructural facilities and, ultimately, profit. Agriculture is the main but by no means the only business that most rural netas are engaged in in Gujarat. In Orissa, the agrarian economy tends to be more subsistence orientated and less given to modern agricultural methods in comparison, with production meant mostly for household consumption. To the extent there is a surplus, it is sold in the local market. The penetration of cash crops and indicators of 'capitalist production relations' such as contractual wage labour is modest by Gujarati standards.

Table 3.5 Cross-tabulation of caste and occupation

Caste	Occupation				
	Owner-cultivator %	Agricultural worker %	Non-agricultural and trade %	Other %	Total %
Gujarat[1]					
High	24	0	67	9	100
Medium	60	16	19	5	100
Adivasi/Harijan	85	8	7	0	100
Total	65	9	22	4	100
Orissa[2]					
High	60	0	34	6	100
Medium	70	2	17	11	100
Adivasi/Harijan	82	14	4	0	100
Total	69	4	20	7	100

Notes: [1] n=131; tau B −0.46; significant at 0.000 level.
[2] n=102; Kendall's tau B −0.18; significant at 0.03 level.

The cross-tabulation of caste with occupation in Surat (table 3.5) reveals a pattern observed by others including Breman.[28] The upper castes, who for ritual and historical reasons do not cultivate the land personally, have instead concentrated on sources of employment outside agriculture, including trade. Less than a quarter of the high castes in Gujarat are owner-cultivators whereas over 66 per cent are engaged in non-agricultural sources, such as trade. The percentage of owner-cultivators goes up monotonically as one moves down the social hierarchy whereas the percentage of non-agricultural occupations and trade decreases as one moves down from the higher social strata. The correlation between caste and occupation is as strong as it is significant. While the same tendencies are present in Orissa, with about two thirds of the local elites from higher castes presenting themselves as owner-cultivators, the picture is relatively less clear, with a correlation between caste and occupation which is neither so strong nor significant.

As regards landownership, the distribution of landholdings among the local elites of Orissa shows greater fragmentation, with a larger proportion of small holdings than in Gujarat (see table 3.6). Orissa's Adivasi/Harijan have a much higher proportion of small cultivators with the size of landholdings in the region of 0 to 5 acres compared to Gujarat. But this observation has to be treated with caution because the Orissa sample as a whole has a larger percentage of people owning land between 0 and 5 acres. The more interesting comparison is that of the lot of local elites from the Adivasi/Harijan category relative to the upper and middle social strata in their own environment. Compared to the sample average, the Gujarat Adivasi/Harijan netas have a relatively bigger probability of being in the lowest landowning category compared to the fate of their counterparts in Orissa. The same holds true for the highest category of landownership as well. On this score, the comparatively greater social polarisation among local elites in Gujarat confirms the observation of others, including that of Jan Breman.[29] The attitudinal implications of this polarisation will be examined in subsequent chapters.

Table 3.6 Cross-tabulation of caste and size of landholding

Caste	Size of landholding in acres			
	0 to 5 %	6 to 20 %	21 acres and above %	Total %
Gujarat[1]				
High	22	56	22	100
Medium	9	70	21	100
Adivasi/Harijan	34	64	2	100
Total	18	49	33	100
Orissa[2]				
High	28	50	22	100
Medium	55	41	4	100
Adivasi/Harijan	45	41	14	100
Total	45	43	12	100

Notes: [1] Tau B −0.31; significant at 0.000 level.
[2] Kendall's tau B −0.16; significant at 0.03 level.

The results presented above confirm the role of caste as an important basis of social stratification within the local elite. It is, indeed, a summary expression of *social class*, seen in the persistence of shared norms.[30] Caste however is not simply an indicator of inherited status. The presence of significant numbers of Adivasis and Harijans among local elites is itself indicative of the upward mobility of the lowest strata on the scales of power. Under the leadership of people of their own community, a caste can play a catalytic role in generating the means of intervention in the social and material environment for the benefit of its members. It also shows the effectiveness of caste associations and the politicised jatis as units of political action because they bring together both the social and the economic faces of local politics in India. In the subsequent analysis we shall use caste as indicative of social class, whose effect provides further reinforcement to the desire for participation and upward mobility by those who have hitherto been excluded from playing a significant role in the political arena.

INTERGENERATIONAL MOBILITY

Conjectures about the incremental addition to the ranks of the local elites or about upward mobility of the previously powerless into elite status require diachronic data for their empirical verification. Survey data can provide only a snapshot view of reality, limited to a given point of time. Village studies, with diachronic data on the rise and decline of powerful families and groups within the community, are a more promising source. Some inferences can however be drawn by comparing the situation and status of the present generation of local elites with those of their parents. Tables 3.7 and 3.8, which compare the level of educational attainment and occupation of the respondents with those of their fathers, present some conjectures on these lines. In relative terms, however, though those who are only just literate also come from an equally backward background, those who have reached the primary level or above tend to do considerably better than their fathers. Though once again it is not possible to find out if the fathers of this generation of local elites were also reputed to be netas as well, their comparatively low educational attainment might be considered as circumstantial evidence to suggest that some of them might not have been.

Table 3.7 Intergenerational mobility in educational attainment

Respondent's education	Father's education			Total
	Just literate %	*Primary/ Middle* %	*Matriculate and above* %	%
Gujarat				
Just literate	79	14	7	100
Primary/Middle	63	35	2	100
Matriculate and above	23	55	22	100
Total	51	38	11	100
Orissa				
Just literate	82	18	0	100
Primary/Middle	58	38	4	100
Matriculate and above	20	70	10	100
Total	51	44	5	100

Table 3.8 Intergenerational mobility in occupation

Respondent's occupation	Father's occupation			Total
	Owner-cultivator %	*Agricultural worker* %	*Trade/ other* %	%
Gujarat				
Owner-cultivator	93	4	3	100
Agricultural worker	0	100	0	100
Trade/other	53	3	44	100
Total	74	12	14	100
Orissa				
Owner-cultivator	83	4	13	100
Agricultural worker	50	50	0	100
Trade/other	62	5	33	100
Total	76	6	18	100

In both Gujarat and Orissa as a whole, the educational attainments of local elites show marked signs of improvement over those of the fathers in the percentage of owner-cultivators over the generations. The overwhelmingly large number of owner-cultivators come from families of owner-cultivators. There is, however, a general decline in the proportion of people born into an agricultural background who stay on. In the case of an appreciably large number of local elites in non-agricultural occupations, the occupational background they have left behind is that of agriculture. In both States, this is more true of the higher castes as compared to the lower, with the percentage of local elites staying on in agriculture going up from 50 per cent for high castes to 74 per cent for the medium and 94 per cent for the Adivasi/Harijan category in Gujarat, and 65 per cent for the high castes in Orissa going up to 76 per cent for the middle castes and 89 per cent for the Adivasi and Harijan groups. Seen across generations, thus, the picture is not entirely static: most appear to stay broadly in the same category, but some rise from a lower category to a higher and others move in the opposite direction. Once again, the conjecture here would fit in with the general trends in occupational evolution in Gujarat and Orissa, where a combination of economic development and occupational diversification together with the increasing pressure on land and state intervention through land reforms have created new, viable non-agricultural economic roles in the countryside and contributed to the growing complexity of the occupational structure of the local elites.

ORGANISATIONAL AFFILIATION AND ELITE STATUS

Once we have identified local elites in terms of their social attributes, we can move in the direction of their political and organisational affiliation. The literature on local politics strongly suggests a close link between elite status and formal leadership of local organisations. The findings from Gujarat and Orissa confirm this relationship between formal association with village organisations and the social recognition of leadership. Both in Gujarat as well as in Orissa, local elites are heavily represented in various organisations in the village (see table 3.9). Organisational affiliation is perceived as an important attribute of power and status. There are relatively few (respectively, 6 per cent in Gujarat and 7 per cent in Orissa) who do not hold positions in any organisation nor have taken the initiative to set up any.

99

Table 3.9 Organisational affiliation of local elites

Organisation	Social class			
	High %	*Medium* %	*Adivasi/Harijan* %	*Total* %
Gujarat				
Political party	24	14	16	17
Panchayat	43	49	74	60
Cooperative	71	47	42	49
Educational organisation	52	47	58	53
Welfare organisation	52	35	45	41
Recreational organisation	24	6	24	16
Caste association	29	24	42	32
Cultural organisation	33	12	31	23
Religious organisation	19	37	42	35
Initiative to form an organisation	71	41	41	47
Neither belongs to an organisation nor formed one	0	12	2	6
Orissa				
Political party	37	6	23	21
Panchayat	59	55	45	55
Cooperative	44	30	23	32
Educational organisation	62	47	36	49
Welfare organisation	47	45	36	43
Recreational organisation	31	23	14	25
Caste association	6	15	9	12
Cultural organisation	28	17	9	19
Religious organisation	9	13	18	13
Initiative to form an organisation	44	21	0	25
Neither belongs to an organisation nor formed one	6	4	14	7

I would like to make it clear here that by organisation I do not imply only or necessarily economic, political or social bodies. Folk culture plays an important role in the life of the village. Organising a *jatra*, or a rival group to the established one in the village, is a key instrument of power for those who aspire to leadership status in the village.[31] Not all organisations are of equal importance. For the sake of statistical analysis, however, all the organisations present in our study villages were given equal weights. Not all organisations however represent the same degree of 'openness' to different social strata, nor do they enjoy the same degree of historical involvement with particular social groups. From the variation in their presence in different kinds of organisations, we could draw some inferences about intra-elite competition as well.

The relationship between caste status and organisational affiliation reflects the different patterns of social mobility in Gujarat and Orissa. The cross-tabulation of caste status and the number of organisational affiliations shows a positive statistical relationship between caste status and organisational affiliation in Orissa where relatively larger numbers of netas from the upper strata are affiliated to more organisations than the lower strata. The same is not true of Gujarat where the membership of organisations tends to be spread more evenly over local elites from all social strata. The statistical relationship between caste status and organisational affiliation of the netas is weak and not significant.

Political parties represent the most visible link between the village power structure and the political arena at the higher level. Both in Surat and Dhenkanal, more people from the higher castes are affiliated to political parties than from the lower social strata. It is important to note, however, that the lowest social strata are not absent from the scene altogether. A little over a fifth of the Adivasi/Harijan local elites in Dhenkanal and a little less than a fifth in Surat are affiliated to parties. Further, in their partisan choice, they do not simply replicate the political preferences of the local elites from the upper social strata of the village. In fact, in partisanship, they might have found a new instrument of struggle. Over 80 per cent of the local elites from upper and middle strata in Dhenkanal expressed a partisan preference for the Janata party whereas only half of the Adivasi/Harijan category described them-selves as Janata supporters, the rest, as Congress supporters, testified to the pro-dalit image of the Congress in the area. The same can be observed in an equally spectacular fashion in Surat where the upper strata are almost equally split in their support of the Congress whereas among the Adivasi/Harijan leaders the Congress(I) enjoyed solid support, with 80 per cent

101

of the local elites demonstrating a partisan preference for the party. Organisational affiliation with a political overtone has been taken to its logical outcome in Surat where the local political arena has been virtually taken over by the Adivasi and Harijan local elites from among whom over 70 per cent are present in one capacity or another in the panchayat organisation. This is no doubt reinforced by their strong involvement in caste associations, with over two fifths of them claiming affiliation. Neither appears to be the case in Dhenkanal, where a relatively larger proportion of the local elites from the upper strata are present in panchayat organisations. To the extent there is any evidence of caste associations, a relatively larger proportion of the upper strata are active in them as compared to the Adivasi and Harijan leaders.

The political success of the local leaders from the lowest social strata in the local arena is not an unmixed blessing for the village arena. As Bjorkman and Chaturvedi have shown from their fieldwork in Rajasthan,[32] once the relentless logic of democracy translates itself in terms of the 'take over' of local political institutions by the lowest strata, the upper strata tend to pull out and invest their energy and capital instead in voluntary organisations, particularly in cooperatives. Unlike the panchayat organisations, there is a financial threshold (usually in the form of a share to be bought) to be crossed in order to gain entry into the cooperative structure. The flight of capital, contacts and influence resulting from the withdrawal by the upper classes lowers the effectiveness of panchayats in the long run. Evidence of this 'penalty of success' can be seen in Surat, where over 70 per cent of the highest strata are present in the cooperative structure. Lower-strata entry into panchayats has not spread in a large way in Orissa yet. There, both panchayats and cooperatives are still dominated by netas from the upper strata.

CONCLUSION

The chapter aimed at identifying a sample of local elites in Gujarat and Orissa for face-to-face interviews on a range of questions relating to social and economic change in their villages. The research design follows from the model suggested in the introduction. The sampling process, for reasons indicated in chapter two, started with the decision to base the field research in Gujarat and Orissa. Next, the districts of Surat in Gujarat and Dhenkanal in Orissa were selected. With the help of aggregate statistics on indicators of development, eighteen villages, representing different levels of economic development and infrastructural facilities available in them, were identified. The application of the reputational method to these study villages yielded a total of 233 rural netas who constitute the sample for detailed interviews.

A subsidiary objective of this chapter was to study the general profile of the gaon ka netas so as to set the stage for the subsequent analysis of their attitudes, expectations and political strategies in order to verify the conjectures made in the introductory chapter. Once the local leaders were identified, the chapter analysed their detailed social profile. Contrary to a common belief among radical students of Indian politics local elites were found to be a socially heterogeneous group in both Gujarat and Orissa. The presence of the lowest social strata among local leaders would possibly encourage a pluralist view of social change in India. But this rather optimistic view needs to be moderated with the persistence of inequalities in the ownership of land, education and social status. The undisputed dominance of the village arena by those born to power, privilege and status is gone. In its place one finds a different power structure where ascription is moderated by achievement as the basis of power and influence.

The substitution of old-style social notables, whose authority derived mostly from ascription, by local elites who have to generate their power in the rough and tumble of the political market place has been one of the most significant achievements of the modern state and democracy in India. This has come about primarily through political competition and the rules of political transaction instituted by the post-independence state, which has placed rural development at the centre of its strategy of the legitimation of power. The induction of new elites and the accretion of power into the hands of local elites are the major sources of change in the local political arena. The availability of vast amounts of patronage, thanks largely to the investment in developmental projects, has given further impetus to local struggle for power, reinforcing political competition in the process.

It is useful at this stage to dwell on the factors that are helpful for the acquisition of the status of a neta and for existing netas to try to retain their position in the face of competition from others. There are clearly several paths available, some of which are overlapping. Higher social status, wealth, power and contacts with the outside world might cause some aspirants to try to acquire elite status within their political arena. As new institutions open up, the elites tend to spread their political influence further by trying to take over those institutions. This strategy is not always able to secure for the local netas exclusive control over all offices locally available both for reasons of law, which increasingly makes some participation by former untouchables, tribals and women mandatory, but also for reasons of political exigency. New institutions and norms of participation have provided some room for manoeuvre to social groups which were hitherto powerless, whose leaders now aspire to and in some cases successfully achieve incorporation into local elite groups in the face of stiff resistance from members of the old guard. In this fashion, closed, stratified social systems based on a system of rigid hierarchy start opening up to the winds of change and are transformed into societies where power and status, rather than being entirely ascribed, become the subject of intense competition.

The social heterogeneity of local elites in Gujarat and Orissa provides some further evidence of the political mobility of social groups that were previously excluded from the exercise of power. A variety of factors, notably including statutory regulations, contrive to induct new social forces into the local political arena. This is how local leaders from Adivasi and Harijan categories in Orissa have secured their entry into the organisational structure at the local level. The data we have generated do not provide much evidence of initiatives in setting up new organisations on their part. Their induction in the institutional structure in Orissa can reasonably be attributed to state policy towards the Scheduled Castes and Tribes. The picture is different in Gujarat, where independent political action by these groups has a longer historical tradition that is accompanied by relatively greater success compared to Orissa.

The analysis undertaken in this chapter has helped us understand the key position of class as a basis of social stratification. It is closely related to other forms of stratification such as education, occupation and landholding. It is also a convenient means of social identification. As such, it provides a natural network for cognition of reality and, possibly, collective action through the formation of political alliances based on caste associations. The survival of castes, long a synonym for social hierarchy and inequality, might create an image of a static reality. This can be deceptive, for the modern caste consciousness is very different from the traditional jati in its ideology and principle of organisation. The dialectics of caste can be quite complex. Itself a product of inequality, caste organisations, by spreading consciousness of this inequality, eventually contribute to the demise of social hierarchy. The organisation along caste lines can thus come naturally to the dispossessed in their search for power and social dignity. The data on the social profile of the local elites have shown caste to be an effective basis of structuring the social reality of education, occupation and land as visible signs of rank. The presence of significant numbers of Adivasi/Harijan among local elites already provides partial evidence to the large-scale change in the local basis of power and influence. In the subsequent analysis we shall examine how social class affects perception of the social reality, consciousness of inequality, and transformation of material deprivation into radical attitudes and collective protest.

We need more evidence, nevertheless, to be able to draw conclusions about the nature of the distribution of power at the local level. This is important because the actual configuration of power does not necessarily reflect the power one might derive from the possession of the normal attributes of power such as land, high social status and education. The political articulation of contentious issues and the rhetoric of development are themselves attempts to question the legitimacy of the existing structure of authority. The leverage that the powerless are able to secure will of course not have any long-term effect on the structure of deprivation if they are not reinforced through the induction of their schedule of preferences into the local agenda of development, and the newly mobilised forces will not be able to generate the requisite power to implement the agenda they have helped expand.

The evidence from Gujarat and Orissa suggests the existence of recursive cycles that give a periodic jolt to the structure of power underlying the political system and the economic structure. The outstanding issues that require further discussion are: how the social groups at the bottom of the pyramid generate power through an alternative political discourse, the rhetoric of development, the repertoire of institutional participation and radical protest; and whether the gain in power by the powerless eventually contributes to the process of broadening and deepening the political arena and to the legitimation of authority. The latter can be explored through the substantive issues and problems that constitute the staple of local politics, the process through which the local political agenda is set and the nature of contacts that local elites maintain with decision-makers at higher levels. These issues will be taken up in the subsequent chapters.

4

SETTING THE LOCAL AGENDA: THE PROBLEMS, PROGRESS AND AGENCY OF RURAL DEVELOPMENT

THE OBJECTIVES

The main objective of this chapter is to analyse the rhetoric of local development, consisting mainly of the views and opinions of the rural netas about the problems they encounter in their everyday life, the solutions they suggest and the agencies they prefer for the implementation of those schemes. However, in contrast to the neo-populist constructions of a kisan movement – a unified peasantry harnessing the forces of the countryside against the city – the findings presented here show considerable heterogeneity in the opinions and attitudes among the rural elites. These ideas emerging from the local level reflect great diversity in terms of region and social class, demonstrating respectively the difference in the level of development across India, and signifying the conflict of interests between social classes. These positions are taken and issues are formulated in the context of the governmental and political structure at the local level. As such, the discussion of elite perceptions of problems, solutions and the possible agencies of implementation starts with an introduction to the panchayati raj structure in Gujarat and Orissa.

Adapting central plans to the local situation and bending them to accommodate their specific schemes are among the priorities of local elites in their dealings with administrators and political leaders. The process is marked by a certain degree of tension, arising out of the 'urban bias' in Indian development. The theme, central to the social philosophy of Gandhi and popular among the students of rural development,[1] has formed a powerful undercurrent of Indian politics from the 1970s onwards.[2] However, the rural netas are concerned just as often about how to take advantage of the new structure of opportunities made available through development plans and projects. The process is naturally contentious, because more resources for some are seen as less for others. The protagonists are all well aware that despite the attempts by government officials and experts to couch development plans in apolitical language, neither the costs nor the benefits of progress are shared equally.[3] The netas of those social groups who face the choice of marginalisation or migration are aware of a range of alternatives, both institutional and radical, that are available to them.

The method of observation elaborated in chapter two identified individual members of the gaon ka netas in Gujarat and Orissa for a detailed study of their attitudes and perceptions. However, at the level of analysis, we have the possibility of examining the interplay of social class and region by grouping them into three clusters in the manner indicated in chapter three. The selection of problems by a particular leader gives some indication of the benefit that he or she and *people in a situation similar to them* expect to gain out of intervention with the process of development. The expected benefits are not necessarily material, but, could range from specific developmental inputs like loans, fertiliser and subsidies to the normative basis of allocation itself. The latter, as the literature of mass protest and collective action gives us to understand,[4] is an important guide to political action and the awareness on the part of the individual of the room for manoeuvre provided by the political system in which they are placed. Thus, the chapter sets the stage for the subsequent analysis of the perception of social conflict caused by the process of development and the range of action, both institutional and radical, that local elites undertake in order to achieve their objectives.

The problems articulated by the gaon ka netas or the solutions they propose for those problems do not, of course, exist in a vacuum. The local political arena is a battle ground of competing issues, ideas and rhetoric with which different sets of political actors seek to give concrete shape to their interests. Within the political arena, development programmes sponsored by the government, despite the advantage that their privileged position gives them, jostle against counter proposals to gain salience and public acceptance. The 'problems', articulated by these articulate members of the rural society, constitute the domain over which individuals express their preferences and form coalitions, to promote their preferred alternatives. The process of setting the agenda provides an entry point to social groups keen on adding their policy goals to the social ordering of preferences. The groups are unequal in size and power; and their success in obtaining the policy outcomes they desire from the political system is variable. But few factions are stable over time. This is why the process of coalition formation has become an integral part of the democratisation of the local political structure.

While democratic politics at the national and regional levels in India, born out of successive stages of transfer of power to representatives of the people and its incremental devolution to regional centres is based on relatively secure foundations, the extension of democracy to the local level is more recent and does not quite enjoy the same legitimacy.[5] In addition, attempts by deprived social groups to promote their collective interest through the political process comes up against the interests of entrenched social groups who seek to obstruct them through force, fraud and manipulation of local institutions.[6] Their efforts are facilitated by the fact that the administrative structure at the local level is not sufficiently formalised and does not have the same constitutional protection as the regional and the national levels.[7]

In the event, the 'felt needs' which pass for the local inputs to the developmental agenda in the jargon of India's Planning Commission are only the visible tip of an iceberg of potential public demands. The less visible parts of this iceberg consist of issues of importance to people at the lower reaches of the power structure. As indicated earlier, collective protest emerges out of the disjunction between the set of demands that get on the agenda and those that are excluded through a variety of stratagems. Since the process of development and, eventually, the legitimacy of the state depend on the success of the relatively less powerful in placing their demands on the agenda and getting the political structure to take them on board, it is important to study local politics from the point of view of the emergence of issues and the institutions and processes that are available to articulate and aggregate these demands.

THE KEY ROLE OF LOCAL ELITES AS OPINION MAKERS

As influential members of the local community, the gaon ka netas are also the local opinion-makers, who reinforce their influence or seek to generate it by formulating local demands. Their views on the issues salient to local development provide us with some indications of the nature and extent of local demands. Some of these may already be a part of the agenda of the local government. There are potential demands other than those that are articulated, but they are kept off the agenda as 'non-issues' by dominant local interests.

The data on which this chapter is based are drawn from responses of local elites to four sets of questions. The first two concern the objectives that local leaders consider desirable in development policy. These are formulated by them in terms of 'problems' that the people of the area who are in the same material situation as the respondent encounter, and the solutions that they envisage to these problems. Related to the first two are two other factors that are also important in their own right: the institutions of state and organisations they consider best situated to implement the solutions they envisage to the problems they have cited; and their evaluation of the material progress achieved over the past years through development plans and projects. The objective of field research here is to collect this information by focusing on the needs and expectations that the process of social and economic change generates in these articulate members of rural society.

The historical and economic context within which the process of rural development takes place has been dealt with at length in chapter two. The focus of this chapter is to develop a comprehensive picture of the problems that are seen as characteristic of the process of development. Since the information on which these observations is based is generated through open-ended interviews with local elites, a caveat is necessary by the way of a general warning to those unfamiliar with the rituals that surround public political conversation in an Indian village. These, for reasons given in the methodological appendix, can be quite complex. Like the smooth contours of a distant mountain range, the Indian village can present the image of a harmonious and self-regulating community to an observer who has recently arrived from outside. The breakthrough for the student of rural society comes with the realisation that the consensual image that the leading people of the village seek to project to the outsider is at least partly false, for the power of the powerful consists in obscuring contentious issues from the public view, especially those that are related to the interests of the relatively powerless.[8]

While our objective is to gain a general view of the local rhetoric on development articulated by rural netas, it is important at the outset to distinguish between the tip of the iceberg that the village reveals to the naked eye and the less visible parts that have to be uncovered through careful investigation. The relationship of that which is revealed to that which is concealed provides an important insight into the local power structure. Which issues are visible depends crucially on whose interests they serve. This phenomenon, not unknown to policy makers at the higher levels of the system, was crucial for the introduction of panchayati raj. The observation by S. K. Dey, Minister for Community Development and Cooperation, Government of India, and one of the architects of the democratic decentralisation of power is quite revealing: 'The so-called harmony that we have in the villages of which we are very proud, is just a harmony enforced by a powerful few on a powerless many.'[9] This remarkably prescient comment by Dey is supported by a wide range of literature in political science dealing with agenda-setting as an exercise in power.[10] Agenda-setting as such, however, has not received the attention it deserves in the academic study of local politics in India. The landmark studies of Reddy and Seshadri, Seshadri and Jain and Iqbal Narain, Pande and Sharma, for example,[11] concentrate mostly on the revealed agenda, inadvertently leaving out of the analysis the crucial area of 'non-decision-making' – 'the practice of limiting the scope of actual decision-making to 'safe' issues by manipulating the dominant community values, myths, and political institutions and procedures'.[12]

In our attempts to go beyond the formal and the 'revealed' agenda on the basis of an analysis of the opinions and issues voiced by local elites, we have made several assumptions. In the first place, local elites do not speak with one voice. In spite of operating within comparable social and economic contexts, the problems they focus on and the solutions they formulate vary widely, depending on the position that the narrator occupies within the political arena.[13] In the second place, despite the importance we attach to the opinions of individual local elites, implicit in the comparison of Surat and Dhenkanal is the assumption that as a whole these local elites represent features specific to two broadly different worlds of development. With the help of these assumptions, we wish to undertake an inter-systemic comparison of the kind of public demands that are voiced by local elites as well as to undertake an intra-systemic analysis of attitudes in order to understand the effects of social class in their identification of the substantive issues of development.

THE SCOPE FOR LOCAL CHOICE IN SOCIAL AND ECONOMIC CHANGE

The social construction of the *problematique* of development requires an operational definition of local development as a sounding board against which competing and complementary images can be assembled. This is easier said than done, for any attempt to define development in terms of a set of desirable end states is liable to stir up a hornets' nest of theoretical controversies.[14] It was common during the post-war years of expansion to use the word to imply modernisation and economic growth. But the confidence with which policy makers used the term gradually lessened as growth has begun to decline and 'pre-modern' values of ethnicity and identity have started crowding the political agenda. The attempts to broaden the meaning of development by bringing in the notion of economic development, as opposed to economic growth only, have had their critics. The extended definition implied 'some kind of structural and organisational transformation of society', but in turn led to 'considerable disagreement as to exactly what the latter implied'.[15] Yet another view understands development 'in terms of progress toward a complex of welfare goals, such as reduction of poverty and unemployment, and diminution of inequality'.[16] Though the most popular of the three views, this is the fuzziest as well. In its attempt to reach a consensus, it mixes up in unspecified proportion both structural change and general welfare. This is an uneasy combination at the best of times, for the two do not necessarily go together. More often than not, the short-term consequence of structural change is a decline in the welfare of vulnerable social groups.

112

The changes that have become increasingly salient in our understanding of the very concept of development also reflect (and are partly induced by) the broader shifts in dominant values in the politics of many post-colonial societies since independence. Under the impact of political competition and the spread of the new values of entitlement, enfranchisement and empowerment of the sections of population previously excluded from participation, the conceptualisation of economic and social change has lost some of its teleological content, derived out of the notion of modernisation. The element of choice has increasingly asserted its presence where the notion of necessity, inevitability and law-like 'stages of growth' had constituted the dominant orthodoxy during the post-war period. The expansion of choice, understood as 'the range of articulated alternatives available to individuals and collectivities',[17] is the operational definition of local development in the context of which we need to understand political competition among rural netas to place their favourite schemes at the top of the local agenda.

The idea of choice neatly combines the subjective element of volition and the objective parameter of the availability of material resources for competing groups of local netas. In most social situations, the allocable resources and values are limited goods, so that expansion of choice, howsoever reasonable in its abstract form, is realised at the expense of identifiable social groups. Those subject to the negative consequences of development can hardly be expected to suffer them gladly. As such, the process of development has an important bearing on politics and public order and the institutional fabric of society. Indeed, as Apter remarks, 'How to control access to choice and promote the sharing of it according to approved rules and conditions of equity has been the special concern of development'.[18] Through its impact on the social and economic issues of development and the salience attached to particular problems, the rhetoric of development, as we shall see subsequently, is also a part of the process of development.

ROOM FOR LOCAL INITIATIVE

The foregoing discussion suggests the essentially political nature of the rhetoric on development. This section will discuss the

113

manner in which local interests are articulated by leaders and their perception of the manner in which they are implemented. Though rhetorical in tone, the opportunity to articulate their opinions is important to local elites and to local democracy. This has critical implications for the process of group formation and social mobility at the local level. Indeed, if the local developmental agenda were purely an extension of a vision of progress from a higher level of the system, delivered to the village through the *diktat* of a bureaucracy, it would be of little interest as a theoretical construct for the purpose of our inquiry. The Indian situation, in contrast to most post-colonial societies, leaves a certain room for manoeuvre to local elites in practice and increasingly in the institutional procedure.

Rural development policies in Gujarat and Orissa, and the organisational structure meant for their implementation at the local level, have gone through substantial changes since independence. The changes in programmes, priorities and institutional modes reflect shifting patterns in regional and national politics. An enduring feature that stands out despite changes in the specific policy concerns is the conflict between state-centred and society-centred rationalities – two major components of local politics which reflect quite different attitudes towards development. The former is projected through planning, national in scope, to be achieved through rational bureaucratic organisations of resources and personnel. The reception of these plans by the rural society can be less than enthusiastic or even hostile, not necessarily because of their novelty but because, often in practice, the plans originating from the state are often antagonistic to rural interests, and some social groups who are left outside the scope of development plans altogether.[19]

While development is high among national priorities, the state in India is not a developmental state in the classic sense.[20] No formal authority is accorded to the bureaucracy or the organisations responsible for developmental planning to initiate the policy process independently of the elected representatives of the people. The power that the Planning Commission has enjoyed in the past was secured through the political support it received from Jawaharlal Nehru, India's first Prime Minister and the leader of the Congress party, which during the first decades after independence held virtually undisputed sway over government in India. This created an anomalous situation in development administration at the local level.[21] The civil servant, down to the level of the *gramsevak* and the *gramsevika* as part of the bureaucratic planning apparatus, had a bureaucratic plan for what needed to be done. But there were few institutional resources to enable him or her to implement on their own the agenda given to them by the state. Under the constitution, they had no power to coerce people into falling in line with the development plan. While the bureaucrats might have had some firm ideas about the specific details of development strategy, they had no authority and little power to tell the peasant what to plant. The situation has become more complicated to the disadvantage of the bureaucracy as the decline of Congress hegemony and the change in the political climate in favour of liberalisation have lowered political support for planning and bureaucratic implementation. Though the state-initiated plans and programmes of development still enjoy greater visibility in the (state-controlled) media, those in charge of implementing them often come against the resistance of those opposed to them at the local level. As a result, often after much publicity in their favour, plans have to be quietly shelved or, more likely, adapted to local interests and conditions. An insight into this process can be gained by understanding the key components of the local developmental agenda.

The awkward situation in which the civil servant finds himself or herself when cast in the role of promoter of change has several explanations. To begin with, though the administration in India is the beneficiary of a long tradition of bureaucratic government during the colonial period, its role has been identified with the functions of revenue collection and the maintenance of order. Corresponding to these two functions, the chain of authority ran along the lines of revenue and land records administration on the one hand and the police on the other. The two chains – of the *daroga*, *jamadar* and *chowkidar* on the one hand and the *tehsildar* and the *patwari* on the other – were combined in the office of the collector and the district magistrate from the district headquarters down to the local level. At independence, the civil service, which provided a readily available national, organisational network, would have been an ideal choice to implement developmental objectives. However, reared in the colonial tradition of vertical chains of command

and administrative rather than managerial tradition, these generalists had neither the technical skills essential to development nor the social vision and aptitude to work with the representatives of the local people in order to achieve the social and economic objectives set by the planning apparatus. Some of these challenges of social and economic transformation have brought to the surface a deep contradiction latent within the bureaucracy in India. As might be expected given its colonial origin, the dominant ethos of the bureaucracy is biased towards the maintenance of order, whereas basic to the notion of development is the upward mobility of lower social groups which necessarily challenges the dominant status of entrenched interests. After independence, the bureaucracy could not maintain its earlier colonial image of power, nor could it continue to exist as a high-prestige class enjoying exceptional privilege. A closer identification with the masses and the shedding of its former paternalistic and authoritarian tone of administration were called for.

> Although the bureaucracy did concede the desirability of such a change on the theoretical and emotional level, yet at the same time it developed a system of rationalisation to justify the maintenance of status quo. A great hiatus persists within the Indian bureaucracy between its emotional awareness of the desirability of change and the willingness to accept it in practice.
>
> (Dwivedi and Jain (1985), p 225)[22]

Following independence, several administrative attempts were made to tide over this difficulty. Creation of the development block – an intermediate unit of development administration situated between the village and the district – was one of the major administrative innovations. With up to fifty villages and on the average about 80,000 inhabitants, the developmental block was parallel to but did not always overlap with the subdistrict revenue units called *tehsils* or talukas, nor with police circles. Each block was expected to provide 'an area large enough for functions which the village panchayat cannot perform and yet small enough to attract the interest and service of its residents'.[23] Present within this new spatial unit of development administration which provided the vital face-to-face contacts between farmers and change agents was the extension staff, a new kind of civil servant with technical expertise, trained in the art of persuasion. Despite the initial expectations, the blocks suffered from their artificiality. Unlike the tehsil or the village, they lacked established identities as territorial units. Furthermore, as the scheme unfolded, the original Community Development Programme became bogged down in bureaucratic rules. Initially intending to encourage popular participation, the Community Development officers patronised the local populace as their colonial masters had once done. The people remained uninvolved and the desired development efforts were not forthcoming.[24] To tide over this difficulty, in 1957 the Committee on Plan Projects of the National Development Council commissioned a special group under the chairmanship of Balwantrai Mehta. The Mehta report recommended that development efforts be expedited through a three-tiered system of decentralised government, intended to elicit local participation and enthusiasm. The result was panchayati raj, a remarkable experiment in democratic decentralisation which was intended to provide for the decentralisation of administrative functions, the politicisation of planning, and the joint implementation of development programmes by officials and local leaders simultaneously.

Panchayati raj is a system of three distinct tiers below the State government. At the grass-roots are the village panchayats or councils. *Panchas*, or members of the panchayat, are elected on the basis of universal adult franchise while the Sarpanch or panchayat chairman may be directly elected by the villagers or indirectly elected by the other panchas. At the block level are panchayat samitis or council committees, whose membership consists of the Sarpanchas and of certain other coopted and ex-officio members – women, representatives of Scheduled Castes and Tribes and leaders of cooperative societies. From among the samiti membership, a chairman is indirectly elected who may be called *Pradhan* or president. These chairmen of the panchayat samitis in any single district comprise the *Zilla Parishad* or district association. Additional members are again coopted to represent women, scheduled castes and tribes in this district level unit. All local members of the legislative assembly (MLAs) and Members of Parliament (MPs) are the ex-officio members of the Zilla Parishad. The Zilla Parishad elects its own presiding officer, called the *Pramukh*.[25]

The political fulcrum of the panchayati raj system is its middle tier, the panchayat samiti. These block-level units are responsible for the development functions, especially for preparing preliminary plans and for implementing the community development schemes. The samiti also controls most of the development resources, including tax monies and material inputs, and how these are allocated and used. The Zilla Parishad on the other hand is essentially a coordinating and advisory body. The powers of the village panchayat are less substantial in comparison.[26]

The initial expectation on the part of policy makers that panchayats would work on non-political lines was not borne out by the subsequent experience. The failure of these institutions to keep politics out reveals the naive expectation and apolitical stance of the post-war hopes of economic growth and modernisation cherished by the Indian development planners who expected to stay above partisan, local politics while intending to bring about radical social change within a democratic political system. Balwantrai Mehta, one of the original creators of panchayati raj, thought that elections might adversely affect these institutions. He wanted some non-official agency to work for bringing about unanimity in elections.

Reddy and Seshadri (1972) have captured the unstated assumptions behind these expectations.

> There were many arguments that politics should not be permitted to enter local institutions where stress should be on developing local potentialities and solving local problems. More particularly, it was argued that political parties should have nothing to do with these institutions because requirements in the local areas like a school, a hospital, a cooperative, a veterinary hospital, a community centre, an approach road, a small irrigation canal, a warehouse, street lights, garbage clearance, sanitation and hygiene, etc. are all the common requirements of any village and the mobilisation of the people need not be tainted by party politics.
>
> (Reddy and Seshadri (1972), p 9)

A scheme was introduced in 1964 in Andhra Pradesh, Rajasthan and Punjab to reward those panchayats and panchayat samitis who could 'elect' their representatives unanimously. However,

This experiment ended where it began. Failure of this experiment also bears out the analysis so far made. Panchayati raj institutions are not humanitarian service institutions but political ones. They are the avenues for local leadership to assert their position and are part of the political pyramid, so to say. The ambitious ones among the panchayat leaders use them as training grounds as well as vantage points to climb up to higher positions. Hence nobody would leave the post uncontested in the altruistic interest of his village.

(Reddy and Seshadri (1972), p 10)

Yet another major innovation in the area of development policy formulation and implementation was the introduction of voluntary organisations, particularly various forms of co-operatives. A history of experiments with cooperatives extended throughout the century.[27] Early cooperatives were primarily intended to provide credit to farmers and to rural agro-industrial ventures. The second Five Year Plan encouraged the Cooperative Movement to add marketing, warehousing, trading and other economic functions to its activities. Following the findings of Sir Malcolm Darling, who was commissioned in 1957 to evaluate the progress of the cooperative movement, it was decided to reinforce their 'popular content' by establishing closer links with the panchayati raj system. In 1958, the National Development Council resolved that cooperatives should be organised from the village level upwards and should become responsible, along with village panchayats, for economic and social development. In the same year the Ministry of Community Development and Cooperation was created to link the cooperative movement with the other ambitious government programme for development. In 1959 the Congress party adopted its famous though controversial Nagpur resolution on cooperative farming. And in the early 1960s, the Ministry of Community Development and Cooperation was expanded to include responsibility for panchayati raj.[28]

The salient achievement of the three innovations, namely the introduction of the developmental block, panchayati raj and the mobilisation of developmental efforts through the cooperative movement, was to distinguish policy formulation from policy implementation below the district level. Under the process of democratic decentralisation, authority and initiative for development policy was to be placed in the hands of the representatives of the people, focused in the panchayati raj institutions, whereas the bureaucracy was given the limited task of implementing the policies adopted by the panchayat samitis. The preeminence of the bureaucracy as the sole embodiment of governmental power was further compromised as the older functions of tax collection, land settlement and records, law and order were dissociated from the administration of development projects and given over to new, democratically accountable government departments. On the other hand, the accretion of real power in the hands of panchayati raj bodies attracted political parties to local elections, creating direct links between the panchayati raj bodies below the district level with ministers and party organisations at the State level.[29] The cumulative impact of these measures was to provide new organisational foci to interests and social groups below the district level, which widened the room for manoeuvre for local elites in their attempts to incorporate their demands in the local developmental agenda. As the knowledge spread that representation in the panchayati raj structure was crucial for a social group to have its objectives put on the agenda, the salience and depth of institutions associated with panchayati raj grew.

The growing penetration of rural society by panchayati raj institutions in the 1960s greatly affected the process of agenda-setting at the local level. In the first place, it institutionalised the provision for a local 'input' into the bureaucratic plans and targets that had hitherto been the most compelling element of the local development agenda. Also, by providing for formal representation of the Scheduled Castes and Scheduled Tribes through the policy of reservation, panchayati raj institutions generated a self-sustaining process of increasing participation. The process also opened up local institutions for use by the lower social strata to put their demands on the local agenda. Under the cumulative impact of these changes, the process of agenda-setting became at least partly accessible to social groups from outside the restricted group of old-style social notables. The process of incremental diffusion of power, achieved in the central and regional political arenas in the 1950s, spread to the local level in the 1960s. Since the developmental plans are at least partly aimed at the groups at the bottom of the social pyramid, to generate the requisite power to implement those plans, those responsible for implementation had to become increasingly sensitive to the wishes of those who were not satisfied with the pace or the direction of development.

This room for manoeuvre in the setting of the local developmental agenda was exploited by the ubiquitous netas who used this role to seek a voice in local politics through the manipulation of the flow of development resources. Conversely, under the expansive logic of political competition, the opening-up of local institutions to local interests paved the way for increasing accommodation of the lower social strata who had hitherto been excluded from effective participation. The process through which the local developmental agenda was formulated and the items that appear on the agenda provide an insight into the local developmental environment, the state of social mobility and the local political arena.

The creation of such political–administrative structures below the district level provides an opportunity for the meeting of the state and rural society. Leaders active below the district level not only voice support for government programmes – their commitment to programme goals and mechanics being a *sine qua non* for policy attainment: they must also forge links between the government and the populace. Along with the traditional political tasks of distributing patronage among supporters and communicating popular grievances to government agencies, netas shoulder the responsibility for new tasks of decision-making, mobilising resources and engendering public support for official programmes.[30] In the same vein, Reddy and Seshadri, in presenting local elites as 'men who would be interested in acting as the conveyor-belt for the policies and programmes of the Centre or the State,'[31] give vent to a desire for rapid modernisation that one finds in the strategic thinking on development of the post-war period. Through their articulation of issues, identification of solutions, and evaluation of the progress and effectiveness of the process of implementation, we can observe local elites at work, making use of the room for manoeuvre generated through the creation of the new institutions of local democracy.

THE CONCEPTUALISATION OF SOCIAL AND ECONOMIC CHANGE

Individual preferences for desirable policy outcomes are the building blocks of local development. They are also instrumental for the expansion of choice and the increase of groups with access to the process of allocation within the rural population. Both are crucial to the pace and quantum of development. The preceding discussion of the institutional constraints on the process of social and economic change provides some insights to the incentives that rural netas have for conceptualising local issues in terms of problems and to articulate them at appropriate levels. In order to understand the extent of choice and the nature of political demands from below in Gujarat and Orissa, we began our survey by asking local elites a series of questions concerning the problems faced by the people in their area and the solutions that they envisaged to them.

In course of their dealings with outsiders, including government officials and politicians at higher levels, local elites are often called upon to formulate their political demands in terms of the 'problems of the people in their area'. The manner in which one articulates these problems varies greatly, going from the most concrete and specific to the abstract and the global, producing in the process a fascinating and somewhat chaotic collection of ideas. These ideas are important as possible keys to the understanding of the response of the people of an area to development projects. And yet, as clues they are useful only if we can place them in the context of meaningful constructs with a social significance. After all, even in a carefully controlled survey environment, how is one to be confident that a 'problem' articulated by a local elite is indeed a deeply felt need with some political significance of its own and not simply a passing whim of little enduring significance?

Political scientists and those engaged in survey research often expect people to have opinions and act out of those opinions without problematising both. In order to construct meaningful chains of ideas out of a cloverfield of issues tossed in by respondents with apparent abandon, we need first to understand the process that must precede the formulation of a problem and its articulation. Our process of inquiry starts with a question: why is a problem a *problem*? We can approach the process of problem formulation and articulation usefully by first taking into consideration the notion of 'recipe knowledge', that is 'knowledge limited to pragmatic competence of routine performance'.[32] In introducing this concept, Berger and Luckmann give the example of the telephone. In most situations, one does not have to master the complex engineering technology nor the organisation which makes the telephone a feasible means of communication. The knowledge of some elementary rules is sufficient under normal circumstances for the specific, pragmatic use of the telephone. The need to know more for most people arises when one comes across a problem with the network of communication, one whose solution lies outside the normal rules of operation. There is, therefore, a critical threshold to the realities of everyday experience beyond which recipe knowledge is no longer sufficient and where political action and knowledge of a different order are called for. Put differently, under normal circumstances, the telephone will not come spontaneously to mind as a problem until it *is* a problem. Once it has registered itself on one's consciousness as a problem, one sets about looking for ways and means of tackling it as well as one can. The solution one is likely to come up with will depend on the seriousness of the problem, the available resources and the scope for intervention provided by the political structure within which one is placed. The hierarchy of solutions might therefore begin with a simple telephone call from a neighbour's home to the telephone exchange. If this does not settle the problem, one will need to move to the more extreme step of contacting the authorities higher in the organisation of telecommunications, and putting pressure on them through a coalition of telephone users from the area to upgrade the local (possibly antiquated) telephone exchange.

Two further concepts are necessary for the process through which social actors formulate problems and solutions. In the first place, the telephone is unlikely to be a problem to a person who is not in a situation where the existence of phones is known or their necessity felt. At the origin of a problem within the individual psyche, there is somewhere along the line a concrete interest, or, alternately, there is the *general situation of the subject in society*[33] which substitutes a subjective necessity for a concrete interest. In consuming better-quality cereals, wearing synthetic fibre and sporting television antennae, the upper social strata create new norms of good living, which, thereafter, become established local norms against which others in the village measure the state of their relative deprivation. This demonstration effect in terms of conspicuous consumption by better-off sections of the rural society is as true of the Gujarat countryside to-day as it is of Orissa.

The second aspect of problem construction concerns the intersubjective communicability of problems. Talking about problems in their capacity as representatives of the local community and shared interests, respondents are likely to exclude the purely personal and private, and come up with problems of reference groups for whom the issues involved constitute shared problems. This is where the catalytic role of the social investigator – whose objective is neither to suggest nor to prompt, but merely to listen actively – becomes crucially important. To make the articulation of problems possible, to quote Berger and Luckmann, the articulator must have some 'knowledge of the relevance structure of others'. As they suggest:

> I know better than to tell my doctor about my investment problems, my lawyer about my ulcer pains, or my accountant about my quest for religious truth. The basic relevance structures referring to everyday life are presented to me ready-made by the social stock of knowledge itself.
>
> (Berger and Luckmann (1967), p 60)

The shared interests which quite conceivably constitute the basis of a political alliance among some local elites and sections of the rural population could create a sense of an 'epistemic community',[34] activated by the investigator through the process of verbalisation of deeply felt needs. Under these conditions and possibly only under these conditions, discourse on the problems of development also becomes the basis of the creation of political communities around competing interests whose discourse, by giving concrete shape to potential demands, helps in the solution to those very problems themselves.

The abstract social psychology of problem formulation can be conceptualised in terms of two macro-political ideal types, situated at polar extremes. On the one hand, there is the equilibrium of the perfectly competitive market where all private demands achieve their just allocation and none needs to be formulated as a publicly articulated problem of the kind described above. This is a model where all transactions are undertaken on the lines of economic transactions or social exchanges. Challenges to the rules of the game, the distribution of power in the political system, or the potential of coalition formation, are not called for.[35] On the other extreme, in the limiting case of a revolutionary situation, every specific social and economic problem is subjugated to the overarching political objective of revolution. The political actors involved in this enterprise construe all actual social situations as intermediate steps towards the dissolution of the distinction between the public and the private in the ultimate *nirvana* of communism.

The framework of analysis more appropriate to rural India is situated between these two polar opposites of a social free market of the kind represented by the ideal type of liberalism and a revolutionary situation conceptualised by Marxist political theory. It provides for both the satisfaction of private needs through the mechanism of the market as well as the possibility of state intervention in a situation of market failure or the non-availability of the market as a mode of transaction. Needs that are best settled in the market place are not normally articulated as public problems. A recipe knowledge of local and regional politics is sufficient for this purpose. As such, the kinds of problems that are mentioned by our rural netas in Gujarat and Orissa provide an important insight into the empirical context from which they arise and about the political profile of the local elites, forming part of specific 'epistemic communities', responsible for them.[36] Alternatively, once we have some idea of the kind of problems that arise within a particular empirical context, we can look for an explanation for the particular constellation of problems in a variety of parameters, including, first of all, the nature of the local economy and the evolution of the market, social mobility and political consciousness.

The hierarchy of problems

In the field situation, when talking to the gaon ka netas who are not accustomed to being interviewed by outsiders, even after an investigator has established his credentials, it is always advisable to start the conversation with a leading, 'warming-up' question. Otherwise, the clash of cultures between the interviewer and the respondent can lead to a quick and disastrous end to the survey. Thus, both in Gujarat and Orissa, a leading, open-ended question regarding 'the most important problem of the people in the area' was asked at the beginning of the survey, both to get the respondent used to the practice of precise and brief formulations to specific questions, as well as to sensitise him about the general objectives of the survey and the respective roles of the investigator and the respondent. This was followed by a series of similarly open-ended questions regarding the solutions that the respondent envisaged to the problems mentioned. The responses to these questions have been used to reconstruct the full range of problems that rural netas, rooted in the life of the village and reflecting it, encounter in their everyday experience of development.[37]

Both as regards problems as well as solutions, the responses were recorded in the order in which they were presented, so that at the stage of analysis we could measure the salience attached to a given problem or solution by looking at its position in the hierarchy of problems formulated by the respondent. The first or the 'top of the mind' item was considered the most salient of all. We also measured the importance accorded to a problem

Table 4.1 The most pressing problem of the people in the area (percentages)

Problem	Gujarat (n=131)		Orissa (n=102)	
	Most salient %	Mentioned at least once %	Most salient %	Mentioned at least once %
Infrastructure				
Irrigation	8	12	56	78
Improvement of infrastructure	10	50	4	59
Agricultural inputs	3	8	0	2
Welfare				
Quality of life	30	53	20	84
Food scarcity	0	1	5	31
Distributive justice				
Redistribution	37	74	6	47
State inaction	7	34	1	7
Social tension	4	12	4	6
None	1	–	4	–
Total	100	–	100	–

by the local elites as a whole by counting the number of persons who mentioned the given problem or solution at least once within the range of items they invoked. Table 4.1 presents the configuration of problems that emerged out of these questions.

Before analysing the results presented in table 4.1, it should be mentioned that the problems suggested by our respondents ran into about 100 different kinds. They were aggregated by putting together items that pertained to a main theme. The Gujarat responses strongly suggest the primacy of the issue of 'distributive justice' – the redistribution of wealth as the major problem of the people of the area, cited by 47 per cent of the respondents as the most salient problem. This general category is created by merging responses such as 'inequitable distribution of irrigation water', 'no water supply for backward sections of the village like scheduled castes and tribes', 'no electricity for Tribals and Harijans', 'non-implementation of minimum wages act', 'unemployment', 'poverty', 'exploitation by the rich', 'harassment by officials' and 'the widening gap between the rich and the poor'.

This is followed by the problems of general welfare and the quality of life, cited by 30 per cent of Gujarat's local elites. This category was created by aggregating responses pertaining to general welfare, such as 'the lack of drinking water facilities', 'poor roads in the village', 'the village not being connected by all-weather roads and bridges', 'lack of post office', 'communal facilities', 'setting up of a police station for protection and safety', 'personal safety from wild animals' and 'street lights'.

The creation of an infrastructure of production came as the third most salient category of problems in Gujarat, voiced by a fifth of the respondents. This included responses with a direct bearing on the production of wealth, such as 'the lack of marketing facilities for agricultural products', 'lack of agricultural storage facilities', 'lack of opportunities for modern farming', 'water-logging', 'inadequate credit facilities', 'poor facilities for goods transport', 'livestock and veterinary centres', 'electricity' and 'irrigation'.

In Orissa, the problems formulated by the local elites are reversed in their order of priority. Irrigation comes well ahead of others, cited by about 60 per cent of the respondents. Next in order is the general quality of life, including items that contribute to general welfare, such as the availability of drinking water, drainage facilities, electricity and medical facilities, mentioned by a quarter of the respondents. The problem of distributive justice comes a distant third, voiced by 11 per cent of local elites.

When compared to 'total sensitisation', where we measure the evidence of some awareness of a given problem among the respondents regardless of the order in which the problems were presented, the order of salience reveals interesting patterns. There is a striking consistency about the ordering of problems in Gujarat. Whether we measure in terms of the 'top of the mind' score or that of 'total sensitisation', the categories of justice, welfare and means of production appear in that order in Gujarat. The picture is much fuzzier in Orissa, where, in the 'total sensitivity' index, the category of welfare moves up to the top, with an astounding 84 per cent citing issues of social welfare or the lack of amenities, indicating a demand for greater public expenditure on social welfare. Irrigation and infrastructure are heavily cited, with the demand for redistribution showing the support of a strong minority of 47 per cent. While the individual need for irrigation facilities and other agricultural inputs are not currently met and hence surface as problems of critical importance to their everyday existence, the consciousness of communal welfare management and just allocation of material benefits is not too far away.

Seen in the context of the aggregate characteristics of the developmental environment presented in chapter two, the formulation of problems by the local elites acquires a logical consistency of its own. With its intensive multi-crop farming, fed by water from the irrigation works of the Ukai project, the Surat farmer worries more about drainage than water shortage, inequitable distribution of resources rather than their availability as a whole. The rural netas of Dhenkanal have a different problem in mind. Major irrigation works planned for the district were still on the drawing board as the survey was conducted. Minor irrigation works still had to contend with the problems of coordination among various agencies responsible for different facets of development and poor quality materials which were not always properly matched to the requirement. The malaise was captured by an independent evaluation of the rural development programme.

The beneficiaries [of minor irrigation] are complaining about the quality of pump sets. The poor quality pump sets require frequent repairing. The repairing facility is not available in Blocks. The dug wells are not able to supply sufficient water during Rabi season for which suitable crop plans are not able to be developed during the season. Due to these reasons adequate number of mandays has not been increased [as a result of minor irrigation works].

(Bhuyan (1987), p 24)

SOLUTIONS

How consistent are local elites about the problems that they formulate? One possible measure of consistency is to look for the relationship between the problems they suggest as the 'most salient for the people of the area' and the solutions that they devise for them. In the order in which they were administered, the two questions are separated by other items. We can therefore expect that, in the event the problems and the solutions are purely random constructions, there will be no relationship whatsoever between them. On the other hand, if problems are the visible tip of an iceberg of a personal agenda consisting of a set of ordered preferences, with a consistent pattern of relationships between the formulation of problems and solutions, then one would expect distinct patterns of relationships to emerge.

As previously, the respondents were asked an open-ended question about solutions that they envisaged to the problems that they had mentioned without reminding them what those problems were. The responses which ran over 100 items were then aggregated into broader categories. The results (see table 4.2) indicate a rich diversity of solutions, testifying to the ability of the local elites to articulate a personal agenda.

Once again, the infrastructure of development dominates the scene in Orissa, followed by the demand that general welfare should be given due attention. Redistribution as a solution appears the last in order for the Orissa sample. In Gujarat, the demand for economic and social reform appears to be at least as important as that of general welfare and both are far ahead of solutions like irrigation, the supply of agricultural inputs and other infrastructure of production.

Table 4.2 The best solution to the most pressing problem of the area (percentages)

Solution	Gujarat (n=131)		Orissa (n=101)	
	Most salient	Mentioned at least once	Most salient	Mentioned at least once
	%	%	%	%
Infrastructure				
Material inputs	6	12	0	2
Infrastructure of production	17	26	63	83
Welfare				
Quality of life	32	52	20	78
Food supply	3	15	7	17
Distributive justice				
Interest of disadvantaged groups	13	42	3	21
State intervention	20	37	2	6
Social tension	2	4	1	6
None	7	–	4	–
Total	100	–	100	–

Table 4.3 The most salient problem cross-tabulated with the preferred solution (percentages)

Problem	Solutions			
	Infrastructure	Welfare	Distributive justice	Total
	%	%	%	%
Gujarat (n=131)				
Infrastructure	44	44	12	100
Welfare	8	66	26	100
Distributive justice	26	18	56	100
Orissa (n=101)				
Infrastructure	85	12	3	100
Welfare	34	54	12	100
Distributive justice	36	55	9	100

When the solutions were cross-tabulated with the problems, the results revealed a consistent relationship between the nature of the problem and the solution proposed to it (see table 4.3).

The importance that local elites in Orissa attach to the improvement of developmental infrastructure is to be seen in the context of the relatively later entry of Orissa into the process of the introduction of improved agricultural methods and the creation of a network of infrastructural facilities essential to rapid economic growth. The local elites demand substantial amounts of investment in irrigation, roads, agricultural inputs – and want most of this done by the government (see table 4.4). The remarkable point here is that though the developments that have already taken place in Gujarat are comparatively recent, in Orissa, thanks to the all-India diffusion of ideas and norms of representation, the local elites of Orissa in a sense are rapidly catching up with their counterparts from Gujarat.

Table 4.4 Social class and identification of problems

Social class	Problems			
	Infrastructure	Welfare	Distributive justice	Total
	%	%	%	%
Gujarat (n=131)[1]				
High	14	10	76	100
Medium	20	47	33	100
Adivasi/Harijan	25	24	51	100
Total	21	31	48	100
Orissa (n=101)[2]				
High	61	29	10	100
Medium	57	27	16	100
Adivasi/Harijan	77	18	5	100
Total	63	26	11	100

Notes [1] Chi-square 14.63; degrees of freedom ; significance 0.005.
[2] Chi-square 3.43 ; degrees of freedom 4 ; significance 0.48.

THE EFFECT OF SOCIAL CLASS

Our analysis so far has concentrated on the examination of the pattern of internal consistency in the formulation of the personal agenda on development through the analysis of the relationship of the problems and solutions. The result of cross-tabulation shows a pattern of consistency. To the extent that social classes contain some features of epistemic communities, we should expect (1) stronger relationships between problems and solutions, and (2) a causal relationship between the kinds of problems that are formulated and the social class of local elites.

In both Surat and Dhenkanal, the lowest social strata among local elites mention infrastructural facilities as the most salient problem of development, though the absolute magnitude of demand for infrastructure is much higher in Dhenkanal than in Surat. Considering the familiarity with the capitalist market in the production system of Gujarat, the demand for economic facilities is more likely to be met there by the market than through state intervention. However, as a rule, this is more likely to be true of the affluent members of society than for the rural population as a whole, the less well-off looking more in the direction of the state to provide them with the necessary facilities. The consciousness of relative deprivation, formulated in terms of the demand for distributive justice in developmental allocation, is very much present in Surat as compared to Dhenkanal. The pattern observed in Surat confirms the observation of others.[38] One thus notices a relatively high awareness of injustice on the part of the highest as well as the lowest strata rather than the middle, who, in fact, are seen as the militant face of rising agrarian capitalism.

The relationship between social class and the perception of problems of development has a consistent pattern in Gujarat, seen in the form of a strong statistical relationship. The responses in Orissa do not exhibit a consistent relationship. Unlike in Gujarat, the middle stratum is the keenest in its demand for distributive justice. Sandwiched between the insistent demands of aggressive Adivasi/Harijan netas, keen on better working conditions and higher wages on the one hand and the absence of the kind of infrastructural facilities that have given a new viability to modest landholdings, the intermediate groups in Orissa are angry, confused about what they could legitimately expect from the state and the market. They are, as a result, without an effective and coherent ideology of development.

In terms of the appropriate agencies to undertake the implementation of proferred solutions (see table 4.5), local elites in Surat give the pride of place to the institutions of panchayati raj whereas the 'government', that is the bureaucracy, gets the top score in Orissa, with practically 70 per cent citing it as the most appropriate agency to undertake the implementation of developmental projects. Though in terms of its salience the government attracts the support of only 30 per cent in Surat, it

Table 4.5 Most appropriate agency to implement suggested programme (percentages)

Agency	Gujarat (n=131)		Orissa (n=101)	
	Most appropriate %	Mentioned at least once %	Most appropriate %	Mentioned at least once %
Government	30	66	69	91
Panchayati raj institutions	60	61	27	46
Voluntary agencies	6	24	0	3
None	4	0	4	0
Total	100	–	100	–

is very much present in the background, with two thirds of the respondents mentioning it at least once among the various agencies cited as appropriate for undertaking the implementation of developmental projects. The corresponding figure for Orissa is an astounding 91 per cent, revealing the relative underdevelopment of alternative structures to the bureaucracy.

The relative prominence of voluntary agencies in Gujarat compared to their virtual absence in Orissa is another significant feature. Though they draw only a modest 6 per cent in the top of the mind score, a respectable 24 per cent mention them at least once in Surat, whereas in Orissa they are not mentioned at all among the first institution cited. Only 3 per cent cite voluntary agencies at least once among all institutions mentioned as appropriate for the implementation of developmental projects. Responses of specific social groups reveal another contrasting aspect of local politics in Gujarat and Orissa. The government as the most appropriate agency draws more support in Orissa among the Adivasi/Harijan leaders, going up to 80 per cent, whereas it is panchayati raj which is preferred by the same social categories in Surat. With its score of 65 per cent among the Adivasi/Harijan leaders in Surat, it is easy to imagine the relative control that they have learnt to exercise over the institutions of local democracy in Gujarat in contrast to Orissa where the lowest strata (like, in fact, the society as a whole, but more so) look up to the government as the ultimate provider.

Interestingly, the only area where the government draws a score almost at the same level as the panchayat in Gujarat is in the provision of infrastructural facilities. The superior funding power of the government which must account for this is much in evidence in Orissa, where, high as the score of the government is, it is at its highest among those who mention the provision of development infrastructure as the most salient problem.

Table 4.6 Preferred solution cross-tabulated with the most appropriate agency (percentages)

Solution	Preferred agency			
	Panchayat	Government	Voluntary agencies	Total
	%	%	%	%
Gujarat (n=131)				
Infrastructure	47	43	10	100
Welfare	72	26	2	100
Distributive justice	62	29	9	100
Total	60	30	6	
Orissa (n=101)				
Infrastructure	23	77	0	100
Welfare	41	59	0	100
Distributive justice	33	67	0	100
Total	27	69	0	

On the whole, the scenario of problem formulation and identification of appropriate agencies in Orissa correspond to Bailey's original observations about the expectations of local-level leaders in Orissa, which mostly consisted in patronage from the government.[39] These elites derive their legitimacy and influence over their clientele by getting things from outside the local arena; not surprisingly, the themes of infrastructure and welfare dominate their range of problems. The Gujarat responses distinguish themselves in two respects. In the first place, redistribution has left far behind that of infrastructure – a need that is taken care of by market transactions. Rather, the problem that dominates the scene is allocation of values and the institutional modes in which market transactions take place. In the second place, the Gujarat elite ascribe a larger role to the local political arena with a large majority identifying the panchayati raj structure and voluntary agencies as appropriate agencies for the implementation of their agenda of desirable developmental programmes.

A GENERAL EVALUATION OF PROGRESS

The formulation of problems and solutions or the identification of appropriate agencies for implementation are not the ultimate objectives of local elites. Faced with competition for developmental allocation they are intensely aware of the fact that their positions are contingent on their ability to deliver the material benefits of development to people in the village. To that extent, it is important to find out how satisfied the gaon ka netas are with the overall rate and direction of development. We shall bring this chapter to a close with a brief look at the general evaluation of progress and its relationship to the preceding discussion of problems, solutions, agencies and social class. The data are presented in table 4.7.

From table 4.7, though there is more discontent in Orissa as compared to Gujarat, in both States according to the vast majority of our respondents there is at least some satisfaction

Table 4.7 Satisfaction with development and welfare of people in the area (village/taluka) (percentages)

	Level of satisfaction			
Social class	Not at all %	Somewhat %	A great deal %	Total %
Gujarat (n=131)				
High	19	62	19	100
Medium	8	74	18	100
Adivasi/Harijan	9	75	16	100
Total	11	71	18	100
Orissa (n=101)				
High	19	75	6	100
Medium	23	58	19	100
Adivasi/Harijan	23	64	13	100
Total	21	64	15	100

Table 4.8 Problem cross-tabulated with development and welfare of people in the area (percentages)

Problem	Level of satisfaction			
type	Not at all %	Somewhat %	A great deal %	Total %
Gujarat (n=131)				
Infrastructure	11	70	19	100
Welfare	2	90	8	100
Distributive justice	15	61	24	100
Orissa (n=101)				
Infrastructure	16	69	15	100
Welfare	34	58	8	100
Distributive justice	27	55	18	100

about the total impact of development programmes on the welfare of the people in the area.[40] Besides, the satisfaction is not confined to any particular social stratum among the elites, but, judging from the non-significant nature of the correlation with social class, is shared widely by elites from all social strata. Nor is the relationship between problem identification and overall satisfaction (see table 4.8) necessarily spectacular. Only 15 per cent of those mentioning distributive justice as their salient problem in Gujarat consider themselves 'not at all satisfied', and the percentage among the same group who derive a great deal of satisfaction from development actually exceeds those not at all satisfied by 9 per cent. On the other hand, the situation in Orissa suggests a closer tie between salience of distributive justice and dissatisfaction with development, with more than a quarter of those citing distributive justice as their most salient problem also claiming that they are not at all satisfied with development, their numbers exceeding the most satisfied by 9 per cent.

The other point to be noted here is the contrast between Gujarat and Orissa when it comes to the cross-tabulation between the most salient problem and dissatisfaction with development. Interestingly, only 2 per cent of those mentioning welfare as their most salient problem among Gujarati gaon ka netas were not at all satisfied with development compared to 34 per cent of local elites in Orissa. The contrast is less striking when it comes to infrastructural facilities (11 per cent in Gujarat compared to 16 per cent in Orissa) and distributive justice (15 per cent in Gujarat compared to 27 per cent in Orissa). One explanation lies in the higher level of provision for welfare in Gujarat, further reinforced by the belief in the market as better placed to provide welfare, unlike infrastructure which is not profitable enough for the market to provide or distributive justice which, being in the nature of a collective good, cannot be provided by the market.[41] Another explanation is the higher expectation of the provision of welfare by the government – yet another indication of the expectation of welfare management by the *sarkar*, reminiscent of Scott's depiction of the moral economy and Bailey's account of the Oriya peasant.[42]

CONCLUSION

The challenge to ascribed status through achieved power is an important aspect of rural development in India. Development, rather than being seen exclusively as the acquisition of 'modern' values and higher levels of consumption, is perceived by local elites primarily as a political process which progressively draws an increasing proportion of rural people into the political arena and extends the social base of institutions, often in the face of resistance from old-style social notables. In the process, traditional bonds of unequal status and privilege are challenged, and are replaced by new norms based on political transaction and new notions of egalitarianism, citizenship and entitlement. The first step in our understanding of this process is to investigate the personal agendas that the local elites, both as participants in the political life at the local level as well as representatives of the interests of different social classes, seek to place on the agenda of development. These problems constitute the visible links of a chain that connects the broad cross-section of local people through their leaders to public and voluntary institutions responsible for the implementation of development projects.

An attempt has been made in this chapter to study the nature of political demands articulated by India's rural netas, the solutions they envisage to these problems and their perception of institutional modes for the implementation of these pro-grammes. Underneath the universe of problems, solutions and evaluations of development agencies, we have sought to understand the differences at the level of region and within each region, on the basis of social class, to which the netas belong and with whose collective interests they are identified. These responses provide field evidence to examine some of the established notions about the nature of interaction between the society and the state in the areas of rural development.

The assertion, consistently made by the planner and the politician and tenaciously held on to by India's left-leaning intelligentsia, that state intervention is the ultimate objective of people at the local level is only partly supported by our data. Further, when people cite the government as the preferred agency of development, the opinion is motivated by objectives not in the nature of material benefits of development but collective goods, relating to the norms of allocation. Thus, in Gujarat, where an active market itself provides the basis for the allocation of infrastructural facilities, the problem perceived on the whole is not that of tangible infrastructural facilities which the market can provide more effectively, but that of distributive justice, which the state and not the market has the authority to provide. The Gujarati netas, used as they are to a more complex set of agencies for the implementation of developmental projects, are able to discriminate between the bureaucracy, panchayati raj and voluntary agencies. In Orissa, where the market is less developed, infrastructural demands are among the most insistent. In the absence of serious alternatives, these demands gravitate towards the government as the only agency capable of undertaking appropriate action.

By and large, one gets the impression from the literature on panchayati raj from the 1970s that local elites have not fulfilled the catalytic role that they were assigned by theorists of development and modernisation. This failure, which has been directed at the local elites as the sole villains of the piece, more interested in their personal gains rather than in the development of the rural society as a whole, should instead encourage us to pose some basic questions to the assumptions that lie at the heart of modernisation theory, shared implicitly by the early writers on panchayati raj.[43] The most important of these assumptions was the reduction of the countryside to an objective state of underdevelopment, which, through the infusion of capital, technology and rational management and the agency of external intervention, would cut loose its traditional roots and set off in the direction of the promised land of the modernist utopia. Development itself was seen by the early modernisers as above partisan politics, which would nevertheless lead to increasing participation, welfare and growth through rational planning and bureaucratic implementation. The political structure within which this model was seen to operate was directly in contradiction with this assumption, because, under the logic of growing participation, the village and local elites as its competing spokesmen were considered autonomous actors, expected in the normal order of things to generate their own agendas. Once we take proper notice of these aspects of development through the analysis of the discourse of the actors themselves, a different general perspective on development begins to replace the views popularised by the modernisation paradigm.

From the identification of problems from their everyday experience of the process of development and the formulation of institutional solutions to those problems by rural netas, we shall next move in the direction of individual action and initiative through institutional participation and radical action. With this intention, we need to relate the overall satisfaction with development on the part of local elites with the salience they attach to problems and the social class whose interests they represent. The picture that emerges both in Gujarat and Orissa is one of enormous complexity. The salience of distributive justice does not necessarily lead to dissatisfaction with development. Instead, one can hypothesise that the formulation of the *problematique* of development in terms of distributive justice is seen as yet another instrument to promote one's position within the arena. For the further examination of these conjectures, we need to look at the sense of financial achievement and satisfaction with development amongst the rural netas and study how these opinions vary according to region and social class. Beyond this, we shall need to study the values and attitudes of local leaders in Gujarat and Orissa towards conflict and the cohesiveness of the local community. These themes will be taken up in chapter five. From what we have understood so far, the relationship between the salience attached to distributive justice and action and attitudes likely to follow from it could be more complex than one might suppose at the outset. This is the basic fact of development at the local level in India in the context of which we have to consider the range of measures adopted by local elites to achieve their objectives. These issues will be pursued in the subsequent chapters.

5

THE SOCIAL CONSTRUCTION OF LOCAL CONFLICT: UNEQUAL BENEFITS, RADICAL PROTEST AND SOCIAL COHESION

THE OBJECTIVES

Growing conflict over caste, community and land has become an important aspect of rural politics in India. Rather than merely indicating the 'decay' of the political system, collective conflict also indicates the growing assertiveness on the part of previously powerless groups.[1] These conflicts involve the use of force as well as institutional methods. They can lead to the creation of political alliances among groups with similar interests. The process of group formation is often couched in the rhetoric of sectional benefits and the ideological objectives of development. The conflict over the allocation of material benefits of development links together the rhetoric through which rural netas articulate their personal agendas and the impact of social and economic change on their interests. This chapter inquires into the larger theme of development and conflict through the specific issues of the relationship between economic change and social conflict; the radicalisation of the local political arena; the social correlates of radicalism; and conflict and cohesion in the local arena. The inquiry then moves on to the implications of these findings for the relationship between radical protest, the process of community formation and political action at the local level. The elites' perception of popular attitudes towards new notions of entitlement and enfranchisement and their impact on conflict and cohesiveness within the local political arena are crucial to the larger theme of social change in India. Though a

141

survey can provide only a still picture of this dynamic process, the chapter will make an attempt to analyse this process by drawing on other sources.

The empirical questions in terms of which this chapter inquires into the interaction between social and economic change and the cohesiveness of rural life include the extent to which different social groups have benefited from development; and growth of radical sentiments and their impact on the structure of power prevailing within the village arena. These issues are examined on the basis of the responses to hypothetical issues such as decision-making by a small group of well-informed leaders as against popular and contentious participation. Some implications for community formation and representative democracy are drawn from this. The comparative method is used to facilitate the analysis of wide regional diversities because the transformation of rural life, initiated by British rule and intensified by post-independence politics, has gone further in some parts of India than in others. Besides, even within the same region, different social strata have been affected by the process of transformation in unequal measures. Hence, in addition to interregional comparison, the data are also analysed according to the social strata from which the local elites are drawn. As in previous chapters, social class is stratified at three levels: high, which includes upper castes; middle, which incorporates cultivating and Backward classes; and low, which includes Adivasi/Harijan netas.

ECONOMIC CHANGE AND LOCAL CONFLICT

Competition over material resources and resentment at being denied what local leaders deem to be their just share of the bounties of the state are often precursors to political action. The problems of development that local elites encounter in their daily interaction with bureaucratic and political decision-makers or with rivals within the local arena create enough potential for tension and conflict over material benefits and norms of allocation. India's villages, the object of state-sponsored development plans and the arena[2] of intense political competition over developmental resources, have been subject to the steady expansion of the market and the colonial bureaucracy for over 100 years prior to independence. The transformation of rural life under the impact of these forces was further exacerbated during the later part of colonial rule through the extension of suffrage. These changes added new layers of administration to rural life. In some cases, British rule innovated new administrative levels, but in others it built on the foundations of antecedent structures. As a consequence, by the end of British rule, the *patwari, chowkidar* and the *dafadar* of the police station had joined the *mahajan* and the Pradhan as key players of the village arena.[3] At a deeper level, new notions of entitlement and enfranchisement, indicating the growing awareness of the 'degree to which an individual or group could legitimately participate in the decisions about entitlement',[4] challenged traditional authority and the cohesiveness of rural society. The achievement of independence, followed by an unprecedented expansion of participation and state intervention, further undermined the authority of traditional social roles and networks. As a result of these changes, conflict over developmental resources, norms of distribution and reformulation of the core values of rural life have become the staple of local politics.

The loss of 'village unity' is a constant refrain in most accounts of the impact of economic development and social change on the local political system.[5] In the coded language of local political discourse, this signifies a decline in public allegiance to the rules and institutions of conflict resolution and material allocation. Field reports inform us of the rise in litigation, factionalism and unstable political coalitions as the village gets integrated to the world beyond its traditional boundaries. Conflict, the overt use of force and 'criminalisation' are increasingly present in the local political arena.[6] The findings from village studies reflect specific instances of general lawlessness and collective violence. Available statistics indicate a steady increase of both.[7] At the root of the growing conflict is the breakdown of the traditional welfare structure of the village and the realisation that political power and social status are closely related to the allocation of the benefits of development. The resulting conflict affects both elite attitudes towards conflict as well as the interlocking social bonds that constituted the basis of the traditional social structure. This leads to the radicalisation of attitudes and the questioning of the values that constitute the moral basis of individual and collective political action, leading to what a number of authors have described as the crisis of authority in India.[8]

Conflicts do not however just exist: they are 'invented' in a way that reinforces one's power over an adversary or helps challenge the power of another person or group. The greater visibility of conflict in the local arena in many parts of India from the late 1960s is due not so much to an increase in the volume of conflict as such, but rather to the qualitative change in the nature of conflict and the sensitivity of the national media to local conflict over land, caste and community. Whereas traditional conflict used to be 'rule-bound' in the sense that struggle for local supremacy or ownership of land, howsoever bitter or intense, was nevertheless conducted according to rules of the arena which themselves remained legitimate, the new form of meta-conflict is based on the same motives as before but the domain of social conflict has been extended through the addition of conflict over rules themselves.[9] The earlier type of conflict could be functional in the sense that it helped maintain the boundaries of the groups by reinvigorating the institutions of rule adjudication and implementation, which, in the absence of conflict, could simply wither away.[10] From this perspective, conflict, at least in moderate degrees, actually contributes to the stability of the social order. Rising meta-conflict, characteristic of social change in India during the past two decades, is at the basis of the reconstitution of community and the structure of political action.

Despite widespread social conflict in India, there is no national pattern as such, nor any scholarly consensus about the social base of conflict in rural India. The change that has come about during the past decades can be seen from the absence of agreement in the scholarly studies conducted in specific regions at different points in time. Bailey's earlier characterisation of Orissa as a homeostatic society[11] is questioned by Mohanty who finds evidence of normative questioning of the traditional rules of transaction.[12] In the same vein, both Morris-Jones and Kothari have questioned the continuing validity of their earlier findings about the normative consensus within which Indian politics, particularly at the local level, operates.[13] Others who have drawn our attention to the increasingly conflictual nature of Indian politics include Brass who has described the trend in terms of the 'criminalisation' of politics, Manor who talks about political anomie and Kohli who points towards the governability crisis that has affected the political system, both at the local level as well as its apex.[14] Similarly, while Breman describes the reconstitution of Gujarat society into the owners of capital and labour, separated by both caste and class, Ghanshyam Shah reports the continued presence of caste sentiments, not in terms of pure nostalgia for past dominance, but as a viable force, contributing to the formation of political communities across the barrier of class.[15]

Though there is no national pattern as such, most commentators agree that dominance of the upper social strata is no longer perceived in India as natural. Under the impact of transactional politics, its residual existence is constantly under challenge. In contemporary India, 'the merest sight or smell of privilege in any area of society instantly provokes an antipathetic response among those who see or smell it. No privilege is inherently legitimate and no authority exists uncontested.'[16] In the absence of another overall organising principle to replace dharma, the result of this great social transformation is a certain anarchy in the terms of discourse and the forms of social organisation:

> Communities form and unform, define and redefine themselves, in relation to this struggle. They exist, essentially, for the purposes of opposing and demanding a share of the privileges seen to be enjoyed by 'others' and dissolve or reconstitute themselves as the context changes and throw up new 'others' for them to oppose. ... In Tamil society, then, all categories of community and identity and, related to them, all evaluations of culture and history are permeated by politics and exist in flux.
>
> (Washbrook (1989), pp 230–1)

The replacement of the reciprocal, personal bonds between employer and employee by a new arrangement resembling a contractual relationship, in some cases overseen by outside forces representing the state, is one of the various factors that have changed the traditional links between the social structure and the local political system. To that must be added the multiplicity of organisations, endowed with some decision-making authority and operating under the legislative requirement of financial and political accountability to an elected committee, which has created an environment that tends to disperse power, bringing in people to a position of influence from outside the limited circle of local notables. Above all, increasing participation in an increasing number of elections has created a new political resource out of the sheer weight of numbers and endowed it on the previously powerless. Though the operation of local democracy is not always smooth nor its direction necessarily irreversible, the combined effect of these changes has led to the demise of the traditional basis of authority inherent in the concept of social dominance, creating a situation of unstable political coalitions within the local political arena.[17]

Since perceived inequality in the distribution of benefits is at the heart of most conflict, our inquiry into the impact of development on rural society started by asking the local elites in Gujarat and Orissa to pronounce on the extent to which various social groups had benefited from development (see table 5.1). The results broadly confirm trends observed by others. Thus, according to the opinion of local leaders, those with capital and connections – big farmers, businessmen and people engaged in 'services' with regular income – emerge as the clear winners in both Gujarat and Orissa. On the losers – the landless, farm servants, sharecroppers and service castes – there is general agreement among rural leaders in Gujarat and Orissa as well. The contrast between the two regions is observed in the categories of medium and tenant farmers and artisans who have done much better in Gujarat than in Orissa. The higher benefits attributed to artisans and medium cultivators in Gujarat are significant, testifying to the better organised and more effective

Table 5.1 Groups which have benefited more than others

Groups	Gujarat %	Orissa %
Landless	12	21
Farm servants	12	10
Sharecroppers	15	6
Service castes	26	20
Small and marginal farmers	40	44
Medium cultivators	44	27
Tenant cultivators	60	27
Big farmers/manager farmers	73	61
Artisans	53	26
Small businessmen	40	54
Big businessmen	58	61
People in services	66	79

credit and marketing facilities, available through the cooperative organisations.

A more subtle aspect of the results is the influence of social class on the perceptions of benefits in Gujarat and Orissa. There is no consistent pattern across the two regions. On the whole, rural leaders from the former Untouchable and Tribal communities in Orissa are more vehement than their counterparts in Gujarat about comparatively less benefits to the landless, the farm servants, marginal farmers and sharecroppers though the difference in perception is one of degree rather than kind. The same is true of the other end of the scale as well. The combined effect of these observations can be seen in table 5.2 where a general question is posed about consequences of development on the society as a whole. In Gujarat, a third of the respondents believe that development has indeed benefited all the social strata whereas the corresponding figure in Orissa is only 9 per cent. Opinion in Orissa is virtually polarised among those who believe that benefits have gone to the well-to-do and those who believe that the poor and needy have benefited. The polarisation on the lines of social class is accentuated by a sense of relative betterment. Further analysis reveals that 75 per cent of the upper strata believe the poor to have done better, and only 15 per cent believe that benefits have gone to the well-to-do. On the other hand, 50 per cent of the Adivasi/Harijan in Orissa believe that the rich have done better compared to 45 per cent who believe that the poor and needy have benefited. One point that emerges above all others is the general belief, shared by 59 per cent of the respondents in Orissa, that the poor and the needy have not been left behind and have managed to corner at least some benefits of development. Though they come disproportionately from different social strata, their

Table 5.2 General distribution of benefits of development

Across the social strata	Gujarat %	Orissa %
All have benefited	32	9
Poor and needy have benefited	27	59
Benefits have gone to well-to-do	40	29
No response	1	3
Total	100	100

relative strength questions the image of helplessness that is sometimes attributed to the poor and the destitute.

There is no consistent and statistically significant relationship between social class and perception of benefits in Gujarat, which, in comparison with Orissa, indicates a certain degree of social consensus in the perception of the wide distribution of development across the social classes. The opinions of the Adivasi/Harijan and the middle social strata closely follow the opinions of the sample as a whole. A degree of concern and *noblesse oblige* can be seen from further analysis of the Gujarati upper strata, where only 9 per cent believe that the poor and needy have benefited from development compared to 48 per cent who suggest that benefits have gone to the well-to-do.

The subjective evaluation of differential benefit has to be seen against the more 'objective' measures of the distribution of the inputs of development (see table 5.3). The higher level of the availability of irrigation facilities and improved agricultural implements signify the generally high levels of these infrastructural facilities in Gujarat compared to Orissa. The marginally higher percentages of improved seeds, chemical fertiliser and bank loans in Orissa can be rather puzzling in view of the less developed character of the district as compared to Surat. The explanation lies in the fact that what is measured here is 'perceived' benefit and not necessarily the total amount of loans, seeds or fertiliser one might consume. As benefits, unlike irrigation facilities, they are procured by individuals in their personal capacity. In Gujarat, one will normally obtain them from the market and the cooperatives, in which case these are not seen as benefits one might have 'received'. The most

Table 5.3 Inputs of development

Has received	Gujarat %	Orissa %
Improved seeds	58	68
Chemical fertiliser	58	63
Irrigation	47	27
House sites	7	6
Land to the landless	2	7
Bank loans	46	55
Subsidy	44	30
Improved implements	28	4
Promotion of small scale industries	6	0

significant difference between Gujarat and Orissa is to be seen in subsidies. The higher percentage in Gujarat can be explained in terms of further analysis of the distribution of benefits along the lines of social class. Whereas about 30 per cent of the middle strata in Gujarat and Orissa have received some form of subsidy, only 9 per cent of the upper castes have benefited from subsidy compared to 31 per cent in Orissa. The most spectacular difference is to be found in the case of the Adivasi/Harijan. The percentage of beneficiaries from among these communities in Gujarat is as high as 73 per cent compared to only 32 per cent in Orissa.

In order to get a general impression of the differential distribution of the benefits of development, a scale was constructed by adding up the number of inputs the respondents had received. The results, presented in table 5.4 in aggregated form, show the very different forms in which social class affects the distribution of the benefits of development in Gujarat and Orissa. The upper social strata in Gujarat are not the chief beneficiaries of the public distribution of the inputs of development, a disproportionate share of which has gone to the Adivasi/Harijan. The situation is the reverse in Orissa, where the leaders of the lowest social strata have fared less well. The overall statistical relationship between social class and the number of benefits one enjoys in Orissa is negative (Kendall's tau B $= -0.17$, significant at 0.02 per cent) whereas in Gujarat it is the reverse (Kendall's tau B $= 0.43$, significant at 0.000 per cent).

Table 5.4 Cross-tabulation of inputs of development with social class

Social class	Number of inputs			
	0–1	*2–4*	*5 and above*	*Total*
Gujarat (n=131)				
High	71	19	10	100
Middle	34	50	16	100
Adivasi/Harijan	9	38	53	100
Total	29	40	31	100
Orissa (n=101)				
High	16	62	22	100
Middle	25	64	11	100
Adivasi/Harijan	41	50	9	100
Total	26	60	14	100

The survey seeks to measure the indirect consequences of development through two questions about personal financial situation (see table 5.5). Continuing the picture of greater dissatisfaction with development in Orissa as compared to Gujarat, half of those interviewed in Gujarat present themselves as fully satisfied as compared to only 13 per cent in Orissa. On the other hand, only 9 per cent of the Gujaratis consider themselves 'not satisfied' compared to about 29 per cent in Orissa. The overall picture is further reinforced by table 5.6 where 77 per cent of the rural leaders in Gujarat report an improvement in the financial situation over the past few years compared to only a quarter of the local elites in Orissa. On the other hand, whereas only 6 per cent of Gujaratis report a net deterioration in their financial situation over the past few years, a third of Oriya netas put themselves in that category.

Table 5.5 Personal financial situation

Level of satisfaction	Gujarat %	Orissa %
Fully satisfied	50	13
Partly satisfied	40	58
Not satisfied	9	29
No response	1	0
Total	100	100

Table 5.6 Financial situation during the last few years

Trend	Gujarat %	Orissa %
Improved	77	25
Remained the same	17	40
Deteriorated	6	35
Total	100	100

The robustness and consistency of the two different measurements of the impact of development on the personal financial situation of rural influentials can be seen from the correlation between the two. Both in Gujarat and Orissa, general satisfaction with the present financial situation is positively related to the impression of overall amelioration over the past few years (tau B in Gujarat 0.26, significant at 0.0009 per cent; in Orissa, 0.36, significant at 0.0000 per cent.) Within the pictures of the overall situations in Gujarat and Orissa, however, the relationship between personal financial situation and social class is more complicated.

In Gujarat, more than 90 per cent of the leaders of Adivasi and Harijan categories report an amelioration over the past few years, contributing to an image of the steady improvement in the material situation of the lower social strata. The correlation between social class (measured from high to low) and amelioration in the financial situation (measured from low to high) is 0.27 (Kendall's tau B, significant at 0.0006 per cent). The measurement in this case involves a comparison of the financial situation of the immediate past, possibly over the span of a generation. However, the measurement of the general financial situation has the situation of others as a reference point. Implicitly, in stating the perception of one's general financial situation, one is also articulating the state of one's relative deprivation. Thus, in striking contrast, when it comes to satisfaction with the present financial situation, whereas 81 per cent of the highest social strata consider themselves fully satisfied, the equivalent figure for the Adivasi/Harijan in Gujarat is only 28 per cent. In terms of the overall statistical relationship, the lower one is placed, the less likely one is to be satisfied (Kendall's tau B = −0.30, significant at 0.0001 per cent). Plainly, while the lowest strata in Gujarat have the satisfaction of noticing a steady improvement in their situation over the past years, they are unlikely to stop pushing for changes in social policy in their favour.

The situation in Orissa presents a double contrast to Gujarat. Compared to their past financial situation, the Oriya Adivasi/Harijan report a net deterioration. However, the picture of misery one might detect in the present financial situation is not specific to any social class and there is no significant statistical relationship between social class and financial situation. Compared to Gujarat, the picture one gets here is general immiserisation. This generality of lack of satisfaction with the financial situation in Orissa also has an amorphous character because no statistical relationship is perceived between the receipt of state subsidies and improvement in the financial situation. Even among those receiving five items or more in Orissa, 60 per cent believe that their situation has remained the same whereas 13 per cent report a deterioration and only 27 per cent admit an improvement. There is no overall correlation between benefits and satisfaction. In a contrasting picture from Gujarat, 90 per cent of those who have got the same level of benefits as in Orissa report an improvement in their situation and only 10 per cent say that their condition has remained the same. None reports deterioration. The overall correlation of benefits and satisfaction is positive (Kendall's tau B = 0.32, significant at 0.000).

RADICALISATION OF THE LOCAL POLITICAL ARENA

Since the legal structure giving concrete shape to moral claims of entitlement has increasingly appeared as an instrument of social justice, we find normative changes in the attitudes towards the legal and institutional structure among the indirect consequences of development policies. Radical protest differs from institutional participation in the sense that it begins by questioning the rules that constitute the basis of allocation of resources within the local arena. These rules are seen as discriminatory because they give a systematic advantage to some groups over others. The rules which come under challenge include not only the rules of normal political transaction but also the normative basis of politics such as the right to property, attitudes towards law and order and membership of the political community.

Some of these issues on which we have examined the radicalisation of local leaders include the attitudes towards the upper limit on the accumulation of property considered legally permissible. While not necessarily destructive of the concept of private property, radical opinion would insist on drastic upper limits on private property. The sequel to the radicalisation of norms is the degree to which people are prepared to extend legitimacy to direct popular action for the implementation of a radical political agenda. Running a close parallel to the theme of justice is the notion that radical action on the part of the poor and the deprived might be disruptive of development, presumably by scaring capital away and by distracting from rational central planning. Having understood the individual position of the rural elites on these contentious issues, we turn to their perception of their immediate environment to study the manner in which the local political arena has responded to the issue of radicalisation of attitudes.

The notion of unrestricted private property finds little favour in either Gujarat or Orissa though opinion on imposing legal limits to private property is more vehement in Gujarat than in Orissa (see table 5.7). However, while there is a large measure of agreement across the social classes in Gujarat on the need for limitations on property, opinion in Orissa is polarised, the lower social strata being more favourable towards limits than the upper. The Adivasi and Harijan leaders are 20 per cent higher in their approval of limits than their counterparts from the highest social class.

Table 5.7 Legal limitation on the ownership of property

Government should	Gujarat %	Orissa %
Limit ownership	87	70
Not limit ownership	12	28
Other	1	1
No response	0	1
Total	100	100

The large measure of agreement on limits to property in Gujarat finds a further articulation in the overwhelming approval to direct political action on the part of the poor and deprived in laying claim to property considered surplus, i.e. over and above the limit authorised by law. The high approval of direct action in Gujarat at 74 per cent (as reported below in table 5.9) is not, however, uniformly distributed over all social strata. Detailed analysis shows the approval rate going up as high as 83 per cent for the Adivasi/Harijan as compared to 55 per cent for the uppermost social class. In Orissa, while the overall approval is lower, the pattern of relationship with social classes is similar, approval being higher among the Adivasi/ Harijan (36 per cent) compared to the upper social class (19 per cent).

Despite the high approval of radical action at the normative level, Gujarati rural leaders are aware of the generally negative impact that political unrest can have on economic growth. Sixty per cent of them agree that protest agitations hinder development, including some who approve of such action on the part of the poor and deprived in the abstract (see table 5.8). The proportion of rural influentials who believe that protest agitations hinder development is higher in Orissa by 10 per cent. In both Gujarat and Orissa, however, the pattern in the statistical relationship between social class and the impact of political unrest on economic growth is consistent: the lowest social strata generally approve of protest and agitation as conducive to development. Kendall's tau B of the relationship between social class and approval of protest agitation is, respectively, -0.26 and -0.16 in Gujarat and Orissa. The percentage of people who believe that protest agitation improves development goes up from 33 among the upper social class to 57 among the Adivasi/ Harijan in Gujarat. The corresponding figures in Orissa are, respectively, 25 per cent and 50 per cent.

Table 5.8 Impact of protests and agitation on development

Impact	Gujarat %	Orissa %
Hinder development	60	70
Improve conditions	38	29
No response	2	1
Total	100	100

The most striking difference in the norms of radicalisation between Gujarat and Orissa, is, however to be seen in the attitudes towards property. A generalised belief in the legitimacy of the 'land grab' – the forcible occupation of 'surplus' land which appeared in several Indian states in the 1960s – was shared by three quarters of Gujarati gaon ka netas, while 14 per cent of those interviewed maintained an ominous silence. Clear disapproval of forcible occupation of private land was expressed by only 12 per cent of the respondents in Gujarat (see table 5.9). The rate of approval of such extreme measures is the highest among the Adivasi/Harijan (83 per cent) but it is shared by a majority of the upper strata as well. The underlying pattern of attitudes is, however, affected by social class, for the relationship between social status and attitudes towards forcible occupation of surplus private land is negative (tau B = -0.15; significant at 0.03). The corresponding figure in Orissa is only a fifth of all those who were interviewed while nearly four out of five disapprove of the forcible occupation of private land. Though disapproval at 81 per cent is the highest among the upper social strata, at 63 per cent it remains high among the Adivasi/Harijan as well. Among the Oriya respondents, sanctity of private property is a generalised belief, for, unlike in Gujarat, there is no significant relationship between social class and approval of the forcible occupation of land.

Table 5.9 Forcible occupation of land and property by the landless

Respondent	Gujarat %	Orissa %
Approves	74	20
Disapproves	12	78
No response	14	2
Total	100	100

On the state of organisation by the poor and the socially disadvantaged, Gujarat has a higher score at about 50 per cent who report 'to a great' or 'to some extent' compared to only 11 per cent in Orissa (see table 5.10). However, the relationship between social class and the state of organisation of the dalit is in the same direction in both States, with the percentage reporting political organisation among the dalit being higher among the Adivasi/Harijan compared to the people taking a similar position among the upper social class.

To what extent is radical organisation by the dalit within the local political arena linked to political organisation at the higher level? Two interesting points emerge from the responses to this question, part of which are presented in table 5.11. In the first

Table 5.10 Political organisation by the poor and the depressed

Level of organisation	Gujarat %	Orissa %
To a great extent	12	0
To some extent	37	11
Very little	48	86
No response	3	3
Total	100	100

place, whereas in Gujarat about a third of the local leaders point out external factors as responsible for radical organisation by the dalits, the corresponding figure in Orissa is a negligible 1 per cent. The comparative absence of external factors in Orissa indicates the absence of regional-level organisation of dalits and the localised and fragmented nature of rural conflict in Orissa. In the second place, the relationship between social class and the identification of the factors responsible for radical organisation by dalits is suggestive of a deeper ideological construction on the issue of social conflict in general. We notice both in Gujarat and Orissa a tendency on the part of the upper strata to blame people from outside who ferment trouble in the local political arena by sowing the seeds of discord and destroying social cohesion by transforming the local community into adversarial groups. The Adivasi/Harijan, on the other hand, newly aware of the political rights and developmental allocations that they are entitled to, recognise the sources of conflict in the inequities prevailing within the local political arena.

Table 5.11 Factors responsible for radical organisation by the poor and the depressed

Factors responsible	Gujarat %	Orissa %
Both external and internal factors	15	0
External factors	31	1
Internal factors	47	46
No response/don't know	7	53
Total	100	100

THE SOCIAL CORRELATES OF RADICALISM

In order to understand the overall extent of radical attitudes and identify the specific social groups that have a more than average tendency to share these attitudes, a composite scale of radicalisation was created by adding the scores from the three specific measures of radical attitudes discussed in tables 5.7–5.9. When measured by this scale, the society in Gujarat appears more radicalised than in Orissa (see table 5.12).

The lower level of radicalisation in Orissa is due in particular to the lower level of approval accorded to 'forcible occupation of the land and property of those with large amounts by people

Table 5.12 Radicalisation of society in Gujarat and Orissa

Level of radicalism	Gujarat %	Orissa %
Low	17	61
Medium	50	30
High	33	9
Total	100	100

with no land and property', where Orissa's approval rate of 20 per cent provides a stark contrast to the 74 per cent in Gujarat (table 5.9). Though the scale of differences is spectacular in this case, the difference in levels of support for radical solutions indicated in the measures presented in tables 5.7 and 5.9, while less extreme, are still in the same direction. Overall, thus, it appears that support for the radical options is greater in Gujarat and preference for the moral and the non-radical course of action is higher in Orissa.

Some explanation for this generally higher level of radicalism in Gujarat can be found in the history of collective protest and popular movements in Surat and Dhenkanal. We learn from Hardiman[18] and Shah[19] of the uprisings in Bardoli, Devi and, more recently, the Nav Nirman movement which have mobilised opinion against social, political and economic injustice. The record in Dhenkanal, while not as rich in popular protest, is not entirely absent. We have already discussed (chapter two) the intermittent struggle against the princely rulers of Talcher and Dhenkanal. But these were mostly in the nature of 'moral uprisings' against rulers who violated the unwritten codes of dharma that would give moral sanction to the authority of the ruler and not against particularly unjust forms of ownership of property nor of dominance by particularly oppressive social customs or classes.

While the above explanation helps to locate the different levels of radicalisation in Dhenkanal and Surat in the context of their historical evolution, we still need to situate these sentiments within the social matrix in order to theorise about the appeal that radical attitudes have for specific social groups in the two regions. Cross-tabulation of the composite scale of radicalisation with social class reveal that despite the difference in historical experience, reflected in the different levels of radicalisation, the relationship between the social strata and radical sentiments are in the same direction in both cases. Those who are more radical tend to be from Adivasi/Harijan background whereas the less radical are usually people from among the medium or high social status groups in both regions. But the percentages and measures of statistical association are more strongly accentuated in Gujarat (tau B of −0.3, significant at 0.0002 between radicalism and social class) as compared to Orissa (Kendall's tau B of −0.18, significant at 0.02). Whereas 64 per cent of the Oriya upper social class is in the lowest radical category, the comparable figure for the Adivasi/Harijan is 36 per cent. On the other hand, while only 6 per cent of the Oriya upper strata espouse radicalism of the highest category, the same is true of 23 per cent of the Adivasi/Harijan. In Gujarat, while the relationship of social class and radicalism is in the same direction as in Orissa, the percentages are more accentuated. Thus, nearly half of the Adivasi and Harijan elites are in the highest category of radicalism as compared to 30 per cent of the upper strata and 17 per cent for the middle strata whereas only 4 per cent of the Adivasi and Harijan leaders express support for the least radical category, compared to 25 per cent of the middle social class and 30 per cent of the highest social class who share these attitudes.

The relationship between radicalisation and other social attributes is less clear. Thus, there is no statistically significant relationship between education and overall radicalism in Orissa. Those in the highest category of education (matriculates and higher) have a higher tendency to be radical than the average rural neta, an observation which is equally applicable to those who are just literate. Those who are at the middle level of education on the other hand are less likely to be radical than others. Overall, therefore, we do not observe a linear relationship between education and radicalism in Orissa. In Gujarat on the other hand, where education is more closely related to wealth and status, those in the highest category of formal education have a lower tendency to espouse radical attitudes (29 per cent) than those with the lowest education (41 per cent). The overall relationship is linear and negative (Kendall's tau B = −0.18, significant at 0.02).

When it comes to age, however, the youngest in Orissa are more likely than their seniors to express radical sentiments (18 per cent as against 3 per cent); inversely, 80 per cent of those who are over fifty or more are likely to be in the least radical category compared to only 24 per cent who express these sentiments. The overall statistical relationship of age and radicalism is strongly negative (Kendall's tau B = −0.35, significant at 0.000). In Gujarat on the other hand, while the young are more radical than the elderly in general, the relationship is not quite linear, with the middle aged coming out almost at the same level of radicalism as those who are less than thirty-four. The relationship is weakly negative (Kendall's tau B = −0.11, significant at 0.08).

The social attributes in terms of which we have tried to draw the social profile of radicalism are themselves not independent of one another. This can be seen from the correlations of radicalism with the social attributes and their correlations with one another, presented in table 5.13. Hence, in a multiple regression analysis which uses jati, satisfaction with present financial situation, age, benefit and education as independent variables in order to explain overall radicalism, only specific variables emerge with coefficients that are significant though the model as a whole explains a respectable fifth of the variance (see table 5.14). The results reveal an important aspect of radicalism in Gujarat and Orissa. The Gujarati radicalism has its origin in relative deprivation, being primarily the outcome of the feeling of having been hard done by in the process of development. In this sense, radicalism in Gujarat is a function of the market and, as such, has a rational basis to it. In Orissa on the other hand, radicalism is at its keenest in the young and low-status groups, the very social groups that Scott and Greenough point out as vulnerable to moral anger at a time of crisis.[20]

Within the constraints of a survey, it is not possible to pursue the social roots of radicalism to more precise sub-groups. The 'lumping' together of the Adivasi and Harijan, however, leads to the loss of differences in attitude of considerable theoretical

Table 5.13 Social correlates of radicalism

	Jati	Present finance	Age	Benefit	Education
Gujarat	−0.3	−0.36	*	0.24	−0.2
Orissa	−0.22	*	−0.37	*	*

Note: * Not significant at 0.05 or less.

Table 5.14 Multiple regression coefficients of radicalism

Independent variable	Gujarat	Orissa
Jati	–	−0.3
Age	–	−0.38
Satisfaction with present finance	−0.32	–
Education	–	–
Benefit	–	–
R^2	0.20	0.21

importance. We learn the extent of greater radicalisation among Harijans – Halpati agricultural labourers in Gujarat who have been outmanoeuvred by Patidar farmers who have 'imported' more docile Tribals as 'scab labour',[21] and the Tribal voters attached to bhadralok households through the Halipratha in Dhenkanal who voted at their master's biddings in 1977 elections, as compared to the more aggressive Panas who managed to break loose from the upper-caste dominance over the village political arena and set up independent political links with political parties operating from outside the village.[22] However, the survey technique helps us understand the other correlates of radicalism, particularly the instrumental use to which it might be put by the protagonists. Once again, the hypothetical expectations arising from the political economy and moral economy debate would be rather different. The rational peasant would be expected to put their political sentiments to the maximisation of economic gain and the expectation would be that of instrumental use of radicalism. On the other hand, to the extent we would notice radical sentiments in the moral peasant, it would be directed against the unindulgent ruler,[23] and inspired by the hope of the successful defence of traditional rights and the resurrection of moral authority. The complexity of the situation obtaining in the field can be seen from the fact that both conjectures appear to be partially supported by the data.

The situation in Gujarat, measured by the positive correlation between radicalism and material benefits of development (Kendall's tau B of 0.21, significant at 0.005, the majority of the radicals being also the beneficiaries of the state sponsored development, lends support to the instrumentality of radicalism, whereas in Orissa there is no systematic relationship between radical sentiments and the benefits of development at all. Both in Orissa and Gujarat, the radicals are not satisfied with their present financial situation. But whereas in Gujarat the radicals, compared to the past, report to be doing better financially, that is not the case in Orissa where no systematic relationship is to be noticed between radical sentiments and relative improvement or deterioration over the past. The difference between the Gujarat and the Orissa situations becomes even starker once we take into consideration the development agendas that the respective local elites articulate. More of the highly radical in Gujarat point out distributive justice at the top of the scale in their problem identification as compared to infrastructural facilities or welfare (respectively, 47 per cent, 24 per cent and 29 per cent), compared to the situation in Orissa where none of the most radical identify distributive justice as the most urgent problem for people in their situation, while an overwhelming majority of 89 per cent suggest infrastructural facilities and 11 per cent look towards state welfare as the most urgent needs.

CONFLICT AND COHESION IN THE LOCAL ARENA

We have so far examined the impact of development on the political consciousness of individuals in so far as it relates to their sense of personal betterment as a result of the process of development. In this section, we shall examine the effect that the radicalisation in individual political norms has on the social and moral life of the individual, seen here as a member of the local political arena. For this analysis, a conceptual baseline can be defined as a situation where the individual, nominally a part of the arena, spends most of his or her life within the relatively restricted world of the jati, kin or tribe, affected by the power structure of the arena but not affecting it. Social cohesion is provided to the arena through the status hierarchy, ritual linkage and economic exchange, referred to as the jajmani system. Political dominance, following the lines of status and rank, is an integral part of this social order. The attempts to build a political community on the basis of equal citizenship and competitive elections have posed a profound challenge to the moral basis of this social order. While the village continues to be a political arena, its relative importance further enhanced because of the availability of developmental resources and the rural vote, the control over this arena is avidly contested. While the real world has moved beyond the baseline, the direction of this movement remains unclear. The relative importance one is prepared to attach to the concept of 'village unity', and the trade off one is prepared to countenance between an individualistic order committed to the rights of the individual at the cost of the collectivity and the interests of the common good even at the cost of the individual, become the space where the battle for supremacy between the competing orders is joined.

Seen in the context of the local political system, the issue of developmental conflict can be specified as follows. In the first place, between the polarities of consensus and dissensus, how do local elites situate the political arena? More concretely, to what extent are they prepared generally to give a free hand to leaders? Alternately, how keen are they to subject major issues to contentious participation, even when the consequence is to slow down the pace of economic development? Moving beyond the general perception of the issues of consensus and participation, what are the rational and moral factors that constrain variation in individual attitudes to these structural attributes of the system within which they operate? The attitudes to these issues of conflict, consensus and dissension in the local political arena are derived out of individual experience with the pace and direction of rural development. In turn, they affect the stability and the representative character of the political system in India.

Overall, the image of dissension, distrust of authority and relentless insistence on subjecting collective decision-making to contentious public scrutiny (even at the possible cost of slowing down the pace of development) describe the turmoil in the political environment of rural Orissa. Some of these findings, which offer a contrast to the undercurrent of village unity in the earlier study of Bailey,[24] are confirmed by more recent field-work in Orissa.[25] From table 5.15, only a little over one third of the local elites value village unity enough to prefer it to development projects that could be divisive. Support for the same theme goes up to 60 per cent in Gujarat. The tendency is even more pronounced in Gujarat among the Adivasi/Harijan than among the upper and middle social classes, with an overall negative relationship between social status and the tendency to agree with divisive development proposals. The situation in Orissa is exactly the opposite, with the tendency to preserve community unity at the cost of development the least pronounced among the Adivasi/Harijan being only 23 per cent, compared to 44 per

Table 5.15 Normative attitudes towards participation

Item	Strongly agree or agree	Gujarat %	Orissa %
1	A good leader should refrain from making proposals that divide the community even if these are important for development	60	38
2	Participation of people is not necessary if decision-making is in the hands of a few trusted and competent leaders	57	41
3	Any decision on an issue, even though important, if likely to alienate a section or group in the community should be avoided	47	51
4	Only those adequately informed on an issue should be allowed to vote on it	47	68
5	In taking decisions a good leader does not wait till all disagreements are fully resolved	59	46
6	Involving many people in decision-making often leads to unnecessary conflicts	70	48
7	Leaders who are over-concerned about resolving conflicts can never carry out community programmes successfully	57	33
8	Participation of as many citizens as possible in decision-making is necessary even if it takes a lot of time and expenditure	47	80
9	If there is a disagreement about a programme a leader should be willing to give it up	60	50
10	Allowing many people to have their say in matters pertaining to the village will only interfere with getting things done	57	44

cent for the upper and 38 per cent for the middle social classes. In the same vein, the second item in table 5.15 suggests that more among the local elites in Orissa as compared to Gujarat are willing to entrust decision-making to the leadership at the cost of larger mass participation. However, further analysis shows that only 32 per cent of the Oriya Adivasi/Harijan are willing to do so compared to 38 per cent of the upper social status group and 49 per cent of the middle strata. In Gujarat, on the other hand, a majority of local elites are willing to entrust leadership to a few 'trusted and competent leaders'. The Adivasi and Harijan leaders, at 64 per cent are the most vocal supporters of this position, though the other social groups are also supportive of this position albeit less strongly. From the third item in table 5.15, a majority of Oriya respondents would like all interests in society to be accommodated in the decision-making process, whereas the Gujarat elites, somewhat more realistically, concede that in practice that may not always be desirable or possible. Another key element is the value people attached to the right to vote, indicative of the empowerment of the previously powerless through enfranchisement. However, not everyone in rural society is positively disposed towards universal adult franchise. Not surprisingly, in item four in table 5.15 a large majority of Oriya elites would restrict the right to vote only to 'those who are adequately informed'. However, these supporters of restricted franchise are more likely to be drawn from the higher social strata and older age groups. Whereas 81 per cent of the upper and 72 per cent of the middle social groups support the restriction of franchise, only 36 per cent of the Adivasi and Harijan leaders take this position.

The consistency in the position of Oriya elites as regards the importance of participation can be seen in their reluctance to allow decisions to be taken before 'all disagreements to be fully resolved', an opinion espoused by a minority of all respondents (46 per cent), a percentage which further goes down to 41 per cent among the Adivasi/Harijan. In Gujarat on the other hand, where the costs of delays in decision-making in terms of the loss of valuable time and resources is more obvious, a majority of 59 per cent approves of a leadership style that is prepared to press ahead even before all the disagreements have been sorted out. There is hardly any difference in the opinions of the upper strata and the lowest. The same tendency is observed in item 6 where a majority (70 per cent) of Gujarat elites agrees that 'involving many people in decision-making often leads to unnecessary conflict', whereas only 48 per cent of Orissa elites (among them, only 32 per cent of the Adivasi/Harijan) take this position. Item 7 reinforces the same range of support for strong, purposeful leadership in Gujarat with 57 per cent of the elites agreeing that 'leaders who are over-concerned about resolving conflicts can never carry out community programmes successfully' as compared to only a third of the local elites in Orissa who take this position. Item 8 brings out the cardinal importance of participation, with 80 per cent of Orissa respondents asserting that 'participation of as many citizens as possible in decision-making is necessary even if it takes a lot of time and expenditure', an opinion shared by a minority of only 47 per cent in Gujarat.

The obverse side of strong leadership is of course the ability and willingness of the leadership to make strategic concessions and appear to be accommodative and consensual in style. The popularity of this style in Gujarat can be seen in terms of the 60 per cent of the respondents who expect their leaders to 'stoop to conquer'. Indicative of the atmosphere of anomic radicalism within which the Oriya gaon ka netas function, there is no clear preference there on this issue, with opinion equally divided on either side. To close the battery of items, we once again find majority support in Gujarat for pragmatic, speedy and efficient management of village affairs even if it necessitates some degree of elitist leadership, a solution opposed by the majority of Oriya respondents and even more intensely by Oriya Adivasi/Harijan, among whom nearly 80 per cent are opposed to this form of efficient but elitist management.

It emerges from the above discussion that, in Orissa, the polarisation of opinion on participation, leadership styles and village unity takes place both on the lines of wealth and status. It is quite likely that the deprivations arising out of poverty and low social status are cumulative. The opinions of those who suffer from this cumulative deprivation are likely to be even more extreme than those who suffer from either. Compared to Orissa, in Gujarat there is greater agreement on the usefulness of strong and purposive leadership, even at the expense of participation. Moreover, unlike in Orissa, the convergence between class, status and deprivation is at best ambiguous. The Adivasi/Harijan in the Gujarat sample (quite unlike their counterparts in Orissa) believe that 'participation of people is not necessary if decision-making is in the hands of a few trusted and competent leaders'. Here, the contrast between Gujarat and Orissa is interesting. There is evidence to show that, compared to Orissa, in Gujarat the lower social strata have greater access to influence, at least at the social level, and proportionately more Adivasi/Harijan own land (and more land) than in Orissa. The Adivasi/Harijan among Gujarat elites can afford to be supportive of strong leadership because, in many instances, the local representative institutions like the panchayats are already being controlled by them – a situation still beyond the grasp of their counterparts in Orissa. State-initiated affirmative action has been relatively more successful in Gujarat, to the extent of earning for Gujarat the dubious distinction of being something of a trend-setter of upper-caste backlash movements.[26]

The Gujarati local elites are at once more managerial, more paternalistic and, within limits, more accommodative. A possible conjecture that could account for this difference is that, rather than social dominance, the upper strata in Gujarat have found a more potent basis of power in their control over the economic arena. There is a convergence of two opposite currents. On the one hand, the successful introduction of new agricultural technology and new means of production (of which diamond cutting, made possible entirely through personal contacts and private financing, is one among many examples) has given these strata a shot in the arm. On the other hand, the political consciousness of the urban bias in India's developmental model has created a psychological necessity among the rural elites to 'hold their troops together' and to be accommodative when necessary and possible. Breman[27] describes the overarching leadership posture that the upper strata adopt for themselves as neo-corporatist. He characterises the political system within which they operate in terms of a new bonding principle:

> A new ideology, which finds support especially in the dominant rural class, also emphasises the unity of farmers and labourers against their common target, the state, which is said to show no concern for those who bear the actual burden of production but instead caters only for urban interests. The *kisans*, an all-encompassing category meant to embrace both large landowners and the landless, must work together to put an end to the neglect and subordination of 'Bharat', i.e. everything that comes from the people and that belongs to the people – as opposed to 'India'.
>
> (Breman (1985), p. xx)

One of the contributory factors to the contrasting ethos of Gujarat and Orissa is the managerial and accommodative elitism and instrumental radicalism of Gujarat which provides a sharp contrast with the dissident and anomic radicalism of the Oriya netas (see table 5.16). From the correlation of overall radicalism with the items presented in table 5.15, it can be seen that the radicals in Gujarat have a significant tendency to approve of leaders who 'refrain from making proposals that divide the

community', are willing to entrust decision-making to a 'few
trusted and competent leaders', whereas in Orissa the situation
is diametrically opposite in so far as radicals are concerned
(items 1 and 2 in table 5.16). Following on this theme, the Oriya
radicals are prepared to stick with issues that 'alienate a section
or group', and are opposed to any restriction of franchise. The
Gujarati radicals are, further, supportive of strong leadership,
willing to put speed and success in achieving community programmes above participation when necessary. However, clearly
from item 9, they expect their leaders to master the art of
accommodation and compromise in practice, if not in rhetoric.
No significant relation of this theme with radicalism is observed
in Orissa.

Table 5.16 Correlation of radicalism with leadership style (correlation coefficient)[1]

Item	Gujarat	Orissa
1	0.27	−0.13
2	0.21	−0.19
3	*	−0.24
4	*	−0.40
5	0.24	*
6	*	*
7	0.29	*
8	*	*
9	0.14	*
10	0.12	*

Notes: * Not significant.
[1] The definition of items is the same as that in table 5.15.

CONCLUSION

Competition for developmental resources, conflict over the rules
of allocation and the radicalisation of rural society are the major
themes of this chapter. It suggests that rather than the actual
occurrence of conflict, attitudes of elites towards conflict are of
great importance to the stability and viability of representative
political institutions in India. The loss of nerve and panic on
the part of the political elites at the higher levels of the
system, anxious at increasing conflict, might provide the needed
signal for an intervention by the army or contribute to the rise
of a Bonapartist movement which promises a panacea to the

breakdown of order in the form of an authoritarian regime. On the other hand, a self-confident elite might use local conflict and protest movements at the lower levels of the system to generate the political momentum to promote the reform of the institutional and legal structure governing the material conditions of life. The chapter has examined this important issue of attitudes of the gaon ka netas towards conflict and participation by drawing on the distribution of the benefits of development, which often provides the most tangible causes of conflict. Less explicit but nevertheless important aspects of the issue are seen in the perception and evaluation of the need for wide, even contentious participation and the extent of radicalisation of attitudes towards unequal benefits and redistribution of property.

The local political arena and attitudes of individuals operating within it provide the empirical basis for our understanding of the process of change that development has produced in rural society. In order to locate Gujarat and Orissa within a general framework of change, a conceptual baseline was drawn at an ideal type of rural society, organised around the dominance of the local arena by the affluent social groups possessing high social status and other material means of political power. Social change, brought about by changes in the macro-political structure which has induced new notions of citizenship, entitlement and enfranchisement, has led to conflict over material resources and the rules of allocation of status, power and wealth. The literature on political conflict and community provides two different models of change. Thus, under the impact of the forces of change, the traditional social structure might give way and be recast in the form of competing political communities where individuals come together on the basis of rational self interest and use their collective power to promote individual interest. On the other hand, the traditional social structure might react as a whole within the framework of a moral community where the lowest social strata, which feel deprived and destitute, might rebel in order to defend their customary rights. Applications of these models to Indian situations shows that elements of both the rational and moral frameworks might underlie behaviour, the key to whose understanding is provided by the local cultural codes. The local structure of cognition, understood on the basis of responses to a series of questions dealing with the values of individual, community and development, help us understand and interpret the contrasting experiences of Gujarat and Orissa.

The fact that we find elements of both moral and rational behaviour among our local elites points towards a larger debate on the normative basis of conflict and community formation between the advocates of moral economy and political economy at a more general level. The argument of the former approach, corresponding to the notion of the caste system (and jajmani relations) as the basis of authority and community in India, is opposed by the advocates of the latter who assume the universal presence of a rational, utility-maximising individual within a given political environment. Thus, for James Scott, most rural households in Asia share a common situation, constrained by 'the vagaries of weather and the claims of outsiders'.[28] Peasant cultivators are conscious that they live near the margin of scarcity. They therefore prefer to avoid risks that would threaten their basic subsistence. Rather than seeking to maximise the well being of themselves and their families, Scott argues, they commit themselves to a moral economy predicated on two principles that seem fairly embedded in both the social patterns and injunctions of peasant life: 'the *norm of reciprocity* and the *right to subsistence*'.[29] Scott views both the norm of reciprocity and the right to subsistence as genuine moral components of the 'little tradition', which applies to peasant culture universally, 'Reciprocity serves as a central moral formula for interpersonal conduct. The right to subsistence, in effect, defines the minimal needs that must be met for members of the community within the context of reciprocity.'[30] For Samuel Popkin, on the other hand, even though peasants may be poor and live close to the margin, 'there are still many occasions when peasants do have some surplus and do make risky investments'.[31] For him, relationships with other peoples are not decided on some general moral principle but on calculations of whether such relationships will benefit the peasant and his family. The concept of the peasant is dissolved by Popkin and is replaced by that of a universal economic man who acts within varying sets of constraints, including those that characterise pre-capitalist agrarian societies and societies incorporated into a global economy. The same dilemma between the moral and the rational is to be seen in studies that characterise rural conflict in terms of categories drawn from political economy such as modes of production and class formation.[32] The persistence of non-economic factors such as caste, tribe, ethnicity and religion in politics continues to defy such strictly economic formulations. The moral approach which uses these factors as categories of analysis has on the other hand to countenance the creation of new communal and associational bonds in response to economic interests and political opportunities.

The perspective of cultural anthropology, which emphasises the role of local cultural codes and historical traditions as domains over which political choices are made, offers a way out of the moral–rational dilemma.[33] Following Greenough, the scale of values that ultimately govern behaviour are derived from local cultural practices and beliefs. In a situation of deeply ingrained belief in the moral economy, one could expect acquiescence in authority in normal times, giving in occasionally to 'just rebellions' where the peasantry rise in revolt against their superiors who have failed in the obligation to provide protection. However, at the time of a severe crisis like in the case of the Bengal Famine of 1943, behaviour no longer conforms to the moral value of the quiet acceptance of authority nor of rebellion. Instead, one noticed the 'cold violence of abandonment' on the part of male heads of families, who, instead of protecting women and children, egoistically kept the precious food for themselves. Greenough's point here is that faced with the likelihood of extinction (after all, a third of the total population perished in the famine), Bengali society reverted to its crisis mode where the local cultural code required food to be saved for the male householder, who, as the biological nucleus of a potential society, was thought to be able to regenerate society when times were better. The male householders were thus not responding to the crisis egoistically but culturally. Once the local cultural code has changed (which is the case with post-independence Bengal), however, behaviour is no longer constrained by this model. Instead, one can then expect intermittent acts of resistance, responding to different levels of risk, new opportunity structures and the precedence of the individual over the group. Using the closed, rigid, stratified social system as a baseline, we can understand the reinvention of the spirit of communal solidarity among Gujarat elites in terms of (a) the achievement by the lowest strata of a reasonable share of the benefits of development and (b) the realisation by all that conflict is bad for development and is to be avoided when possible. In Orissa, on the other hand, the combination of radicalised, under-achieving lower strata and the overall lack of conspicuous development of the region creates fragmented, anomic radicalism, leading to attitudes supportive of localised conflict rather than communal solidarity.

At the level of attitudes towards the issues of leadership, participation and delay in decision-making as a consequence of having to reconcile conflicting interests, the implicit anger and bitterness of the Oriya elites express themselves strongly in favour of a form of anomic (as opposed to instrumental) radicalism, likely to create a fragmented, even anomic political culture.[34] The Gujarati local elites, on the other hand, confidently choose community as the political context of action and perception of benefits. They are aware of the trade off between participation and delay in decision-making, potentially leading to the loss of precious time and future benefits. This collective preference for a consensual and managerial style is consistent with their perception that development has benefited all – which is in stark contrast with the perception of social polarisation by Oriya elites. From their perception of groups that have not benefited from development as well as in the overall perception of benefits, the Gujarati elites are aware, nevertheless, that some less fortunate members of the society have fallen through the safety nets. Hence the expectation that leaders would take the interests of these hapless citizens into account in their decision-making.

Finally, local conflict, exacerbated by rapid social and economic change, has itself become an engine of further change. Rather than treating conflict as necessarily destructive of stability and legitimacy, the chapter has suggested that radicalisation of local politics can help reorder social and political relations. The process is neither smooth nor uniform across the whole of India. Instrumental radicalism of the kind noticed in Gujarat is more conducive towards the functioning of democratic political institutions than the anomic and fragmented radicalism that the Orissa data convey. The availability of a macro-political system, and the legitimate authority of the state which intervenes between different regions and accounts for inter-regional knowledge-sharing, are of crucial importance for representative democracy in India.

The findings reported in this chapter have some larger implications for representative democracy in developing countries which are in the midst of rapid social and economic change. In general, to the extent that the political process provides room for manoeuvre to competing elites who become a bridge between the modern state and the traditional society, the political system gains in depth, breadth and legitimacy.[35] This has been made possible in India through a fortuitous combination of the legacy of high institutionalisation under colonial rule, pre-independence experience of elections, continuity of leadership after independence and a broad-based mass party. What gave it substance after independence, however, is the momentum generated by competing local elites, increasingly drawn from the underprivileged social groups who have mobilised potential beneficiaries of state intervention through a combination of electoral, institutional and radical strategies.

What is the implication for political action that emerges out of our understanding of attitudinal changes brought about by social and economic change in rural India? Once again, we shall attempt to understand the scope for political action and the forms that such action takes in Gujarat and Orissa within the context of the general theory of the behaviour of people placed within similar conditions. The consequences of action for the state are of great importance to the legitimacy of its authority, the stability and growth of its institutions and its scope for intervention in the process of social change. These issues of room for manoeuvre by local elites will be taken up in the next chapter. This will provide the empirical base for a concluding discussion of how the radicalisation of the local arena affects the state and the role that institutionalised conflict plays in the resilience of constitutional democracy in India.

6

INSTITUTIONAL
PARTICIPATION AND
RADICAL PROTEST: THE
STATE, SOCIETY AND
ROOM FOR MANOEUVRE
IN THE MIDDLE

THE OBJECTIVES

Our inquiry into the politics of rural development has so far concentrated on the contrasting positions of local elites on the nature of social change and its impact on the cohesiveness of rural life. This chapter extends the study to the range of action that the gaon ka netas undertake to influence decision-makers at higher levels in order to achieve their development goals. The chapter inquires into the nature of this interaction between village netas and bureaucrats and political leaders through a range of specific questions. How frequent are the meetings between rural netas and bureaucratic and political decision-makers? Are these encounters merely routine and formal, or do local elites view these meetings substantively rewarding? Do local elites act merely as intermediaries between the citizen and the state, or do they, as one might expect of the gaon ka netas themselves take the initiative in contacting higher-level decision-makers? Is the interaction between local elites and decision-makers confined to the normal, legitimate and orderly political process, or is there an element of coercion and threats to public order implicit in the political strategies of local elites? What is the new relationship between institutional participation and radical protest? Further, are contacting higher-level decision-makers or taking matters into one's own hands through 'direct action' merely a posture that local elites adopt to suit their rhetoric, or are these methods successful in obtaining results?

173

Political action takes place against the background of different ensembles of local infrastructure, political and organisational networks, different levels of resource endowments and links between local, district and regional levels of the government. Some of these factors have already been discussed in earlier chapters. As before, we assume that behaviour of local elites is constrained by a multiplicity of factors, the focal points of which are, respectively, region and social class. From the difference in the level of economic development between Gujarat and Orissa already discussed in chapter two, one would expect a significant difference in the scope of political demands in the agendas of local elites from Gujarat and Orissa. The difference in the range of organisational infrastructure available to the netas in Gujarat as compared to Orissa and the different historical experiences of radical protest significantly affect elite attitudes and behaviour.

The question of motivation behind action is of equal importance. There is not one clear motive behind the efforts of local elites to intervene in the process of developmental policy making and its implementation. They are individually concerned about their own welfare and keen on improving it through their contacts with civil servants and political leaders from outside. They are also beholden to their supporters within the village to use these contacts to bring in more resources to the village and particularly to the social strata with whose interests they are identified. Finally, the gaon ka netas are expected to look after the well being of their local community by virtue of local tradition even as the customary pressure on them to do so is itself on the decline because of the larger process of social and economic change. Some of these theoretical assumptions and the structure within which political action takes place have already been referred to in the previous chapter. Before we examine the range of methods employed by local elites to achieve their goals, we need briefly to look at some of these macro models of action.

THE RATIONAL, MORAL AND CULTURAL MODELS OF ACTION

Using the concept of a closed, rigid, hierarchic social system as the baseline of analysis, we have attempted to measure the social and economic change that has taken place in Gujarat and Orissa

174

during four decades since independence. It is not the case that traditional society contained no notions of entitlement or power, but the political competition specific to universal adult franchise and citizenship have radically altered the meaning attached to them.[1] They have in some cases exacerbated traditional conflict, created new forms of conflict over the rules of allocation, reinforced social networks and, in some cases, ruptured traditional patron–client relations and led to the formation of new political communities. The empirical questions on the basis of which we intend to measure their impact are based on two basic assumptions: the first suggests that rural netas are conscious of the structure of opportunities and resources potentially available through successful intervention; and the second that the state, when pressurised, yields the required resources.[2] These assumptions are not universally supported in the literature on peasant societies. The first assumption, similar to the notion of peasant rationality,[3] is questioned by moral economists and others who see Indian behaviour as necessarily fatalistic, attributed to predominant cultural values of dharma and karma or to the risk-averse, subsistence basis of material existence.[4] The assumption of a responsive state is questioned by those who see in the bureaucratic apparatus of the post-colonial state a tendency[5] and a structural incentive to exact a form of bureaucratic rent rather than respond to social pressure emanating from organised interests.[6]

Recent Indian village studies literature provides plenty of examples of the interplay of both moral and rational norms, typically the effect of the latter on the former being seen as a source of social and economic change. The moral image of Indian society, which still survives in European perceptions of India, has had a long evolution. Two observations on popular reactions to famine in Bengal before the onset of colonial rule and one just before independence when the Ministry of Food was at least partly controlled by Indians, help illustrate this scepticism about the applicability of rational norms of political action to India. As reported by Greenough,[7] Bengal was stricken by a great drought–famine in 1770; one third of the population, perhaps ten million persons, are said to have died. Numerous Europeans witnessed this disaster, and a discussion of their accounts by the Abbe Guillaume Raynal in the 1780s[8] includes the following observation:

175

But it is still more remarkable . . . that amidst this terrible distress, such a multitude of human creatures, pressed by the most urgent of all necessities, remained in absolute inactivity and made no attempts whatever for their self-preservation. All the Europeans, especially the English, were possessed of magazines [i.e. stores of grain]. These were ever respected, as well as private houses; no revolt, no massacre, not the least violence prevailed. The unhappy Indians, resigned to despair, confined themselves to the request of succor they did not obtain, and peacefully awaited the release of death. Let us now represent to ourselves any part of Europe afflicted by a similar calamity. What disorder! What fury! What atrocious acts! What crimes would ensue! How should we have seen among us Europeans, some contending for food with their daggers in their hands, some pursuing, some flying, and without remorse massacring each other! How should we have seen [them] at least run their rage on themselves, tearing and devouring their own limbs, and in the blindness of despair, trampling underfoot all authority as well as every sentiment of nature and reason!

(Raynal (1969), p 847)

Despite its dubious historiography, Raynal's rhetorical excess correctly expresses the French revolutionary discourse of his own time: 'hungry men rebel'. His informants just as clearly saw that hungry Bengalis did not. Nor is the observation of such quiet despair and resignation to fate unique to this intrepid French traveller. The unrelieved 1943 Bengal famine, with its toll of two million or more deaths,[9] showed the same features to European observers: 'passivity' and 'fatalism'. An English medical officer testified before the 1944 famine inquiry commission:

A In Bengal they died in front of bulging food shops.
Q Bulging with grain?
A Yes, they died in the streets in front of shops bulging with grain.
Q Because they could not buy?
A Yes, and it was due to the passive, fatalistic attitude of those people that there were no riots and they were dying.[10]

This pattern of victimisation had nothing in common with European traditions of rage and revolt. In Europe famine violence was turned 'outward' against offending landlords, merchants, and officials; in Bengal the tradition was to turn violence 'inward' and 'downward' against clients and dependents. This was the cold violence of abandonment, of ceasing to nourish, rather than the hot violence of bloodshed and tumult. In Europe the quasi-legal notions of subsistence 'rights' and the 'just price' gave legitimacy to food riots, a legitimacy sometimes conceded by officials, who refused to punish enraged looters and leaders of hungry crowds.[11] In Bengal such legal notions were absent; the demands made by starving dependents upon their destined providers were purely moral and customary, and abandoned victims did little more than to beg and dramatise their helplessness in the hope of stimulating a flow of benevolence. Hence mendicancy, imploring gestures, cries and wails; hence the passive encounter of starving victims with the well-fed in front of 'bulging' grain shops.

Greenough's interpretation of the behaviour of Bengali peasants faced with famine does not indicate uniform passivity in the face of imminent death. As the crisis worsened, the earlier charity shown by those with surplus grain towards the indigent stopped abruptly. Food (particularly rice, which in Bengal is more than just food; being full of life giving substances, it is more like an approximation of the sacred: it is Lakshmi, the goddess of plenitude) was set aside by the male, upper-caste householder for his personal consumption. Was this merely rational, egoistic behaviour on their part? If so, why would the victims – those used to the customary largess shown by the powerful, the rich, the husband and father to the dependent subjects, wives and children – acquiesce in this grossly unjust (at least from their point of view) act? Greenough finds an explanation in the 'cultural meaning of subsistence',[12] in this case, the values of indulgence which the powerful show to the powerless, and in return for which they can expect abundance from the goddess Lakshmi; these are the cultural codes with which one needs to understand Bengali forbearance in the face of a tragedy of this proportion. It was in that sense 'action' of a perverse kind, an 'involuted form of victimisation', which explains the absence of popular rebellion.

While cultural anthropology is enormously helpful in understanding behaviour which is not completely explained by either the rational choice or the morel economy models, there is an implicit danger of giving an enduring character to values and a cultural context that are temporally specific. The cultural model, used in exclusion of others, denies a residual role to history and the political structure which in their own ways provide a context to culture. State–society relations in a political environment based on popular sovereignty and accountability, compared to the colonial state of Greenough's study, are essentially different. The institutional apparatus and process of democracy, which during the four decades since independence have promoted new notions of entitlement, have affected the basic terms of discourse and the values which govern behaviour. How far has the post-independence 'citizens' state' helped in transforming the structural and moral basis of action? Some evidence of these changes will be discussed in the rest of the chapter.

LOCAL ELITES AND THE DEVELOPMENT ENVIRONMENT

The gaon ka neta, as we have already seen above, is not merely a fixer – touter, pyraveekar, a facilitator or a commission agent – who would deliver any service for a fee. They are leaders of the village and, as such, are aware of playing a role, creating, challenging and providing legitimacy to social norms and helping in the specification of the local developmental agenda. However, though they are usually better informed about the ways of the wider world and have occasions to encounter influential people from outside, the typical gaon ka neta is not a politician in the proper sense of the term. Relatively unconstrained by a party line on matters of policy and unbeholden to a party organisation regarding the distribution of patronage, the neta is a comparatively free agent.[13] Such freedom brings opportunities. They are sought out by competing political leaders, civil servants and others, who desire to influence them and, through them, the people of the village. They are in demand and can, under some circumstances, name their price. But freedom from above also implies the lack of a guaranteed and secure political relation with the powers that be. To retain their position of influence or to get the better of local rivals, the neta is under constant pressure to take the initiative to contact decision-makers at higher levels.

The social vision of rural netas and the range of actions they are prepared to undertake in order to give their personal agendas concrete shape are affected as much by their personal motives and social background as by the infrastructure and the climate of popular consciousness that surrounds them. The climate of opinion is constituted by the extent to which ordinary people take an interest in development, the nature and extent of communal efforts that are available for collective projects and the extent to which they actively pursue their developmental objectives. Not all factors that lead local elites in the direction of higher-level decision-makers, of course, are imbued with the spirit of service to their clientele. In their private capacity as farmers, traders and artisans, the gaon ka netas have need for outside contacts with political and administrative decision-makers.[14] A variety of reasons thus intervene to cause them and representatives of the political arena at the higher level to meet.

Judging from the data presented in table 6.1, the rural netas in Gujarat and Orissa are not greatly impressed with the extent of popular interest and involvement that they encounter in their everyday experience of development. Only a few in Gujarat (and exclusively from among Adivasi and Harijan leaders) report 'a great deal of interest'. Interestingly, more local netas from among the Adivasi and Harijan communities in Gujarat report 'least interest' or 'indifference' than members of other social strata. Since the measurement in this case is a self-anchoring scale in the sense that every person defines the extremities of their level of interest, other things being equal, those who expect a high level of interest (for reasons of their own interest and involvement) are also the ones likely to find less of both in others. The high level of commitment of the Adivasi/Harijan elites in Gujarat to the ideology of development might account for their simultaneous reporting of 'great deal of interest' and 'least interest' or 'indifference'. In Orissa, on the other hand, where the mantle of development leadership falls, if at all, on the upper social class, it is there that we observed the most admission of least interest, more than that in other social classes.

Economic development and social change affect the internal political structure of the village. The changes thus brought about also influence the political environment within which the gaon ka netas function. A leading question on this theme asked

Table 6.1 Elite perception of popular interest in development
programmes

Popular interest and involvement in development works	Gujarat (n=131) %	Orissa (n=101) %
A great deal of interest	2	0
Not much interest	51	81
Least interest/indifference	32	17
Any other/no response	15	2
Total	100	100

the respondents to describe the political environment in terms
of 'a community in which different groups of people cooperate
with each other in any programme of development' or 'the kind
of community in which there are two or three groups which
generally oppose one another in any programme of development'. Despite the changes that have come about, including the
rupture of the traditional patron–client relations and creation
of new political communities, the gaon ka netas in both Gujarat
and Orissa appear to get by reasonably well. At about 70 per
cent, the results (see table 6.2) show a fairly high degree of
cooperation of different groups of the village in development
projects, with a significant 28 per cent reporting active opposition in Gujarat and a non-negligible minority of 13 per cent in
Orissa reporting inaction and apathy as the general state of
communal political life as regards development projects. The
cross-tabulation with social class reveals the extent to which
leadership of the development ideology has passed into the
hands of the Adivasi/Harijan in Surat. As the group in the
position of leadership, 80 per cent of the Adivasi/Harijan in
Surat claim the existence of an atmosphere of cooperation
compared to 67 per cent for the highest and 61 per cent for the
medium social class. In Orissa, on the other hand, the highest
social class, secure in its social and developmental leadership,
reports a confident 72 per cent of cooperation and a condemna-
tory 25 per cent of apathy but only a complacent 3 per cent of
opposition and dissension. When it comes to detecting opposition in the environment, Gujarati upper and middle castes, at
29 per cent and 39 per cent respectively, feel more contention
in the air than the Adivasi/Harijan (18 per cent). In Orissa,
on the other hand, the Adivasi/Harijan, still very much the

Table 6.2 Nature of interaction among different groups within the community

Nature of group relations within the community	Gujarat (n=131) %	Orissa (n=101) %
Active cooperation	70	72
Active opposition	28	15
Apathy	2	13
Total	100	100

underdogs, feel the weight of opposition (23 per cent) more than the middle (19 per cent) or the upper social classes (3 per cent). In Orissa, those who are more radical, notice more apathy; in Gujarat, the radical report more opposition.

The next item to be looked at is the nature of messages that local elites receive from the environment they are placed in and the way in which they respond to them. Placed as they are between the state and the wider body of the citizenry, rural leaders are often the first line of contact for the people seeking the redressal of a grievance or looking for support to reinforce a local initiative. Netas themselves are rarely more than catalysts in the process of authoritative intervention, their role being that of facilitator. With this caveat, as we look at the battery of structured items presented in table 6.3, three broad avenues of possible redressal appear.

In the first place is the state itself, represented by its officials who have maintained the time-honoured custom of Indian kings, of receiving petitions from ordinary people directly in the *durbar*. The British collector touring villages on horseback and

Table 6.3 Elite perception of the means of popular participation

People in the area generally	Gujarat (n=131) %	Orissa (n=101) %
Contact officials	90	85
Contact panchayat leaders	95	94
Contact MLAs, MPs and Ministers	72	56
Contact leaders of the ruling party	62	54
Contact leaders of the opposition	43	15
Resort to direct action	14	14

their contemporary successors negotiating the same terrain by the ubiquitous jeep have lived up to the same image – *mai bap* – to the people, though this image of benevolent authoritarianism has greater resonance in Orissa than in Gujarat. But, even in Orissa, the residual traces of a moral economy can be misleading in so far as elite-initiated contacts with higher authorities are concerned. In both Gujarat and Orissa people contact officials when they are unhappy and dissatisfied with the course of development. The rural netas in both States are nearly unanimous on this point.

The second possible avenue of redressive action is the range of intermediate structures, in this case, the leaders of the local administration, and members of political parties and elected legislative bodies. Two points emerge clearly from the data. One notices the comparatively higher incidence of resort to these institutions in Gujarat (see table 6.3), signifying both the longer history of their implantation in Gujarat and the richer associational life of Gujarat. However, both in Gujarat and Orissa, as one goes higher in the level of the secondary institution, the number of people taking recourse to them drops off. A less obvious point is the impact of social class on the perception of the local elites. Both in Gujarat and Orissa, fewer Adivasi/Harijan (respectively 74 per cent and 41 per cent) believe that people contact ministers and members of legislatures compared to the higher social strata (respectively 81 per cent and 75 per cent) whereas, when it comes to 'panchayat leaders like Sarpanch', the percentage of the lowest social strata is practically at the same level or higher than that of the highest social class.

Yet another possibility for political action while remaining within the range of institutional structures is to take one's grievances to the opposition parties. Not only do far fewer local netas in Orissa do so compared to Gujarat; the Oriya resort to opposition leaders is more in the nature of registering a grievance than seeking redressal. This would appear from the fact that there is no significant relationship between radicalism and resort to opposition leaders in Orissa, whereas in Gujarat 63 per cent of the 'highly radical' resort to opposition leaders compared to 47 per cent for the sample as a whole.

The third category of action that people take recourse to belongs to the range of techniques collectively referred to as direct action. Though the proportion of people taking recourse to direct action is lower than the other categories of action, significantly, they are roughly at the same level in the two States. Equally significantly, the percentage of elites reporting the resort to direct action is higher among the upper social class than among the Adivasi/Harijan being, respectively, 38 per cent and 2 per cent in Gujarat and 22 per cent and 9 per cent in Orissa.

So far in the study we have assumed that local elites perform the role of intermediaries between the state and society. In order to put this crucial assumption to test, we asked a structured question with a battery of items: 'There are occasions when people take their grievances and complaints to leaders like you. In such situations which of the following do you generally do and which do you not do generally?' This is a multiple-choice question in the sense that one course of action does not necessarily exclude another. In practice, local elites are likely to receive supplicants for a broad range of issues and resort to action appropriate to the specific nature of the task. The responses to the question (table 6.4, details in the appendix) provide strong evidence of the intermediary role of the netas. That the question is meaningful is seen from the generally low rate of non-response. A fairly large number of local elites are able to take the matter to relevant officials, panchayat leaders and 'upper level leaders like MLAs and MPs', the higher figures in Gujarat being suggestive of the greater sense of efficacy of the Gujarati leaders as well as the more entrenched nature of intermediate structures in Gujarat. This is supplemented to some extent by the resort to 'involving party leaders' where Orissa has a marginal edge over Gujarat. In both States, the incidence of local leaders resorting to direct action in order to draw attention to local grievances and complaints is rather low.

Table 6.4 Elite responses to popular grievances and complaints

Action generally taken in response to grievances	Gujarat (n=131) %	Orissa (n=102) %
Take up the matter with the relevant officials	93	78
Refer it to panchayat leaders	94	81
Represent before upper-level leaders like MLAs, MPs	69	63
Involve party leaders	54	58
Resort to direct action like morcha, dharna, etc.	9	6
Handle it personally	84	88

Within a broadly similar picture of an active intermediate layer to politics in both Gujarat and Orissa, the role of social class presents a rather contrasting scenario. With regard to involving members of higher-level legislative bodies, the Adivasi and Harijan leaders of Gujarat are ahead of their upper-caste counterparts, the lowest score being the lot of the middle social class. Fifty-two per cent of the middle social class elites take up local complaints with MLAs and MPs and 36 per cent of them involve party members as against, respectively, 81 per cent and 70 per cent of the Adivasi and Harijan elites for those items in Gujarat. In Orissa, on the other hand, local elites from the upper social strata are far ahead of the lowest, with, respectively, 81 per cent as against 50 per cent and 83 per cent to 55 per cent in those items. However, though they are less active when it comes to institutional intervention, the Adivasi/Harijan of Orissa (like their counterparts in Gujarat) are quite able to hold their own with regard to personal intervention in the case of local complaints. More than 80 per cent of the respondents among the Adivasi and Harijan elites in Orissa 'handle it personally' when a complaint is made to them. But even in this respect, the Orissa upper strata, at 90 per cent, are ahead of them, unlike in Gujarat, where the proportions are reversed, with the Adivasi/Harijan elites at 84 per cent and the highest social class at 71 per cent, though, the biggest score in this case lies with the middle social class at 90 per cent.

THE NATURE OF ELITE INITIATIVE AND EFFICACY

Local leaders are reactive as well as pro-active. They meet other political leaders and government officials at their own initiative to articulate local grievances and seek state intervention. Table 6.5 presents the responses of local elites in Gujarat and Orissa to a battery of items that asked them about the frequency of their contacts with the political system and the administrative machinery of the state. One notices at once that the frequency of contacts decreases monotonically as one moves up the administrative hierarchy in both States. There are, however, subtle differences between Gujarat and Orissa. At the lowest or village level, for example, the Orissa leaders appear more active than their Gujarati counterparts. This can be explained in terms of

Table 6.5 Frequency of elite contacts with decision-makers

Often contacts	Gujarat (n=131) %	Orissa (n=102) %
Village leaders	67	78
Village officials	67	76
Taluka leaders	49	40
Taluka officials	54	56
District leaders	21	12
District officials	21	8
State leaders	9	6
State officials	7	2

the linkage between local institutions and social formations.

Reference has already been made to the progressive penetration and control of the institutions of local democracy at the lower levels by the more numerous lower classes in parts of the country, notably including Rajasthan and Gujarat.

Under the pressure of local democracy, local elites from the upper social classes in Gujarat have tended increasingly to move to higher levels of the system to make contacts and seek intervention. Thus, when asked about the frequency of their contacts with village leaders, 81 per cent of the Adivasi and Harijan netas claim that they contact them frequently, compared to only 57 per cent of the leaders from the upper and middle social classes. The statistical relation (Kendall's tau B = 0.19, significant at 0.009 level) suggests that the lower the social class, the higher the frequency of contacts with village leaders in Gujarat. The same scenario (with an even stronger statistical relationship) holds for contacts with village officials. Statistical relationships of the same order between social class and frequency of contacts with leaders and officials are observed at the taluka level, the next on the hierarchy. However, as one moves up to the district level and beyond that to the high politics of the State capital, no straightforward statistical relationships are to be found, though in terms of percentages we find more upper and middle social class leaders contacting officials and leaders than the members of the Adivasi/Harijan. In Orissa, on the other hand, no statistical relationship is observable between social class and the frequency of contacts with leaders or officials at the

185

village level, with fairly high numbers of all social classes reporting frequent or occasional contacts. However, as one moves up higher, a trend, not always significant but nevertheless robust, of greater upper social class contacts with decision-makers is discernible.

What transpires when the gaon ka netas contact political leaders and government officials? Table 6.6 presents the responses to a question on this theme where the respondents were asked to describe their interlocutors in terms of those that were 'consistently most helpful' and those that were 'least helpful'. Once again, as with the statistics regarding the frequency of contacts with leaders and officials, there is a linear drop in the efficacy of these contacts as one moves up the ladder. Again, as before, at the aggregate level Orissa has a slight edge over Gujarat in the efficacy of contacts at the village level though the picture changes to the advantage of Gujarat as one moves up the hierarchy. The explanation is to be found in the comparatively negative experience of the Gujarati upper and middle strata about the efficacy of contacts at the village level. Around 75 per cent of the Gujarati upper classes find village leaders helpful compared to 93 per cent for the Adivasi and Harijan leaders. The same trend holds for village officials as well, with 52 per cent of the upper classes reporting them helpful compared to 91 per cent for the local elites from Adivasi/Harijan categories. Though the relationship between social class and efficacy is less significant in Orissa at the village level, there is a tendency nevertheless for greater efficacy for lower social strata compared to the upper and middle social classes. However, the trends reverse as one goes up, a clear trend being discernible by the time one reaches the level of the district. Fifty-seven per cent of local leaders from the highest strata in Gujarat find district leaders helpful compared to only 29 per cent for the Adivasi/ Harijan. The experience of contacts with district officials produces a level of efficacy for the different social classes in the same direction. The comparatively more negative experience of the lowest social class in Gujarat in their contacts with leaders and officials at the district level and beyond is replicated in the experience of Orissa local leaders as well.

Not surprisingly, what transpires when a local influential contacts a leader or official is closely related to the frequency of such contacts. It would be counter-intuitive to expect rational

Table 6.6 Institutional response when contacted

Most helpful in getting things done	Gujarat (n=131) %	Orissa (n=102) %
Village leaders	82	87
Village officials	81	83
Taluka/block leaders	72	62
Taluka/block officials	83	77
District leaders	30	10
District officials	29	14
State leaders	12	5
State officials	10	4

actors to behave otherwise. The behaviour of local elites is further constrained by their perception of their clientele and the frequency with which people approach them for their intervention, either in their personal capacity or as mediators between the ordinary citizen and the authorities. Also, from previous discussion of the role of organisations, the extent to which local leaders are involved with social, cultural, economic or political organisations is likely to affect their sense of efficacy and the frequency of their contacts with higher authorities. Above all, structural variables like social status, age and education are likely to affect their level of involvement and sense of subjective efficacy. In order to test these conjectures, the batteries of items used to measure aspects of each of these attributes were first merged to form Guttman scales and then their intercorrelation was worked out. The scales are listed in table 6.7.

Table 6.7 Frequency of participation by local elites: percentage scoring 'high' on aggregate indicators of participation

Item	Gujarat (n=131	Orissa (n=102)
Citizen initiative	40	13
Leadership response	41	51
Contacts with leaders	26	15
Contacts with officials	23	11
High satisfaction with leadership contact	30	10
High satisfaction with official contact	29	13
Organisational involvement	29	18

Perhaps not surprisingly, Gujarat scores higher than Orissa on all of these indicators of participation. Her elites perceive people to be more active in seeking out leaders and officials in order to pursue their developmental objectives, though, interestingly, the Gujarat netas are a little more circumspect about the responses of 'leaders like themselves when contacted by the people': on this factor, Orissa leaders are 11 per cent ahead of Gujarat. However, when asked about the frequency of contacts with leaders and officials who are at a higher level, and presumably have the authority to take decisions, Gujarat comes ahead of Orissa on both counts. But most important of all, not only do Gujaratis contact higher-level decision-makers more often, they have a much higher sense of efficacy about these contacts, for nearly 30 per cent of them feel highly satisfied with the results of these contacts compared to only 13 per cent who feel similarly in Orissa. The combination of all this is seen in organisational involvement, where Orissa, at 18 per cent, is once again behind Gujarat's 29 per cent.

Though Orissa is behind Gujarat in the scores achieved by their elites in the aggregate indicators of participation, do Oriya and Gujarati leaders respond to the same *structure* of participation? The structure of participation is a certain mental clustering of attitudes which places actions, anticipated or based on past experiences, in a certain logical order. One would thus expect those who have a tendency to contact leaders for decision-making purposes also to do likewise with civil servants. One would expect a sense of efficacy about these meetings, or else it would be meaningless to continue them. 'Active' elites would tend to perceive more active citizens around them than less active elites. Finally, the active and efficacious local elites would not stop merely at ad hoc meetings with decision-makers: they would get involved with a range of development organisations and continue their efforts through those organisations as well. Some of these expectations are borne out in the intercorrelations of these variables reported in table 6.8.

While most of the actions undertaken by the gaon ka netas in order to promote their agendas fall into conventional methods of participation, not all actions are necessarily or exclusively within the bounds of 'normal', institutional politics. There is considerable enthusiasm for and approval of conventional forms of participation, but, when it comes to radical action, the

Table 6.8 Intercorrelation of leadership perception, efficacy and contacting

	CITIACT	LEADACT	LEADCONT	OFFCONT	LEADEFF	OFFEFF	ORGN
Gujarat (n=131)							
CITIACT	1.00						
LEADACT	0.39	1.00					
LEADCONT	0.33	0.45	1.00				
OFFCONT	0.22	0.45	0.72	1.00			
LEADEFF	–	0.25	0.39	0.40	1.00		
OFFEFF	0.24	0.29	0.48	0.49	0.57	1.00	
ORGN	0.34	0.38	0.22	0.18	0.19	0.19	1.00
Orissa (n=101)							
CITIACT	1.00						
LEADACT	0.56	1.00					
LEADCONT	0.39	0.60	1.00				
OFFCONT	0.46	0.54	0.52	1.00			
LEADEFF	0.16	0.24	0.33	0.42	1.00		
OFFEFF	0.26	0.27	0.44	0.50	0.49	1.00	
ORGN	0.47	0.47	0.45	0.47	0.26	0.37	1.00

Notes:
CITIACT = Citizen initiatives
LEADACT = Leadership response
LEADCONT = Contacts with leaders
OFFCONT = Contacts with officials
LEADEFF = Sense of efficacy about contacting leaders
OFFEFF = Sense of efficacy about contacting officials
ORGN = Organisational involvement

pattern is more complex. Such 'hard' forms of direct action as non-payment of taxes and gherao (surrounding a decision-maker and holding him until a favourable decision is obtained), with larger potential costs in terms of individual penalty, carry less support than 'softer' forms such as morcha (a procession intended as a show of force). Only small, determined minorities can be expected to approve of radical collective action in most cases.

Many of the forms of radical protest are 'spontaneous' in the sense of not being organised by established political organisations and being individual rather than collective in character. But, invariably, they have deep roots in the history of collective grievances behind them. They share their origin in social protest with what Scott calls 'everyday forms of peasant resistance – the prosaic but constant struggle between the peasantry and those who seek to extract labour, food, taxes, rents and interest from them'. The typical examples of this form of resistance are 'foot dragging, dissimulation, desertion, false compliance, pilfering, feigned ignorance, slander, arson, sabotage' – which require 'little or no coordination or planning; make use of implicit understandings and informal networks; often represent a form of individual self help'. Most important of all, however, they 'stop well short of outright collective defiance'. The image of guerrilla warfare as compared to conventional battle occurs frequently in Scott's account of the everyday forms of peasant resistance for, above all, the peasants 'typically avoid any direct, symbolic confrontation with authority'.[15]

Everyday forms of peasant resistance are for Scott a constant parameter of peasant societies, a 'constant, grinding conflict over work, food, autonomy, ritual'. In Scott's metaphor, the standard form of this battle is guerrilla warfare of a ragtag band trying to protect traditional rights against an expanding state and market more than a disciplined army of dissidents fighting for outright victory. 'In the Third World it is rare for peasants to risk an outright confrontation with the authorities over taxes, cropping patterns, development policies, or onerous new laws.' Despite some similarities, the main thrust of these observations are at variance with the findings from Gujarat and Orissa. The Indian netas, with an eye to the media, a sensitive ear for the political vulnerability of the authorities and the presumed sympathy of the party in power at the regional level which will define the limits of police tolerance for the disturbance of law and order, have increasingly resorted to local protest movements as a political instrument. We posed two further batteries of questions to local elites on the full range of action people engage in. One of them relates to the participatory acts engaged in by the people – seen here as the constituents of the village netas – and the other requires of them their normative evaluation of each of these modes of participation. From table 6.9, both in Gujarat and Orissa, popular participation in the relatively easy and legitimate acts of participation such as signature campaigns, attending meetings, contacting important leaders and officials are widely practised, with Gujarat having a small edge over Orissa. However, when it comes to more contentious methods such as demonstrations, morcha and processions, strikes and non-payment of taxes and gherao, there is a progressive drop in the number of people engaging in them frequently or occasionally. Further, in each of these items, Gujarat comes well ahead of Orissa.

Table 6.9 Elite perception of popular participation

People engage frequently or sometimes in	Gujarat (n=131) %	Orissa (n=102) %
Representations like signature campaign or memoranda	84	82
Joining demonstrations	18	16
Attending meetings	86	84
Morcha and processions	32	9
Gherao	8	2
Strike	20	1
Non-payment of taxes	11	2
Contacting important leaders	87	79
Contacting important officials	83	76

The perception of higher incidence of popular involvement in the more contentious methods of participation in Gujarat can be attributed, first of all, to the greater incidence of riots, demonstrations and other acts of collective protest in Gujarat. However, there is also an element of greater awareness of these acts in Gujarat, which is expressed on class lines. Thus, the elites from Gujarati upper classes tend to report more extensive participation in radical protest than is the case in Orissa. That, by itself, is however rather ambiguous, for higher reporting could arise out of completely different motives as well. It is possible that the upper social-class leaders have a lower tolerance threshold for such activities so that they tend to report an act of public disorder whereas those more tolerant of such activities would see otherwise. The second possibility is for the elites of the upper strata to include collective protest as a legitimate element in the armoury of protest from below, whereas the lowest strata, in view of their deference to authority, tend to under-report such activities. To test the validity of these two different conjectures, we posed the same battery of elements to the local influentials for their normative evaluation.

The responses, presented in table 6.10, offer some explanations of the puzzles encountered in the perception of popular participation. To begin with, when it comes to the peaceful and legitimate methods of participation, the relatively high reported incidence of these acts in Gujarat and Orissa are replicated in the equally high approval of them by all social classes in both States. However, when it comes to the more contentious ones, the approval rating in Orissa tends to be on a par with Gujarat, or, in some cases, even higher. The explanation for this comes from the fact that the Gujarati upper classes have a significantly higher rate of approval for these acts than the Adivasi/Harijan. The latter, with their numerical preponderance among the village netas and lower rate of approval of radical protest, lower the overall rates on the whole. In Orissa, however, the lowest social classes have an approval rating of radical protest at the same level as the upper social classes.

Table 6.10 Normative evaluation of methods of participation

Respondent approves of	Gujarat (n=131) %	Orissa (n=102) %
Representations like signature campaign or memoranda	93	94
Joining demonstrations	20	39
Morcha, processions	37	31
Gherao	7	12
Strike	12	16
Non-payment of taxes	10	8
Contacting important leaders	95	98
Contacting important officials	94	98

SOCIO-STRUCTURAL AND POLITICAL FACTORS IN THE BENEFITS OF DEVELOPMENT

Having already examined some particular indicators of attitudes towards conventional and radical modes of participation, we shall now offer a more systematic examination of this process. This is done by first identifying the implications of a situation where there is no 'room for manoeuvre' for vulnerable social groups and social class is the only determinant of participation in development. The hypothetical expectations arising out of this situation can be summed up in a structural equation which suggests that the higher the social class of local elites, the greater are the gains one might expect out of development. This model is specified in terms of a simple equation:

Equation 1

Economic benefits of development $= f$(social class)
where, $f > 0$,
    social class is measured
    by caste status.

As before, benefits of development are measured in terms of a variety of 'objective' indicators, pertaining to material resources such as agricultural inputs and developmental loans. We expand this definition by including the more subjective 'satisfaction' with development as well as improvement in the overall personal financial situation. From the foregoing, we can conceptualise the 'routes' one might traverse to reach these desired goals. The first of these requires the least amount of political or organisational effort. This route, of 'participation without politics',[16] is secured through the normal operations of the market. *Ceteris paribus*, those with the necessary initial advantages of wealth, social standing and education are likely to be the normal beneficiaries of participation without politics as implied by equation 1.

There are, however, other routes to participation that are more political in character. These consist in contacting leaders and officials at higher levels, getting involved in organisations and taking direct action. While they are conceptualised in the abstract as independent paths, in the real world of politics they are likely to operate in complex combinations. To measure their

193

independent and joint contributions to participation in development, we can specify a structural–political model in terms of a second equation:

Equation 2

> Benefits of development = *f*(social class, organisation and contacting, attitudes to collective protest)
> where, *f* > 0,
>> social class is measured in terms of caste status
>> organisation is measured in terms of the number of organisations with which the respondent is associated
>> contacting is measured in terms of the frequency with which the individual contacts decision-makers at higher levels,
>> and,
>> attitude to collective protest is measured in terms of the local elites' approval of direct action.

'Benefits of development', the major dependent variable in this analysis, is measured in terms of a scale created by adding up responses to items such as improved seeds, chemical fertiliser, irrigation, house sites, 'land to the landless', bank loans, subsidy, improved agricultural implements and government aid for promotion of small industries. For the purposes of construction of the scale of benefits of development, those who have received any of them during the 'past couple of years' score one point on each item, and those who have not score zero. Considering the relative levels of development of Orissa and Gujarat, the results do not come as a surprise. Whereas in relatively backward Orissa only 14 per cent of the local elites have received six or more of the items of the scale, the corresponding score for Gujarat is 30.5 per cent. Both in Gujarat as well as in Orissa, benefits of development are closely related to satisfaction with improvement in the financial position of the respondent (the correlation is 0.4 and 0.18 in Orissa) and the general satisfaction with development of the area (the correlation is 0.21 in Gujarat and 0.27 in Orissa). The subjective indicators themselves are positively correlated, giving both measurements of development a reasonable degree of internal coherence.

Having specified the parameters used in both the structural

and the structural–political models, table 6.11 presents the
results of the multiple regression to examine the implications of
equation 1. Thus, the negative coefficient of caste status in
regression equation 11.1 (in table 6.11) in Orissa confirms the
hypothetical expectation that the lower the caste of the local
elites, the less are the chances of their getting any development
inputs. Though the model explains only 6 per cent of the
variance, the statistical relation is in the predicted direction.
High multicollinearity, caused by the strong correlation between
land, caste and education, reduces the significance of the coefficients of education and landholding. However, turning next
to results from Gujarat in regression equation 11.1 (see table
6.11), it is immediately obvious that rather than low-caste status
reducing the chances of obtaining development benefits, the
strongly positive coefficients suggests that it actually improves
them. The variance explained at 11 per cent is modest but
higher than that explained by the same model in Orissa. Moving
over to equation 11.2, we notice that the model does not
produce any significant coefficients in Orissa. However, in
Gujarat, the implications of the model are somewhat contradictory. Those owning land are more likely to be satisfied with their

Table 6.11 Structural factors associated with the benefits of
development (standardised beta coefficients)[1]

Independent variables	Material benefits (11.1)	Present financial situation (11.2)	Finance compared to past (11.3)	Overall satisfaction with development (11.4)
Gujarat (n=131)				
Social class[2]	0.31	0.20	0.33	–
Education	–	–	–	0.23
Land	–	0.24	–	0.26
R^2	0.11	0.13	0.09	0.12
Orissa (n=102)				
Social class[2]	0.25	–	0.31	–
Education	–	–	–	0.31
Land	–	–	–	–
R^2	0.06	0.01	0.10	0.08

Notes [1] Only coefficients significant at 0.05 level or less have been reported.
[2] Social class is measured in terms of caste status, scaled as follows: Adivasi/
Harijan 1, Middle castes 2, Upper castes 3.

present financial situation; but, the higher the caste, the opposite is likely to be the case. From equation 11.3 in Orissa, the lower the caste, the less one is satisfied with one's present financial situation, whereas the opposite is the case in Gujarat. Finally, as regards overall satisfaction with development, in Orissa the more educated are less satisfied. In Gujarat, on the other hand, the higher the education and the size of land-holding, the more one is satisfied with the pace and quantum of development.

What happens when people do not receive the benefits to which they believe they are entitled? In order to account for the contrast between Gujarat and Orissa, we need to add some political and organisational variables as additional explanatory factors through equation 2. We know from chapter 5 that more Gujaratis believe in the efficacy of protests and agitation than the local elites in Orissa. Moreover, belief in the efficacy of development in Gujarat is not simply normative. It seems to have a firm basis in the development experience of the Adivasi and Harijan elites in the two States as well. Both in terms of the tangible benefits of development and general financial situation, these historically underprivileged groups have a more positive record in Gujarat as compared to Orissa. An impressive group of 60 per cent of the netas in the Adivasi/Harijan category in Gujarat are in the highest category of the composite scale of the benefits compared to 9 per cent of the uppermost social class and 16 per cent of the middle social class. The corresponding figures from Orissa are, respectively, 9 per cent for the Adivasi/Harijan, 11 per cent for the middle and 22 per cent for the upper social class local elites. Even more spectacularly, 91 per cent of the Adivasi/Harijan report an improvement in their financial situation over the past 'ten or fifteen years' in Gujarat, whereas none among the Adivasi/Harijan in Orissa reports having experienced an improvement of their personal financial situation over a similar period.

Among other factors that further enhance involvement with and benefits from the process of development are contacts with leaders and officials at higher levels, involvement with a range of intermediate organisations and psychological preparedness to engage in radical behaviour to promote development. At the level of partial correlations, each of these factors is positively related to developmental benefits in Orissa (respectively, 0.15,

Table 6.12 Contribution of structural and political factors to the benefits of development (standardised beta coefficients)[1]

Independent variables	Dependent variables (regression equations)			
	Material benefits (12.1)	Present financial situation (12.2)	Finances compared to past (12.3)	Overall satisfaction with development (12.4)
Gujarat (n=131)				
Social class[2]	0.28	–	0.33	0.33
Education	–	–	–	–
Land	–	0.3	–	–
Contacting[3]	–	–	–	–
Organisation[4]	–	–	0.22	0.22
Radical norm[5]	–	–	–	0.21
R^2	0.13	0.18	0.18	0.19
Orissa (n=102)				
Social class[2]	0.24	–	0.32	–
Education	0.28	–	–	0.32
Land	–	–	–	–
Contacting[3]	–	–	–	0.20
Organisation[4]	–	–	0.24	–
Radical norm[5]	0.21	–	–	0.20
R^2	0.14	0.02	0.14	0.15

Notes [1] Only coefficients significant at 0.05 level or less have been reported.
[2] Social class is measured in terms of caste status, scaled as follows: Adivasi/Harijan 1, Middle castes 2, Upper castes 3.
[3] Contacting is measured by adding up the frequency with which local elites contact leaders and officials at higher levels (Never 1, Rarely 2, Sometimes 3, Frequently 4).
[4] Organisation is measured by adding up the number of organisations and associations with which the respondent claims to be involved.
[5] Radical norm is measured by adding up the approval of modes of protest behaviour: morcha, gherao, strike, non-payment of taxes (Approval 1, Non-approval 0).

0.14 and 0.22). In Gujarat on the other hand, only organisational involvement is positively related to benefits and radical attitudes are expressed by those who have not been successful in securing benefits.

Let us now consider the regression results presented in table 6.12. Although the addition of these variables causes the variance explained to go up modestly, their contributions are not significant. In regression equation 12.3, whereas organisational involvement in Gujarat contributes positively to the improvement in the financial situation compared to the past, the opposite is the case in Orissa. One explanation for this is the considerable number of local elites from the Adivasi/Harijan in Orissa who are involved in a range of organisations but who complain bitterly that their financial situation compared to the past has definitely worsened. Radical sentiments are expressed by those from the upper social strata in Gujarat who have not seen any improvement in their financial situation over the past (12.4 in table 6.12). However, those who are satisfied are also likely to take radical action to achieve their ends. In other words, the political repertoire of developmental participation in Gujarat includes institutional as well as radical action, used in an optimal combination. In Orissa, on the other hand, anger and frustration are the expression of a sense of personal inefficacy, more likely to be the rebellion of the deprived than a potent instrument in the hands of resourceful political entrepreneurs.

THE RELATIONSHIP OF INSTITUTIONAL PARTICIPATION AND RADICAL PROTEST

The existence of a multiplicity of methods of participation in India, ranging between voting and armed insurrection, has been reported by several authors including Hardgrave and Kochanek[17] and James Manor.[18] However, the interrelationships of the modes of participation are not explored at sufficient depth. The general tendency in the literature is to conceptualise protest demonstrations as acts of despair rather than as elements of a complex repertoire, used by rational actors on appropriate occasions for the most effect. Despite its paucity, the evidence from comparative literature is more helpful.[19] Commenting on the relationship of the conventional or 'orthodox' modes of participation and acts of collective protest, Marsh suggests,

> Active partisans will signal their discontent and demands for redress of political grievances through a mixture of political methods. For example, a demonstration may conclude in a lobby of parliament, or an unofficial strike may occur to provoke the intervention of officials.
>
> (Marsh (1977), p 4)

Similarly, Suzanne Berger, using French data, shows the adroit use of protest demonstrations by French peasants to prevail upon the state to continue its protectionist policies in favour of French agriculture. Scott, putting on record everyday forms of peasant resistance, says as much.[20]

The evaluation of the various methods which people adopt in order to bring pressure on decision-makers is itself derived from a cognitive structure that arranges the behavioural norms under a core set of basic attitudes towards authority. The room for manoeuvre in the middle consists of the complementarity of radical and institutional behaviour. However, when society is polarised into antagonist camps, we would expect a negative correlation between attitudes towards institutional and radical modes of action. Elite perception of the nature of the state is crucial to this relationship. The image of the state as a manipulable source of bounty will encourage attitudes closer to a transactional model. On the other hand, a state which is perceived as distant and paternalistic would not lead to a sense of individual efficacy. There, authority is more likely to be allowed a higher threshold of acquiescence by those subject to it. When pushed beyond this, the affected groups might break into violent protest.

The questions asked to measure the perception and evaluation by the gaon ka netas of the range of activities relating to participation have already been discussed. The relationship between institutional and radical modes of action was tested on the basis of a factor analysis of modes of participation. The factor analysis was carried out on the sample as a whole as well as on the netas of Gujarat and Orissa separately. The results of the analysis on the full sample (see table 6.13) points to the existence of two principal factors, explaining 46 per cent of the variance. On the basis of the factor loadings, we can identify two principal factors. Factor 1 represents the institutional dimension of participation, consisting of personal approval of signature campaigns, contacting important leaders and officials. Factor 2, with high loadings on various forms of coercive and direct action, constitutes the radical dimension.

The factor correlation between the institutional and the radical dimensions of participation is a relatively weak but positive .06. However, when carried out at the regional level, the model reveals interesting regional variations. In Gujarat, the factor correlation between the institutional and the radical dimensions is positive, and, at .2, is stronger than that of the

Table 6.13 Factor analysis of the modes of participation (with oblique rotation)

Respondent personally approves of	Factor 1	Factor 2
Representations like signature campaign or memoranda	.36	.11
Joining demonstrations	.18	.65
Morcha, processions	.11	.43
Gherao	.16	.90
Strike	.04	.77
Non-payment of taxes	.14	.57
Contacting important leaders	.99	.06
Contacting important officials	.83	.21

correlation on the total sample. In Orissa the factor structure is slightly different. The radical dimension is composed of the same items as in Gujarat. The institutional dimension appears as two distinct but positively related factors, with signature campaigns appearing as a separate dimension. The correlation between the first dimension, composed of contacting leaders and officials and radical dimensions, at −.26, is quite strongly negative.

In so far as both the radical and the institutional dimensions derive their specific characters out of a certain disposition towards authority, the perception of the state is crucial to the analysis of their relationship. The perception of the state as a manipulable source of bounty would encourage attitudes closer to a transactional model. On the other hand, a state which is distant and paternalistic would brook no such robust confidence in the reasonableness of order. There, the government is more likely to be allowed a higher threshold of toleration by those subject to it. When pushed beyond this, collective protest is likely to manifest in explosive, no-holds-barred rebelliousness.

CONCLUSION

The field data presented in this chapter indicate the extent of involvement, efficacy and initiative that one can find in India's rural leaders. One of the remarkable aspects of this finding is the fact that, though separated by levels of economic development, the Oriya elites are not lagging very much behind their Gujarat counterparts when it comes to manipulating the state in order to bend the flow of development resources in the direction of their villages. To some extent, this is the outcome of the diffusion of the egalitarian ethic of the modern state, brought home to local elites all over India through national schemes aimed at target populations, a welfare and development bureaucracy and the demonstration effect of the more advanced regions whose prosperity, thanks to the rapid expansion of telecommunications, has vastly raised the level of expectations of material affluence. The potential availability of resources acts as a catalyst for the demand for them, with local elites acting as the mouthpiece for these expectations from below. The need for democratic accountability to popular representative and control from above both politicises and bureaucratises the process of development.

In a different context, Clay and Schaffer have provided a number of valuable insights about the scope of effective action by vulnerable social groups and the conditions under which this is feasible.[21] In the first place, two limiting situations exist where there is no room for manoeuvre. The 'over-developed state' is one where the bureaucracy, sometimes in association with the rational planner, decides on the right course of action and has the requisite political power to implement this course of action without having to accommodate the views of those affected by bureaucratic planning and implementation.[22] The second scenario is provided by a polarised political situation where power, knowledge and capital are so completely concentrated in a narrow social base that the destitute are totally without any scope for intervention in the making of decisions that vitally affect them. In a situation of this kind where social groups are polarised across a great political divide, class war rather than room for manoeuvre within a model of incremental development and redistribution would appear to be the only way ahead. The scope for intervention arises in societies which fall outside these categories. In these societies, the room for intervention by a broad range of interests arises with the realisation on the part of some members of the policy community that 'something needs to be done and can be done'.[23] Concrete shape and depth is given to the room for manoeuvre with the raising of specific questions, for instance, 'is there an opportunity to choose different policies?'

The assumption underneath the interaction between ordinary people and policy makers, mediated and initiated by local elites, is that there is an awareness of the need for and scope of such intervention in India. These norms of participation have been institutionalised through the decentralisation of power from the central government to the regional and local levels. The creation of a development bureaucracy, accountable to elected representatives at various levels of government, has reinforced this process. India's local elites have themselves helped the process gain momentum through their complex repertoire of institutional participation and radical protest, based on culturally recognisable categories and sanctified by the halo of Gandhian satyagraha. The combination of these factors have provided a counterweight to the joint legacy of colonial authoritarianism, grafted onto a closed, rigid, stratified social system, now in the throes of democracy and rapid social and economic change.

The existence of local elites, placed at the crucial meeting point of the state and society, who are aware of the scope for intervention and have the political and organisational means of intervening, helps activate these potential resources and create an effective room for manoeuvre in the middle. Field data analysed in this chapter show that both in backward Orissa as well as in more advanced Gujarat, with a much longer tradition of popular participation, local elites are aware of the room for manoeuvre. In both regions, we have convincing evidence of frequent contacts with political and bureaucratic decision-makers by local elites. Though the aggregate indicators of participation are higher in Gujarat than in Orissa, local elites in both regions engage in lobbying and contacting, operate within the same structure of participation and feel satisfied with it.

While most of the strategies which local elites bring to bear in their attempts to generate pressure on the decision-makers belong to the realm of institutional participation, they are by no means exclusive to legitimate or non-coercive methods. Mobilisation of protest and such radical methods as gherao, dharna, boycotts, rasta roko campaigns and no-tax campaigns are also present within the political repertoire of local elites. In a factor analysis of the range of methods employed by local elites as a part of their repertoire of participation, methods of radical

202

protest emerge as a distinct and separate dimension both in Gujarat and Orissa. However, the relationship between the institutional and radical dimensions is different in the two States, a differential pattern the origins of which go back to the separate evolution of the two regions.

The positive relationship between the institutional and the radical dimensions in Gujarat point to the complementary use of the techniques of bargaining and coercion to which Gandhi gave concrete shape in the form of satyagraha. While the Gandhian spirit of satyagraha may not always be present, the form has certainly taken root and acquired wide popularity in Gujarat as indeed in large parts of India. This has given legitimacy to the notion of rational protest where political entrepreneurs can be relied upon to bring into play one technique or another depending on the structure of opportunities available at a given time and place. A wide range of empirical evidence, particularly the growth of a new social group of what the Rudolphs have called 'bullock capitalists'[24] – peasant proprietors from previously low-status groups who use family labour, high-yielding varieties of seeds and modern techniques and, increasingly, take resort to direct political action to press their demands for greater subsidies – provide further support for this combination of radical and institutional methods.[25]

Unlike Surat, Dhenkanal, like most of Orissa, has not experienced the excitement of the great non-cooperation movements of the 1920s. During the post-independence period, in the absence of State-wide organisation of vulnerable interests, Backward Castes movements or the kisan movements characteristic of northern and western India, Dhenkanal presents a situation where political consciousness has overtaken political organisation. One consequence is the growth of institutional and radical dimensions as separate entities where the radical dimension helps mostly to emphasise the inadequacies of normal politics and serves as an outlet for the ventilation of collective anger rather than as an instrument of political intervention. Once again, anecdotal evidence from Orissa suggests elements of a moral economy, where the popular conception of the role of government is that of a provider, of an agency which can legitimately be expected to look after the weak and vulnerable. It is also realised that times have changed and that, in the new political situation of competitive politics, power is essentially instrumental and maximisation of self-interest is the new governing spirit. One consequence is political anomie and an abrupt, violent edge to the normal politics of the region.[26]

Where does this leave us so far as the rational, moral and cultural models are concerned? The data presented here make one conclusion inescapable: the tragic scene of desperate poverty combined with hopeless inaction so effectively sketched by Abbe Raynal and Greenough[27] are probably a part of history. There is every indication of action, collective as well as individual; at lower levels as well as higher levels of the system; engaged in by the upper strata of society as well as the lower orders. Nor is the action restricted to the members of a specific jati. Political alliances and caste associations are the order of the day. It may seem a little paradoxical that political actors, driven by such 'modern' desires as the promotion of individual and sectional welfare, should fall back on such 'traditional' identities as caste. But the relationship between caste-consciousness and the caste system is dialectical. Caste associations are a vehicle to promote material welfare. Their very success at generating power and resources through the pooling of numbers also challenges the exclusiveness of the isolated, traditional jati and leads to the opening up of the traditional closed, stratified, rigid social system and the formation of broader communities.

The method of survey research with the scope it provides for measuring attitudes, supplemented with secondary information from the observational data of intensive village studies, are helpful in this context. The findings reported in this chapter indicate strong support for 'rational' choice, if by this we mean behaviour guided by a desire to achieve the stated objective – of material resources and influence. But this does not necessarily lead to the individual leaving the group behind in his pursuit of his private gain. The quest for personal gain has led to the rediscovery of communal solidarity in Gujarat, a phenomenon widely observed in areas of successful green revolution in India. Community formation, in the form of the growth of caste associations, or the use of ethnicity and communal networks as vehicles for material interests that a social group seeks to achieve by building a political alliance, is very much the prevailing method of political action in Gujarat. The Oriya local elites are also guided by the same desire for more material resources for rapid development as in Gujarat, but their radicalism, in contrast with their counterparts from Gujarat, tends to be more anomic than instrumental. We learn from diachronic studies of both Gujarat[28] and Orissa[29] that the cultural codes of behaviour have changed greatly in both. However, beyond the spread of the new, democratic notions of entitlement, enfranchisement and empowerment, the regions of India have evolved differently in terms of the organisation of the beneficiaries of development, the social groups who are, at least in the short run, its victims and the actual levels of improvement in material well being. The absence of horizontal alliances of social groups on the basis of collective interests is both a cause and a consequence of this difference. The origin of the separate trajectories on which different regions are set goes back into the history of economic development and the growth of representative institutions. The state of political consciousness of the present set of local elites has been affected by the different patterns of historical development.

7

CONCLUSION: THE TWO FACES OF DEVELOPMENT: PROTEST AND PARTICIPATION IN INDIA

THE PROBLEM RESTATED

Parts of this book would be familiar territory for students of political science. These sections deal with questions about the location of the village within the levels and arenas of power that together constitute the state; the people who run the institutions of the village; and the manner in which they are appointed. A political scientist with an interest in the discourse of development would venture even further and ask: How do social and economic change affect the distribution of power and the allocation of public resources within the village? What strategies do competing coalitions employ to promote social change or to thwart it as the case may be? And what ideologies and rhetoric do competing elites use to maintain their cohesiveness as political groups? Other parts of the book, steeped in the intimate, face-to-face world of rural social networks, ties of ritual and social obligation, belong more properly to the domain of cultural anthropology. Is it possible to comprehend the full text of the narrative through a common language of social science?

The problem as I understand it is two-fold. In the first place, we are attempting to study the life of a moral community through the tools of methodological individualism. It is important to recognise here that the distinction is not merely spatial, with the rural and urban being interchangeable with the moral and the rational. There have been over four decades of intermeshing of the rural and urban spaces in India. This has been brought about through state-sponsored diffusion of modern norms, market transactions and electoral coalition building across social groups. The two worldviews – moral and rational – are thus intertwined, present at every level of the system. There is not, however, as yet, a set of general rules from which these specific rules could claim a common ancestry. Mass politics emphasises the differences between the moral and the rational. The idealism embodied in the constitution, common citizenship and the modern state project their commonality. But there is still no common political language with a standard syntax.

In the second place, the problem of cross-paradigm discourse is not merely linguistic or methodological. It is also a substantive problem, related to the historical origin of modern political science and cultural anthropology and their application to the politics of post-colonial societies. The basic concepts of political science such as methodological individualism, liberal democracy, political parties and constitutionalism were formulated to create a sense of order out of the chaos resulting from rapid social and economic change in industrialising Europe. Cultural anthropology, which also came to its own during the same period, looked for the antithesis of the new world and discovered it in the little communities outside the pale of industrial Europe. Between these two disciplines grew the multi-disciplinary field of modernisation which described the transformation of the moral to the rational and held up the promise of a future for mankind when the language of rationality would become a common medium of discourse. The transposition of these concepts to contemporary India is problematic for both political science and anthropology. Politics in post-independence India, rather than being driven by economic and social change as was the case in Europe during the period of rapid industrialisation, has become the space where the forces of modernity and tradition are locked in battle. Politicisation and mass participation have taken the competing norms to every corner of the society so that political discourse even at the lowest level of the system sports elements of both the moral and the rational worldviews.

Seen from this angle, the fusion between the modern and the traditional in order to create an endogenous modernity is among the main problems that face India today. What do the gaon ka netas do to provide local roots to alien forms and create

207

a political environment in which the creation of new institutions that are responsive to local and regional needs becomes an inescapable necessity?

The anomaly that results from the simultaneous existence of rational and moral modes of politics has been reported on at length. Morris-Jones initially alerted the students of Indian politics to the three idioms – modern, traditional and saintly – of Indian political discourse.[1] Satish Saberwal attributed the roots of the crisis to 'social blanks' that define the void between traditional India and modern institutions.[2] James Manor has reported widespread prevalence of anomie at the level of the individual, caught between the cross-currents of tradition and modernity.[3] While I agree with these authors in their characterisation of the problem, my disagreement arises from the inference they draw from it. In the normal functioning of the political process in India, I see the possibility of a fusion between the modern and the traditional in a manner where both undergo a metamorphosis, out of which are born modern institutions that are also endogenous to the society and a society which is a partner of the modern state rather than being its supplicant. This is the lesson that emerges from the dual roles and dual lives of over 200 gaon ka netas – rural elites placed between the state and society – whose biographies provide the basis of my narrative.

The rhetoric and strategies of the local elites in Gujarat and Orissa are focused on the broad theme of social change and political action. My point of departure here is the conclusion that Barrington Moore drew from his cross/cultural and historical analysis of modernisation of peasant societies which has since become part of the received wisdom on the subject.[4] In the inevitable clash between modernisers and the forces of tradition, Moore had no doubts about the likely outcome. 'The tragic fact of the matter is that the poor bear the heaviest costs of modernisation under both socialist and capitalist auspices.'[5] Whether through the masked coercion and dispersed violence of capitalist agriculture, the centrally directed violence of the 'Stalinist squeeze' or the more surreptitious but no less brutal forms of agrarian fascism, the peasantry is marginalised, crushed and reshaped into the disciplined foot soldiers of the modern state and the modern economy. My objective is to move away from Moore's dismal conclusion which many have accepted as both natural and necessary. The field data presented here question the apparently supine and abject surrender of the peasantry by drawing upon their ability to manipulate the environment to their benefit;[6] to engage in a covert guerrilla war against their enemies with 'weapons of the weak';[7] and even to find allies within the state structure who devise policies that seek to balance central planning with local knowledge and welfare.[8] Analysis of the Indian case provides an opportunity to examine some of these revisionist theories of the politics of social and economic change by drawing on the institutional participation and instrumental radicalism of India's rural netas.

Another way to examine the effectiveness of pressure from below is to study the direction of social and economic policy at the highest level of the political system. India's experience with development over four decades since independence has seen a shift in policy from an exclusive preoccupation with economic growth and industrialisation to one more oriented towards agriculture and small and intermediate technologies. There has been a growing concern with the welfare of former Untouchables and the Tribal population who have been given constitutional guarantees of preferential treatment. The latest claimant to the status of potential beneficiaries of positive discrimination are the Backward Classes, an issue which has been at the centre of Indian politics. Analysis of field data which reflect some of these concerns is important not only for the larger understanding of Indian politics per se, but for the politics of development in post-colonial societies as well, for the Indian case remains a significant exemplar of attempts to achieve 'economic transformation through constitutional means'.[9]

It was suggested in the introduction to the book that the major changes in developmental policy in India since independence have come about within a political system whose relative stability and high degree of participation have made her appear as rather exceptional among post-colonial states. However, as recent developments in Punjab, Kashmir and Assam and the earlier spell of authoritarian rule under the Emergency of 1975–7 indicate, India's status as a stable democracy is not entirely secure.[10] The fact remains though that, unlike in many parts of the world, the Indian electorate still enjoys free and largely fair elections. In addition, Indian netas have developed a complex repertoire of politics that effectively combines institutional participation with radical protest.[11] They have done this through such tactics as dharna, gherao, boycotts, rasta roko – methods which take after the Gandhian satyagraha of the 1920s – and other forms of popular struggle, which combine the ideological aspirations of modern politics with the indigenous idioms of protest. Notwithstanding caste conflict and terrorist violence, the basic stability of the state (in this context, the institutionalisation of power as opposed to personal rule) within the broad framework of constitutional democracy remains largely intact.[12]

The legacy of public services, high institutionalisation at independence and continuity of leadership have no doubt contributed to the stability of the post-colonial state in India. These factors provide the macro-political context for the universe of India's local elites who, by promoting protest and participation, play an important role in the growth and legitimation of authority of the state. This achievement has been made possible through protest and participation which are but two facets of the politics of development in India.[13] Earlier attempts at theorisation have treated them as distinct and contradictory forms of action. In contrast, the view proposed here suggests that under certain conditions, institutional participation and radical protest are perceived as complementary forms of action. Under those circumstances, a state which is linked to society through multiple channels of articulation can expect greater legitimacy compared to others in a similar situation which treat participation and protest as strictly separate and favour 'normal' forms of participation to the exclusion of all manners of radical protest. These propositions have been examined through the perception of the range of alternatives open to rural netas in India in their dealings with the developmental bureaucracy and political leaders at higher levels.[14]

The crucial intermediaries in this process of social change and developmental transformation of the economy are local elites, or gaon ka netas as they are generically referred to in India's rural setting. They are political actors, situated at the interface of the modern state and traditional society. They use the double language of the state and society, of modernity and tradition and of individual rationality and group solidarity. They are engaged in a two-way interpretation of norms and political demands. Their methods range between acting as brokers in national, regional and local elections, lobbying and contacting the bureaucracy and higher political elites for the allocation of material resources and seeking to bolster their demands through rhetoric and occasional spells of radical protest. Their 'room for manoeuvre' is created when bureaucrats, political decision-makers and the law of the land accept the legitimacy of multiple modes of participation from below. This, in turn, contributes to the expansion of the social base of the state through the involvement of a broader range of citizens in the process of social change. The ability of India's local arenas to draw newly emerging social forces, whose leaders challenge and occasionally replace the existing group of netas, into the political and the policy process, and to exclude those old-style notables who fail to adapt, has cast them as a conveyor belt for political mobilisation and extension of participation in the post-colonial state.

ORDER, DEVELOPMENT AND THE POLARISATION THESIS

The propositions made in this book on the basis of field data from Gujarat, with its long history of economic development, and Orissa, where the stimulus for large-scale social and economic change became available only after independence, are at variance with the early comparative literature on conflict, protest, stability and the strategies of development. Under the influence of such seminal works as Huntington, Gurr and Moore,[15] the relationship between collective protest and legitimacy of state power has been considered to be generally negative.[16] On the basis of the findings of Hoselitz and Weiner,[17] Huntington[18] suggested that rapid economic development in societies with inadequate institutional infrastructure can lead to violence, unrest and loss of legitimacy. The theoretical linkage has been further reinforced by Gurr's notion of relative deprivation which suggests precisely why discontent is felt at its most intense in areas and among people experiencing rapid change.[19] This general conjecture, suggested in the introduction, can be recast in the form of a series of linkages among economic development, protest and loss of legitimacy. This can be specified in the form of a 'polarisation' model (see figure 7.1).[20]

211

(1)		(2)		(3)
Economic development	→	inequality relative deprivation	→	political conflict	→	weakening of legitimacy

Figure 7.1   The 'polarisation' model

The assumptions and implications of the polarisation model[21] have been brought into question by Lichbach,[22] who reports on the basis of a comprehensive review of the literature that no conclusive evidence of a relationship between economic inequality and political conflict exists. Recent historical research has also challenged many previously well-established assumptions about the reaction that developmental change was supposed to invoke in peasant societies. Rather than the spontaneous outburst of righteous, even mindless, anger, one is more likely to witness strategic protest from the 'rational' peasant, trying to combine the institutional and radical tactics to achieve their objectives. As Barkan and Holmquist suggest in their study of Kenya,

> No longer regarded as passive actors in the state–peasant equation, peasants are now seen as rational actors seeking to maximise their individual, class and community interests within the multiple constraints of the social structure, the market, ecology and state policy.
>
> (Barkan and Holmquist (1989), p. 363).[23]

What are the implications for the relations between protest behaviour and legitimacy (figure 7.1(3)) once we introduce policies of economic growth and redistribution, undertaken by a state responding to pressure from below, as intervening factors? Is it not plausible to argue that the availability of an extremist party or group speaking in the name of the deprived, poised Janus-like at the fringe of the system with an anti-system public face but a private face organised around conventional lines, actually reduces bigger threats to the legitimacy of the 'system'?[24] These speculations are given greater validity by the findings of Powell who suggests that 'riots and protests are less likely to appear under these conditions, perhaps because of the opportunity for protest leaders to work within the system'.[25] These conjectures can be put together as an alternative 'rational protest' model (see Figure 7.2).

In the first instance, unequal distribution of the benefits of

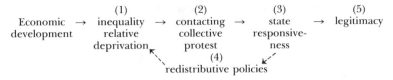

Figure 7.2   A 'rational protest' model of participation

development, causing relative deprivation, intensifies pressure on the existing institutions and decision-makers for accommodation of the demands arising from the newly mobilised social groups (figure 7.2(1)). This pressure can take the form of contacting, lobbying and protest action (figure 7.2(2)). One of the critical determinants of the form and intensity of protest is state responsiveness (figure 7.2(3)): the more unyielding the state, the more radicalised collective protest gets, whereas, through the accommodation of some strategic demands, the state can enhance its legitimacy and take the wind out of the sail of revolution (figure 7.2(5)), bring pressure to bear on its functionaries at lower levels to remain responsive (figure 7.2(3)), initiate redistributive policies (figure 7.2(4)) and reduce *perceived inequality* (figure 7.2(2)).

Our field data show how the rural netas act as intermediaries between the state and society for the purpose of political transaction. Their ability to combine institutional action and radical protest, though of critical importance to the process of social change, is little understood in cross-cultural studies of development. These local busybodies have been either villified or ignored by both the rival groups of classic development planners as well as advocates of peasant revolution. The former, top-down theories of development have routinely assumed that knowledge, technology and capital accumulating at the top of the system will trickle down to the bottom in due course through the process of modernisation. The failure of the nature and course of economic development to live up to these expectations is blamed on the meddlesome middlemen who obstruct the functioning of rational plans. On the other hand, the advocates of radical reform see an ally of repressive structures in local elites who defend 'backward' and social and economic systems. The main thrust of development theory avoids mentioning local elites altogether, except to point them out as the enemies of economic development and social change.

The literature of protest too is silent on the dual role of local elites. Scott,[26] one of the most influential among contemporary writers of this genre, recognises neither the internal differentiation of elites at local, regional and national levels which makes competitive coalition-building an inescapable fact of India's political life, nor does he consider the implications of a responsive state where, through a combination of bureaucratic design, training and the entry of new social classes into civil service, some genuine interest in development and welfare among decision-makers is discernible.[27] Under these circumstances, Scott's concluding remarks about the inability of even revolutionary change 'to deliver the petty amenities and minor humanities that animate the struggle of its subjects'[28] appear overtly and perhaps needlessly pessimistic. Scott justifies his pessimism[29] in terms of the historical experience of both revolutionary states as well as non-revolutionary contexts and draws from it a general lesson for the victims of change in their ultimately self-defeating struggle to maintain a life of dignity and some material comfort:

> If revolution were a rare event before the creation of such states, it now seems all but foreclosed. All the more reason, then, to respect, if not celebrate, the weapons of the weak. All the more reason to see in the tenacity of self-preservation – in ridicule, in truculence, in irony, in petty acts of noncompliance, in foot dragging, in dissimulation, in resistant mutuality, in the disbelief in elite homilies, in the steady, grinding efforts to hold one's own against overwhelming odds – a spirit and practice that prevents the worst and promises something better.
>
> (Scott (1985), p. 350)

The field data presented in this book should help modify the unmitigated pessimism of Scott and Moore[30] regarding the fate of the little man pitted against the tidal waves of social and economic change unleashed by the process of modernisation. However, the vital role of local elites in capturing some of the momentum of the same waves and turning them to the advantage of themselves and people whose interests they represent, and thereby acting as a bridge between the modern state and traditional society, remains inadequately understood in the academic writing on the subject. Though a number of studies of panchayati raj in India have analysed the role of local leadership and institutions, the dynamic aspect of their character is lost because most of these studies identify rural elites exclusively with those occupying positions in the panchayati raj structure. One exception here is the study of Esman and Uphoff which shows the room for manoeuvre at the local level through the creation of new institutions.[31] On the basis of a cross-national analysis of Asian experience, they conclude that effective local organisations, 'accountable to the local people, and involved in rural development functions, generally accomplished rural objectives more successfully with respect to the available resource base than those with less rural organisation'.[32] However, like the panchayati raj studies already referred to, the absence of the ground-level actor denies this study the full representation of the dynamism of the local political process. While their analysis draws attention to the scope for significant intervention at the local level, the focus on formal bodies shifts attention away from the local netas who are the real actors behind much of local and district-level politics. The results presented here show that it is possible to go beyond these limitations through the use of reputational technique for the identification of local elites and by concentrating on their rhetoric, strategies and normative perceptions of social change.

Though rural elites in India are the subject of our study, no attempt is made here to make a case for the uniqueness of India. The rational protest model, which is central to the room for manoeuvre in the middle, is potentially applicable outside developing societies as well. Indeed, even in great Britain, that epitome of stable democracies,

> protest behaviour, far from being the occasional outbursts of a hopelessly alienated minority, is an integral part of political consciousness and is viewed, under a variety of circumstances, as a legitimate pathway of political redress by widely differing sections of the community.
>
> (Marsh (1977), p. 39)[33]

Cross-cultural support for this view is provided by the efficacious rather than deviant character of 'unconventional political behaviour',[34] 'disorderly politics'[35] 'deliberate defiance of the law'[36] and the efficacy of protest movements as complementary forms of political action in France[37] or the anti-poll tax campaign in the U.K. which generated enough political momentum to bring about a change in policy. Further supportive evidence for these conjectures, which would radically challenge the dismissal of protest behaviour, seen as destructive of the legitimacy of the state, is provided by Powell who reports extremist party support to be associated with both cabinet instability and citizen turmoil, but not with 'deadly violence or the overthrow of democratic regimes'.[38] The difference in the Indian case lies in the sheer magnitude of the problem of change, of the numbers affected and, thus, the implications of local politics for the political system as a whole.

SITUATING THE MODEL IN THE INDIAN CONTEXT

Though India is not unique in providing a role to local elites in the transaction between levels of governance, the fact remains that, compared to industrial democracies in Europe, the gaon ka netas are much more in evidence and regulate a much higher proportion of public transaction in India.[39] In order to analyse the greater salience attached to their role, we need first to place them within the larger structure of the modern state in India. In contrast to the origin of the modern state in Europe, the state in India is neither the product of a rising bourgeoisie leading an industrial revolution nor of the revolutionary seizure of power by political forces committed to a socialist revolution. The leaders who took over the mantle of the state after independence had perfected the art of political transaction during colonial rule through competition and collaboration with the British Raj. Independence further expanded the scope of the bargaining political culture which had become the hallmark of the Congress party. The post-colonial state in India has become a catalyst of popular participation and protest. Development, understood as a generic expression for a series of mostly government-sponsored activities – the construction of roads, bridges, public utilities, more generally social welfare, subsidies and rapid economic growth – became the *leitmotif* of the political discourse of post-independence India. Political formations of the left, the right and the centre confronted one another in successive general elections with their specific interpretations of the 'developmental imperative'. Under growing political pressure, the state in India intervened in the social process by creating new legislation. Whereas in Western Europe during the formative phase of capitalism the state behaved very much as the 'executive committee of the bourgeoisie', the state in India after independence adopted a more complex posture. Like the *avatars* of Vishnu,[40] it reserved for itself a multiplicity of roles – of accommodation, extraction, production and repression, stepping in as the inevitable intermediary when the conflict between social forces became threatening to public order. The intermediary role of the state offered room for manoeuvre to vulnerable groups.

The strategy of bestowing official recognition on a thin layer of social notables as contact points with the vast hinterland of rural peasantry had formed the cornerstone of the colonial edifice in India. Successive degrees of incremental devolution of authority in the form of local and district boards gave institutional recognition to the role of local elites as intermediaries. Competing with the colonial government for the loyalty and allegiance of these important social groups was the Congress party, which by the early 1920s was able to 'demonstrate a capacity . . . of running a regular "ticket" in local elections and maintaining a small body of committed Congressmen on the municipal and district boards of most localities in the United Provinces, Bihar and East Punjab'.[41] The growth of Congress organisation in Gujarat and Orissa was comparatively slower, but even there it followed the national strategy of combining institutional politics and the distribution of patronage with the omnipresent potential threat of resorting to direct action in the form of collective protest. The implicit *pas de deux* between the Congress and the British Raj helped create a political environment where increasing involvement by lower social classes became necessary and possible. The British took advantage of the division in the ranks of their putative adversaries but, in the process, forced the Congress elites to evolve a continuous stream of progressively accommodative rules of transaction. The obverse side of the British 'divide and rule' was the Congress solicitude to 'unite and rule', which, in turn, became the mainstay of its post-independence strategy of ruling through political accommodation and social consensus. In the short run it meant more jobs for elites from lower social ranks but in the long run it led to greater representation of the lower social orders.

The process of state formation in India is characterised by the 'superimposition' of a centralised political system on 'acephalous local arenas', where the centre seeks to accommodate those who wield social power rather than attempting to replace them.[42] As a consequence, the local political process is marked by the conflicting demands of a modern state and a resilient traditional society. The regional variation in this process can be explained with reference to differences in the geographic location, the length and depth of colonial rule, and the integration of the local and regional markets with the national and international markets. Some of these factors are highlighted through the contrast of Gujarat and Orissa. However, the rural netas, situated though they are within and at the fringes of the local arena, are increasingly aware of their counterparts in other regions of India. The result is a form of regional knowledge-sharing, a process strongly encouraged by the development bureaucracy and national leadership through the export of successful regional experiments to other parts of India. This explains another paradox of development in India which, simultaneously, exacerbates regional differences and reduces them through the diffusion of norms, new institutions and material resources across regions.

THE FIELD STRATEGY FOR IDENTIFYING RURAL NETAS

Since the general statements made here hang crucially upon the local elite, devising a field strategy for their identification and measurement of their attitudes is of utmost importance. Previous Indian research is of limited utility here. Based often on studies of single villages, they provide insight but are not helpful to answer theoretical questions nor to draw general inferences. Studies of panchayati raj (village councils) which utilise survey methods are more promising but not very helpful in terms of illuminating the political world of local leaders because, more often than not, they are based on interviews with those holding elective office – a restricted group compared to the broader and more important group of rural netas.

A decision was therefore taken at the beginning of fieldwork to utilise the reputational technique to identify local elites. Thus, in each of the eighteen study villages, five informants were asked to list the gaon ka netas in order of their influence. These lists, compiled independently, were then compared and the names appearing on most lists were retained as a working list of local elites in a particular village. In this process, a sample of 233 people, drawn from the ranks of those who form part of the panchayati raj structure (village and area councils), cooperatives, school boards, school teachers or village-level workers (who as government employees are not entitled to dabble in local politics but do so all the same) and people in a leading position in the caste networks, were identified. These leaders were interviewed on the basis of structured and open-ended questions on a range of topics starting from the problems faced by the people of the area, the solutions they considered desirable, the agency that they thought was best placed to implement these solutions and the methods they pursued to influence decision makers at higher levels. The interviews, conducted during 1978–9 simultaneously with a larger survey of the cross-section of the population[43] in the study villages, were undertaken by the author with the help of a collaborator and two research assistants, and were conducted in the local languages.[44]

Any study purporting to generalise about India must come to grips with India's regional diversity. State responsiveness and the bargaining political culture are more likely to be present in those parts of India which are more advanced in terms of economic and infrastructural development. A second contributory factor to this diversity is the length and depth of British colonial rule. The 'due process of law' and limited political participation which the British made available to their subjects even under colonial conditions was not applicable to the natives of princely states. In the empirical specification of the model, therefore, the regional dimension is incorporated through the selection of two regions of contrasting character – Gujarat, with a longer history of participation and economic development, and relatively backward Orissa, large parts of which were ruled by Indian Princes and were integrated with mainstream politics and the market only after independence.

The sample for the survey was chosen from Surat and Dhenkanal districts, respectively from Gujarat and Orissa. Using a quasi-experimental research design which controlled for village size, nine villages situated at high, medium and low levels of development were chosen in each district. Surat district in

South Gujarat has a long history of capitalist development. The rural scene has been virtually transformed from subsistence agriculture to one where capitalist farming provides an important but not the primary source of occupation. Dhenkanal, on the other hand, provides a contrasting rural scene, where sporadic attempts to introduce new agricultural technology have created isolated islands of modern farming surrounded by a vast hinterland of subsistence agriculture. There is nevertheless a sense of movement in the labour market owing to the rapid growth of rural industries undertaken by the Orissa State government. These activities have been drawing away some agricultural workers, creating resentment among employers and strains within the traditional social structure where a *halia* (farm servant) used to work for a given master through the year on the basis of an annual contract. As such, the situation is one of radicalised workers, often pitted against employers operating within a relatively traditional economy.[45] Despite changes in the high politics of Delhi, recent studies have confirmed the enduring nature of the contrast between the two regions.

THE RHETORIC OF LOCAL DEVELOPMENT

Like other residents of the village, the gaon ka netas are also affected by the attempts of external forces including the state, market and voluntary agencies to transform the social and economic structure of the village. To the extent that these outside interventions are perceived as inimical to local interests, the netas resist attempts to 'develop' 'their' village, through a number of coping strategies. The most ubiquitous of these is also the least discernible. Development experts, planners and bureaucrats who are aware of its existence refer to it as foot-dragging, dissimulation, bottlenecks or recalcitrance. With the exception of an occasional 'incident', this is routine guerrilla warfare between the bureaucrat and the peasant, each trying to manipulate the other in the interest of his or her preferred state of the world. To call this a battle of wits between the agenda of the state and the counter-agenda of the society would, however, be attributing rather more consciousness, organisation and sense of direction than one is likely to encounter in the rhetoric of rural netas. But this is not to suggest that the demand for participation from below has no clear agenda of its own. Our data reveal the urgent desire for more material benefits of development and resources, particularly irrigation, in Dhenkanal whereas, in Surat, the just allocation of resources appears as the most pressing problem. These 'problems of development', strongly supported by suggested solutions in the same direction, no doubt reflect the reaction of the gaon ka netas to the structural constraints within which they operate. However, through their very articulation of these problems in a survey situation, they demonstrate their ability to provide local variations to the main theme of the centrally devised notion of progress, and to modify and adapt it to local needs.

Not only are the netas aware of the needs of 'people of the area such as themselves' and articulate them, they have clear ideas as to which agency – the governmental bureaucracy, the panchayati raj officials, political leaders or voluntary groups – they can approach in order to take their specific demands about development into account as well. Once again, the differences between the institutional structure in Gujarat and Orissa are evident from the higher preference for voluntary agencies in Surat as compared to Dhenkanal where they are either not known to exist or, when they do, their credibility and efficacy are at such a low level that the netas do not even bother to cite them. But the most important finding is that in *both* regions, local leaders are aware of the room for manoeuvre. They also demonstrate clear evidence of acting on this knowledge by frequently engaging in negotiation with decision-makers at higher levels. Nor does their repertoire of participation end with contacting. Occasionally, though less frequently, they bring pressure through popular mobilisation, signing of petitions and, eventually, the disruption of public order.

REGION, CLASS AND THE FORMATION OF POLITICAL COMMUNITIES

Region and social class are among the major sources of variation in Indian politics. Both play a key role in affecting the behaviour of rural elites. For the purpose of statistical analysis, social stratification is measured in terms of caste status. The 'elite castes', especially Brahmins, traders and writer castes (so called because of the reliance on them by the British Raj to act as intermediaries which facilitated their entry into the professions,

221

government services and legislatures), have been designated in this analysis as upper social class. The cultivating castes, corresponding to *sudras* in the ritual hierarchy, referred to in Indian constitution as the 'Backward Classes', are grouped together as the middle social classes. The former Untouchables and Tribal population have been designated as the lowest social class and referred to as Adivasi and Harijan categories. It is true that there is considerable heterogeneity within this group in terms of their racial origin and social practices but the small size of sub-groups does not permit separate analysis. Besides, their status as the lowest social status category itself has led to their being grouped together as the beneficiaries of the policy of 'reservation', meant as a part of state-sponsored affirmative action.

From the perspective of the polarisation model discussed above, economic development affects the three social classes quite differently. Those with contacts and adequate capital (in this case, the upper and the middle castes) can be expected to do rather nicely out of development, whereas the Adivasi/ Harijan are vulnerable to a rapid erosion of their standard of living as their living space is 'enclosed' by a rapidly advancing capitalist economy and the sources of supplementary income are steadily removed by the more rational book-keeping of the modern economy.[46] The polarisation model would lead to the expectation of greater relative deprivation among the Adivasi/ Harijan than the upper castes but the hypothetical expectations of the rational protest model would be more complex and variable according to the structure of opportunities provided by the particular context. Further, the expectation arising out of the polarisation model would be that of intense relative deprivation, conflict and loss of legitimacy whereas the rational protest model would channel relative deprivation towards political action. The rational protest model would witness extensive use of contacting and all forms of social and political leverage including various forms of radical protest.

The empirical evidence presented in this book shows that while structural parameters like high social status, education or superior financial position are conducive to greater access to developmental benefits, in some cases political organisation and radical action by those bereft of such resources can act as a countervailing force, and bring some rewards to the underprivileged as well. This room for manoeuvre in the middle is more effectively present in Gujarat where the leaders of Adivasi and Harijan groups (as indeed other sections of the society) have become well versed in the political repertoire of protest and participation. In Orissa, on the other hand, radical protest, while not entirely unknown, tends to be anomic and without clear political objectives rather than instrumental and organised as in Gujarat.

It emerges from the field data that despite the mitigating effects of empowerment of the poor and socially underprivileged groups through affirmative action, caste status continues to affect one's life chances. What then is the impact of development on social hierarchy? Though beyond the scope of the specific empirical puzzle addressed in this book, the question nevertheless is central to the politics of development in India. It can be argued here that by creating a new source of power in numbers, institutional participation and radical protest as against the old regime where ritual rank attached to occupation and status was the main avenue to power in society, the politics of development has provided an incentive for the transformation of the caste system itself.

Traditionally, the caste system has derived its strength and tenacity from its material base in the occupational structure embedded in an agrarian economy. As long as, generation after generation, members of the same jati plied the same occupation, they were inescapably conscious of belonging to the same social niche which in turn contributed to the resilience of a traditional society and its moral economy. The remarkable achievement of the politics of development has been to sever this traditional link between caste, occupation and power. The change that has come about at the level of popular consciousness is quite significant. Thanks to new notions of entitlement, enfranchisement and state action born out of political necessity, the 'Untouchables' of yesterday can aspire to become the lawyers, doctors and ministers of tomorrow. Some actually do, more in some regions of India than in others, but the fact remains that the centuries-old illusion that people born in a particular jati are fit for and ought to pursue only one specific occupation is most definitely dead.

Seen across India as a whole, the process of interpenetration of norms of centrally diffused egalitarianism and local social hierarchy is marked by contradictions and paradoxes. Thus, the fate of the same social group might differ dramatically from one region to another and even within a given region. Similarly, in trying to sever the link between caste, status and wealth, the policy of reservation which makes caste the criterion for the allocation of material benefits of development might, at least in the short term, rejuvenate caste consciousness. However, in the long run, by creating new communal solidarities which are perceived as instrumental for the securing of material benefits, caste consciousness destroys the moral basis of the caste system. By severing the link between a caste and an occupation, the policy weakens its material base. When caste is dissociated from its material base, the consciousness of caste becomes purely formal. It then joins region, language, ethnicity, religion or class as a badge of politically convenient self-classification, to be manipulated and waived when necessary and discarded when it ceases to be useful.

> An 'untouchable' [today] does not automatically and in-
> stinctively think of himself as an untouchable; rather he
> now presents himself as one to secure certain advantages.
> His being is detached from his self-consciousness and that
> is a remarkable gain. Caste-consciousness is a ladder one
> uses to climb out of a social cul-de-sac, and having got to
> the top he kicks the ladder away. The dialectic of reserva-
> tion is far more subtle than is generally appreciated.
>
> (Mitra (1987), p. 307)

The critics of caste as the basis of positive discrimination point out that the policy of reservation, by skimming off the natural leaders of Harijans and Adivasis, might leave the non-elites of these communities even worse off. Freeman's narrative of Muli, a *bauri* who belongs to the 'underclass' among the former Untouchables of his village in Orissa starts with a poignant reminder of these questions:

> The memory of Muli's humiliation stayed with me. I
> recalled similar incidents in my own country, and I
> wondered if the responses of untouchables to discrimina-
> tion paralleled those of minorities in other countries. Was
> Muli indifferent to the insults he bore in silence? I hardly
> thought so; but I wondered how an ordinary untouchable

like Muli survived economically, socially and psychologically as a member of a despised group at the bottom of society. What were his joys, aspirations, and triumphs, as well as his humiliation? What would provoke someone like him to question the treatment he received from upper-caste people, to fight back?

(Freeman (1979), p. 3)

Muli, the Orissa untouchable, turns out to be a Razak-like figure whom readers of Scott[47] would remember as a master of the art of coping and surviving under conditions of great adversity. To all appearances, he is a physically weak, infirm and thoroughly unreliable person who is the object of pity and contempt by his social superiors and subject to derision by his peers, the other Harijans of the village. But in reality, he is also a survivor who not only somehow manages to eke out a living at the margin of destitution and social degradation. He is also a master of the art of manipulation who, at least once, comes within the reach of a window of opportunity which might have seen him out of poverty had he not, in his blind desire to earn the esteem of his upper-caste customers (among his other dubious occupations is also a part-time pimp, supplying bauri women to his bhadralok clientele), squandered his money in trying to live like them.

The point behind the anecdote is the tremendous complexity of the social situation in contemporary India which is not easily put into neat little theoretical boxes on the lines of conflict, revolution or theories of modernisation. By this I do not mean that micro reality is necessarily indeterminate or incomprehensible in terms of macro theory. Rather, my intention is to question the teleological assumptions that propel both the radical and the liberal theories of development, from the traditional and moral to the pre-determined and, in a curious way, apolitical goals of modernity and the rational, utility-maximising individual. The process is also part of the product. The future is affected by the past, economy is influenced by history and the shape of development is affected by the dialectics of politics and culture. Seen merely as lone operators, Freeman's Muli, Scott's Razak or Breman's Halpatis[48] are all losers but there is a pattern in their attempts to manipulate the environment. Their efforts are not entirely without consequence. The satisfactory comprehension of each case requires the local knowledge of both value, social distance and configuration of power and the rules that provide the link between the local political system and the arenas at the district, regional and national levels. Rather than applying categories derived from context-free macro-economic categories for the perception of the local actor and his or her motives, what is needed here is local knowledge of value and information about the structure of power in the local and regional political systems for a proper understanding of the local situation and its specification within a larger problem of development.

In the narratives of Freeman and Scott, Muli and Razak are lone operators, surviving on the basis of skilful use of their knowledge of conflicts and divisions within their localities and public and private sources of sustenance. Field evidence from Gujarat and Orissa provides other examples of such individual initiative in pursuit of personal benefit as well as collective efforts to obtain group benefits. A report in the Gujarat press, publicising the 'rights of tribals', draws our attention to these victims of 'unrestrained industrialisation and unbridled consumerism' which has 'dispossessed tribals of their lands, deprived them of their accesses to and command over natural resources, uprooted their communities and forced them to disappear as rural migrant labour or urban slum dwellers':

> They [Dangi tribals] have been fighting for full occupancy rights over lands cultivated by them, regularisation of other lands occupied by them, ownership rights over trees on their lands, re-transfer of their lands illegally transferred to others, minimum wages, employment opportunities for the landless, basic facilities like schools, health roads and protection from exploitation and repression by police and forest officials.
>
> (Times of India (1991), p. 6)

The author is critical of government response to the protest movement by tribals, 'The only response of the government is *lathi*-charges, police firing, indiscriminate arrests, false criminal cases and massive misinformation campaigns'.[49]

The larger picture that emerges from the aggregation of the local incidents from Gujarat, Orissa and other parts of India is one of an incremental, secular change, leading to a situation where social privilege, rather than being conceded as natural, is considered essentially contestable. The means of power in rural India are increasingly dispersed rather than being concentrated in the old-style notables who commanded status, power and wealth. One of the most remarkable aspects of cross-regional comparison of social change in India is the rapidity with which differences in the level of radicalisation of the lower strata disappear with time. The slow progress of economic change has now been overtaken by the rapidity of mass communication and the television which carry news of caste violence, conspicuous achievements by former Untouchables in terms of ministerial positions and social movements for or against positive discrimination all over India. Thanks to the diffusion of information, export of institutions found useful in one region to others and the commitment of the state to egalitarian values, backward regions like Orissa catch up with the more advanced ones, at least in the area of the radicalisation of the poor. Marguerite Robinson's data from Medak district in Andhra Pradesh about this 'creeping revolution' complement our findings from Gujarat and Orissa.[50] Using field data over a decade she contrasts the exercise of force and physical coercion as instruments of power, before and after the mid-1970s. Her research also provides an important insight into the changing social location of power.

One comes across the most unexpected instruments of power at the disposal of the downtrodden and lowly, which, thanks to the asymmetry of the link between status and power, can suddenly overturn the ideological basis of dominance. Marguerite Robinson's example of the power of the polluting touch of Untouchables is an interesting example. She cites 'who beats whom' as an index of power in rural India where 'fathers beat their sons, husbands their wives, mothers-in-law their daughters-in-law, teachers their pupils; village elders beat any offending youth of the same or lower castes'.[51] Before the mid-1970s, in extreme cases, where the potential threat of physical force was not sufficient, a landholder would have his adversary beaten by a Harijan, retained for this specific task, whose polluting touch would further enhance the loss of status and humiliation of the victim. However, through a few incidents during the 1970s, both Harijans and their employers learnt that a single Harijan, refusing to beat his master's adversary as instructed or even turning in the direction of his master, shoe-in-hand, with obvious intent, can quickly turn the scales of power and not only destroy one of the major props of local power but actually acquire a part of the power lost by the master.[52] Robinson concludes that 'by 1977 landowners had to compete with government credit sources, the Harijans, who had learnt to employ the awesome threat of force including the beating of an upper-caste person with leather shoes to their own advantage and a no longer supplied force on demand'.[53] Beatings had not been abolished from the arena; they were merely democratised. By then, beating-generated power, which under the perverse logic of the system was equal in direct proportion to numbers and in inverse ratio to one's position on the scale of ritual pollution, had become available to the previously powerless Harijans and greatly changed the nature of power relations in the local arena.

GENERAL IMPLICATIONS OF THE MODEL OF THE TWO FACES OF DEVELOPMENT

Judging from the evidence presented here, the social composition and political linkages of local elites are critical determinants of the pace and direction of social change. Several empirical scenarios are possible. Competing local elites, operating within institutions that have at least a modicum of political autonomy, are representative and accountable to a larger constituency, and can act at the cutting edge of an expanding, liberal state. On the other hand, to the extent that they are able to control local institutions, old-style notables, who manage to cumulate the advantages of wealth, high social status and physical force, can use local autonomy to reinforce their authoritarian political dominance. Two critical factors in this context are, first, the nature of the state, which can be responsive or authoritarian, and, second, the character of local institutions which might be representative and accountable to a larger constituency or authoritarian and oligarchic. Many commentators on rural India appear to be closer to the second view. Hence the scepticism about the ability of the state to extend its norms of social equality and political participation into the domain of the (traditional) society. Thus, for the purpose of economic development and social change:

Institutional changes, in particular, would have to be implemented in the villages through the existing local authorities, that is, the very rural elites against whose power they were directed. At the villages, the loudest voices still belonged to leading members of the dominant landowning castes.

(Frankel (1978), p. 547)

In contrast with this image of a socially cohesive elite, dominating rural life through its control of the means of production and political power, our field data indicate that local elites are far from being socially homogeneous and politically cohesive. Allocation of developmental benefits in the local political arena is not the result of social dominance but is the outcome of a complex process based on bargaining and political competition, however imperfect. Thanks to the state structure and the political process that characterises it, discontent and relative deprivation arising out of unequal allocation of developmental benefits do not necessarily result in apathy, anomy or powerlessness. Instead, people engage in political contacting and various other forms of direct action. All forms of intervention in the process of development allocation, ranging from contacting decision-makers at higher levels to direct action of indeterminate legality such as gherao, are seen as shades of legitimate political action. All these forms of action, related through normative approval and participation, constitute a complex repertoire. The strategic choice of a particular form of action is contingent upon the local configuration of power and the issues at stake. Their actual and potential availability within the political system extends the set of relevant players, the developmental agenda as well as the political arena within which the issues of allocation are settled.

Political trends in various States of India provide variations around this basic model. Both in Gujarat and in Orissa, the lowest social strata are very much present within the local political arena. But, whereas in Gujarat, the former Untouchables and Tribal leaders are part of a wider network, similar organisations and political linkages are not available in Orissa. The absence of these institutional and political links and slower rates of growth of the rural economy have combined to slow down the pace of the accommodation of lower-class interests in

Orissa. On the other hand, in Gujarat, the consequences of a rapidly expanding rural economy, combined with radical and organised lower-class politics, can be seen in the relatively more successful accommodation of the interests of the lower strata in the political agenda of the State.[54]

There is a certain degree of indeterminacy to the outcome of a fusion of the modern and the traditional when both are allowed to interact in a manner that resembles something like parity. The Indian experiment at granting universal adult franchise and admitting to the political arena the full range of social forces had drawn considerable scepticism of which Selig Harrison's *India, The Most Dangerous Decades* was the most celebrated.[55] Unreconstructed imperialists and cultural anthropologists whose scholarly reputations are based on the internal life of micro-communities, pointing to the failure of constitutional experiments in the vast majority of post-colonial societies, might argue that cross-cultural export of good practices is essentially a neo-modernist pipedream. But the Indian case does offer a lesson for those seeking, *simultaneously*, to achieve both stability of the state and some measure of economic growth within a democratic political structure. The Indian case demonstrates that the room for manoeuvre for vulnerable social groups, created through decentralisation of power and active political participation at the local level and legal and administrative tolerance for protest behaviour, can contribute to the legitimacy of the state.

Some caveats need to be specified here regarding the cross-cultural generalisability of the model of protest and participation underlying our findings. In the first place, India's federal structure and the knowledge-sharing at the regional level are important points of reference and leverage for local elites. In the second place, it is not being suggested here that there is a unique 'Indian' model of development, which is equally applicable all over India, or that there is a linear path of development where we could locate Gujarat and Orissa at different 'stages' of development. Gujarati society today is significantly different compared to the situation before the introduction of sugarcane. Less significantly, but nevertheless quite evidently, Oriysa society today has changed greatly compared to only a generation ago. For an outside observer to comprehend these changes, some knowledge of the prior situation is as indispensable as the *common* changes like the introduction of panchayati raj (in politics) and the high-yielding varieties (in agriculture). In both situations, development is thus the outcome of a dialectic of the local 'cultural given' and the exogenous intervention from national and even international sources. The consequences of reaction to similar forces may thus be strikingly different. While the local elites of Gujarat have mastered the art of balancing negotiation and bargaining with radical protest, their counterparts in Orissa still perceive them as separate strategies. But in each case, it is important to remember, development is the unfolding of forces implicitly present within the social and cultural matrix of the region. Finally, local values and the responsive/authoritarian character of the macro-political system are the boundary conditions within which one needs to locate the specific cases.

The high responsiveness of the Indian state, itself the outcome of a particular history of state formation, is a limiting factor on the cross-cultural generalisability of the room for manoeuvre as a panacea for political legitimacy. The accommodative nature of the state in India facilitates the spread of transactional values which constrain the behaviour of all actors engaged in the game of political bargaining. This specific attribute of the state in India originated with the success of the colonial state in linking its authority to the 'elite entrepreneurial network' that characterised Indian society during the high noon of the Empire.[56] The Congress party, product of the *pas de deux* between the Empire and the Indian middle classes, was eventually linked to the peasant base of the society under the Gandhian non-cooperation movement, an enduring legacy that helped institutionalise participation as a cardinal value in modern Indian politics.

Within the boundary conditions stated above, results presented here would question the general validity of the assertion of the polarisation thesis, and early modernisation theories that protest behaviour necessarily lead to the decline of the legitimacy of the state besides posing an obstacle to development. It is more appropriate to think in terms of critical but variable thresholds of tolerance for protest behaviour as a helpful factor for political legitimacy. To this end, a post-colonial state might find it prudent to concede enough authority to local elites so that they may develop a stake in the institutions of the state. On the other hand, too much local power at the expense of the political centre can obstruct the induction of new elites from previously power-less groups, causing in the process the transfer of authority from the state and the political arena altogether to those who have little patience or need for democratic niceties.

THE STATE AND LOCAL DEVELOPMENT IN INDIA

Since the mediating role of the state is a critical determinant of the behaviour of local elites, we shall further explore the effectiveness and continuity of the transactional state in this section. Data on the norms and attitudes of rural netas from Gujarat and Orissa point towards unresolved issues relating to the resilience of the state in India. Does radical protest, emerging out of a sense of injustice, diminish or extend the legitimacy of the state in India? Further, what are the *limits* of the political repertoire that effectively combines protest and participation? Where does institutional participation end and protest begin? If the political repertoire is a combination of protest and participation, then which social, political and historical attributes influence the relative proportion of these rather different components? In the same vein, what are the upper limits on protest and participation by the lower social orders beyond which the state needs to react with overwhelming force rather than accommodation? Finally, what cross-cultural inference about the integration of the two faces of development might one draw from the Indian experience? Some of these are practical problems that are best left to pragmatic politicians from the real world. My reason for raising them within the confines of a theoretical exploration is to draw attention to important political developments in the national and inter-national arenas that might require further refinements of the model that I have suggested here.

To recapitulate the findings from the perspective of state theory, our data show that, contrary to the postulates of Alavi and Reddy and Hargopal,[57] local leaders, acting as double agents, provide a bridge between the state and society. Their insistent demands, under the impact of the growing radicalisa-tion of the rural society, contrary to the lines suggested by Huntington and Gurr,[58] enhance the legitimacy of the state rather than leading to its collapse. Why is it, then, that the political unrest in Punjab, Kashmir and Assam has proved so intractable and destructive of the legitimate authority of the state?[59]

Though separated by geography and the history of political development prior to independence, these three cases share some common attributes. Each has several insurgent political groups, operating mostly outside the law, following violent tactics in order to achieve separate statehood. At the fringes of these groups are people who might share with our rural netas their dual lives, but the analogy is more metaphorical than literal. The rural elites of Gujarat and Orissa are skilful political operators who are engaged in political transactions for material reasons. The mainstream of political insurgency in Kashmir, Punjab and Assam is concerned with the issue of a separate identity for whose protection nothing short of a separate territorial state would suffice. But outside of the hardcore militants and their political sympathisers are ordinary people, who share with the ordinary people of Gujarat and Orissa their belief in the effectiveness of protest and participation. And yet, many of them would support a political cause that ultimately denies the legitimacy of the constitutional democracy which stands as a guarantee for political transaction through institutional participation and radical protest.

Recent incidents in Assam which I have summarised from press reports, though less well known than Punjab and Kashmir, are illustrative of the trend. Following 'an escalation of violent activities such as extortion, kidnapping, assault and murder', the 'entire State of Assam was declared a "disturbed area" under the Armed Forces Special Powers Act'; several insurgent camps were raided and many were captured. The move was publicly declared to be motivated by a desire to make the army help the civil authorities to 'control the situation, bring confidence to the people and restore law and order'. A private objective of the state might have been to remove some key leaders of the insurgency from the field of action and use them as pawns in the bargaining with the rest. This strategy does not appear to be effective, as was found after the release of 'about 500 activists arrested under the Terrorists and Disruptive Activities (Prevention) Act which failed to have any impact' on the insurgents who 'increased their demands and pressed for the release of several detainees who are facing serious charges'. The government of the State, having found the situation 'very grave', reserved the option of inducting more troops. For all its trouble with insurgency, the government of Assam was criticised by the members of the opposition in the Indian Parliament for not having consulted it before troops were sent and they 'painted a picture as though an Army had been sent to "invade" another country'. The Assam government defended its action in sending for the army without first announcing it in the Parliament on grounds that point only to the extreme gravity of the situation. On previous occasions it was found that there were people sympathetic to the insurgency within the legislature and the administration who alerted the insurgents so that the element of surprise, vital to such military operations, was lost, which reduced their effectiveness severely. The government also produced evidence linking the insurgency in Assam with support from China, Pakistan and Bangladesh.[60]

Insurgencies are different from local protest movements in their goals, tactics, organisation and political linkages. But their presence affects the political environment in a manner that reduces the room for manoeuvre for local elites and the flexibility with which the government would otherwise be prepared to confront them. In order to understand why the complex repertoire that combines protest and participation does not function as effectively, either by providing acceptable solutions or be making insurgency unnecessary, we need to reexamine the assumptions that have gone into the making of our model.

The state in India is based on the joint assumption of a constantly expanding core which attains legitimacy through increasing participation and distribution of the benefits of economic development. One situation where the model would lose its effectiveness is the capture of political power by an emergent agrarian class with capital and connections. The historical parallel here is Moore's 'marriage of iron and rye',[61] reinforced with the support of violent retainers maintained for the purpose of restraining landless agricultural workers, former Untouchables, Tribals or zealous civil servants with too much enthusiasm for social justice. The scenario, all too familiar to the readers of the left-wing *Economic and Political Weekly of India* and the *Journal of Peasant Studies*, has been sketched vividly by Breman:

The prevailing climate in the central plain of South Gujarat is anti-labour, and the social-Darwinist mentality of the members of the ruling class in the rural areas provides a fertile soil for an emergent brand of fascism. 'Peasant interests' has become the banner around which these sons of the soil rally, although their economic behaviour is that of rural entrepreneurs pure and simple.

Breman hints at dark implications of these developments at the local and regional level for the state in India.

It is important to establish that the direction of such tendencies moves upwards from below and not the other way around. The reaction of the state to the harsh regime which is currently prevalent close to the grass roots might be a pointer to the kind of development India is likely to see in what remains of the twentieth century.

(Breman (1985), p. xv)

Kisan movements as a form of demand group, led by sections of the upper and middle farmers, have become a common feature of the Indian political scene, both at the local and the regional level.[62] That they aspire to power at the national level became fairly obvious during the short period of rule by Charan Singh as the Prime Minister of India, who championed agrarian interests. The power of the 'rich peasant lobby', as radical students of Indian political economy like to point out, is alive and well, wielding considerable influence within each of India's major political formations. Others have hinted more darkly at the surreptitious use of power by a coalition of big business and the farm lobby ('the marriage of wheat and whisky') under the aegis of a populist left–centre party of coalition in power at the centre. Some of the tendencies described by the authors we have cited above are undoubtedly present in Gujarat and elsewhere in the country. But the suggestion that a fascist–authoritarian leadership is likely to take over seems unlikely in view of the complexity of the Indian political system which renders a take-over bid by a conservative coalition (or for that matter, a radical coalition) very difficult. The complexity in question refers to a multiplicity of levels – local, district, regional and national – at which power is exercised, to the multiplicity of political contenders available at each level, and to the shifting coalitions

235

of political forces that stretch both vertically and horizontally through the system.

The character of the national political arena as a 'stalemated class-conflict'[63] or multiple groups and coalitions balancing one another[64] explains why attempts to overturn the system by forces operating outside the political arena (most recently in Punjab) have so far yielded few concrete results. Efforts at creating political change through terrorism by older brands of Indian Maoists, commonly referred to as Naxalites, have not been successful. Even for forces like the kisan movements which operate largely within the norms of the system, attempts at moving faster than the rest are likely to bounce back as the counter mobilisation by dalits in Western India demonstrates. Under the implicit rules of India's state-dominated and 'involuted' pluralism,[65] political competition and the availability of a plurality of political forces, including the movement of the 'nonparty' (or grass-roots) political movements[66] ensures that deprived social groups find an outlet to articulate their demands. In spite of the impressive demonstration of strength by the emergent agrarian forces, it is unlikely that the rural poor would go down in front of the storm-troopers of the green revolution, not at least without a struggle. A stalemated class-conflict at the macro level and coalitions of forces ranging from the centre–left to the centre–right in the regional arenas is the more likely scenario for the near future.

A theoretical problem of a different order is raised by the increasing salience of issues of identity, community and religion as compared to the narrow concerns with allocation of the benefits of development. Will this become the one language of discourse, which, as in British politics, functions as the multi-political idiom within a political arena bounded by Englishness within which class-conflict can take place, or the formation of French identity which, as Le Pen reminds us, is far from complete?[67] Rather than merely asserting a hierarchy of needs, as Weiner appears to be doing,[68] one should problematise it. The neo-modernist vision of Nehru, shared by academic social science during the first decades after independence,[69] was that the rational will become the common link among the little communities which will eventually burst open, pouring their contents into the national body of citizens of modern India. Nobody seriously took into consideration the possibility that the little moral communities could also invent a larger moral bond outside the common objective of economic development for the same purpose of national integration.[70]

Once we turn our attention away from the politics of development in rural India to the urban (and increasingly peri-urban in Punjab and Gujarat), politics turns more violent and beset with communal conflict. Though these are beyond the empirical issues raised in this book, they have implications for the rational protest model on which it is based. The transactional model has been called into question by at least three distinct though related phenomena. In the first place, at the institutional level, the decay of Congress dominance has removed from the scene the organisational mechanism that provided an overarching scheme for the resolution of conflicts at the local and regional levels. Meta-conflict over the rules of allocation rather than competition over scarce resources within a framework of rules over which there used to be a political consensus has become a dominant theme of politics in India from the 1970s onwards. The process has been expedited through positive discrimination – a series of legislative initiatives through which material benefits and preferential quotas in matters of recruitment are extended to the Scheduled population. National leadership and the institutions of state which used to be perceived as relatively autonomous of competing social forces have become increasingly involved directly in regional and local struggles for power. In the third place, the twin legacy of the turbulent 1960s – the large-scale induction of the Backward castes to the political arena and the introduction of new forms of political struggle such as gherao, dharna and other forms of radical protest – significantly altered the style of local politics, which has become more conflictual than before. These developments at the macro level and the phenomenal increase in the quantum of resources available for rural development have vastly expanded the scope and range of rural politics. Kothari and Morris-Jones,[71] who had applauded the ability of the state in India to mediate between competing social forces during the first decades of the post-independence period, have described this in terms of the decline of the moderate state and civil war, resulting from attempts by political actors to obtain results more expeditiously or to resist attempts by the state to encroach on customary rights. The unprecedented increase in both the scope and range of politics has rendered the transactional model somewhat inadequate. In its place, we require a more comprehensive model capable of incorporating the multiple methods that local influentials employ to bring pressure to bear on the political system.

Conflict over the issues of religion, ethnic identity and community formation rather than the allocation of material benefits of development dominate the agenda of Indian politics in the 1990s. What role if any can transactional politics play in national politics? We can usefully elaborate here on arguments made in an earlier study.[72] These conflicts which have caused considerable despair both among practitioners and theoreticians of Indian politics were not totally absent during the comparatively tranquil 1950s and 1960s. The state solved issues of language, ethnic identity and religion by creating new political arenas which institutionalised those values within the rules that described those arenas. Thus, language became less contentious as an issue once linguistic States were created; Naga or Mizo identities became enmeshed in the more worthwhile if boring task of the allocation of material resources within Nagaland and Mizoram, and the creation of the Malapuram district in 1969 (following almost a decade of cooperation between the Muslim League with the Congress and the Communists) gave enough of a sense of security and identity to Kerala Muslims for their representatives to be able to participate in the transactional politics of the region. The point that needs to be made here is that transactional politics of allocation and transcendental politics of identity, ethnicity and values can coexist in India if political actors are able to explore the full range of institutional alternatives.

The findings presented here can contribute towards the specification of a more general model which incorporates the national state and the international arena, which in our model of local politics were left as part of the political environment. As before, we assume that the behaviour of local elites is constrained by a multiplicity of factors, the focal points of which are, respectively, region and social class. From the difference in the level of economic development between Gujarat and Orissa already discussed in chapter two (tables 2.1 and 2.2), one would expect a significant difference in the scope of political demands to characterise the agenda of local elites. The difference in the range of organisational infrastructure between Gujarat and Orissa and the different historical experiences of radical protest significantly affect elite attitudes and behaviour. Oriya identity and the issue of Gujarati language have ceased to be contentious issues of politics following the creation of political arenas coterminous with linguistic identities. No region of India is however totally impervious to conflict imported from other areas. To that extent, the Muslims in Orissa or Gujarat will perhaps continue to have outbreaks of violent conflict for reasons unrelated to regional politics. Regional politics in India, therefore, cannot be fully understood without reference to the national arena.

Transactional politics in the regional and local political arenas however does not necessarily exclude the potential for surreptitious, covert and limited authoritarianism at the macro level. Paradoxically, such attempts at authoritarian leadership from the national level might strike a sympathetic chord in social segments at the regional and local levels, who resent their loss of power and prominence as the result of transactional politics in arenas where they used to be dominant. Two developments point that way. As the radicalisation of the rural poor and their political mobilisation have paved the way for their entry in greater numbers to the institutions of local democracy, so the affluent have fled from the political arena at the local level, concentrating their energies instead at the sub-district and the district levels. In what appears to be the ultimate 'penalty of success', the very success of the leadership of the majority poor in capturing positions of power at the local level has caused a steady withdrawal of the upper strata from the institutions of local democracy. Instead, they have increasingly sought refuge in organisations operating within the voluntary sector such as the cooperatives to which an obliging bureaucracy has shifted credit and the more important economic functions from the village panchayat.[73] The success of the lower strata in capturing local political institutions, denuded of their influence and resources, could thus at best amount to a Pyrrhic victory, while the more prosperous sections, divested of political power and marginalised in the local arena, may look up to the national arena for authoritarian and nominally apolitical and technocratic but essentially elitist leadership.[74] In the second place, as the radicalised rural poor have intervened more and more in the local political process, the political systems at the local level have been paralysed through intense dissension. In a situation where decisions need to be reached rapidly, a paralysed political system caused power either to seep away to the local bureaucracy or to gravitate upwards. Both trends, resulting in a loss of power for local democracy and the rural poor, are present in Orissa. It would of course be unfair to blame only Congress-run States. Even in States ruled by parties of the opposition who protest vociferously against attempts by the national government to reduce their power, it is commonplace to come across the superseding of local democracy by the district administration, or of not holding panchayat elections altogether. As our discussion of normative attitudes towards conflict and social cohesion suggests, elements of the upper strata in Gujarat and Orissa would not be averse to a dose of authoritarian leadership if it helped in the better management of the local economy. Judging from normative attitudes of elites towards conflict and participation per se, the local roots of the liberal state in India are not yet completely secure.

Finally, from the despair of the elites from the lower stratum about lack of personal financial achievments by Harijan and Adivasi netas in Dhenkanal and the undertone of class hostility of the lowest strata in Gujarat (the only region in India so far to have had a Tribal Chief Minister outside of the North-Eastern Hill States where regions were carved out on the lines of Tribal Identity) we can infer the upper threshold under which transactional politics operates. Pointing to the causes of these limitations, neo-Marxist scholarship on the state and legitimacy suggests that limits to lower-class participation and protest comes from upper-class hegemony, which is both ideological and institutional. Though, as Scott[75] points out, no hegemony is in fact invulnerable. The middle ground between hegemony and resistance in the local arena is the scene of constant battle. The structure of power at a given point in time is more one of shifting sand than a rigid and immutable brick wall that separates the oppressors from the oppressed. In the short run, however, obstacles to open, collective resistance are many indeed. Breman's example of the eventual defeat of Halapati agricultural workers demanding higher wages at the hands of Patidar sugarcane growers through the orchestrated migration of poor Tribals, willing to work for lower wages,[76] provides a

Gujarati parallel to Scott's example of the marginalisation of recalcitrant agricultural workers through the strategy of mechanisation by the rich peasants. In both cases, larger changes in the political economy achieve 'a gradual bulldozing of the sites where class conflict has historically occurred'.[77]

The other limit to transactional politics is state repression, particularly the political use of policing. The recent case of torture and blinding of prisoners under trial in Bihar, with active collusion by prominent citizens of the area, is a case in point. Finally, as the anti-reservation movements of Gujarat and the more recent anti-mandal movements demonstrate, protest is not the monopoly of lower classes. The fear of individual reprisal and collective upper-caste backlash can dissuade potential beneficiaries amongst the lower classes from staking their claims to benefits they are entitled to under the law, in the process restricting the potential of the transactional model.

Orthodox defenders of political stability for whom any protest is anathema might read at least a mild form of 'Huntington's revenge' in India's undistinguished record of economic growth compared to the economic miracle of the newly industrialised countries (NICs) of East Asia. By accelerating the entry of new social forces into the political arena, protest behaviour can overstretch governmental capacity, besides cluttering the political agenda with unrealistic demands. All of these contribute to the reduction of political coherence of the system, leading to a governability crisis.[78] The rapid mobilisation of the intermediate castes in the 1960s caused similar crises in many of India's regional governments. However, this experience of the efficacy of protest might have provided the confidence and organisation with which the opponents of Mrs Gandhi's Emergency in 1975 united in their opposition to authoritarian rule.

In the last analysis, an important explanation for the resilience of Indian democracy is found in the complex political repertoire of her local elites and their remarkable blend of institutional participation and collective protest. There is of course a price to pay for the solution that India has adopted in balancing democracy and development in the form of the rise of regional bosses and populist leaders like Haryana's Devilal and freewheeling god-men intermediaries like Chandraswami whose presence is a threat to the continuation of constitutional democracy in India. Further, the combination of radical rhetoric from below and populist policies from above can seriously compromise the prospects of sustained growth.[79] Under these circumstances, rapid political mobilisation without institutionalisation can only contribute to governmental instability. The unhappy outcome is political paralysis, the wages of which are paid in the form of petty tyrannies at the bottom and 'popular' authoritarianism at the top.

Following independence, India enjoyed two decades of democracy moderated by the hegemonic role of the Congress party and two decades of heady populism. A touch of variety was added to this experience through the half-hearted authoritarianism of Mrs Gandhi's Emergency. As India enters the turbulent 1990s, her intelligentsia and those who specialise in the study of Indian politics will need to raise the unresolved issues of order versus representation, communal identity and constitutional democracy, and economic growth as against distributive justice and environmental degradation, which will gain increasing salience. These issues of universal significance will need to be raised in an idiom that makes sense within the parameters of Indian culture and tradition.

APPENDIX

THE BACKGROUND OF
THE SURVEY

The survey, funded by a grant from the Indian Council for Social Science Research made to the Centre for the Study of Developing Societies, Delhi, was carried out in 1978–9. The samples for the survey were chosen from Surat and Dhenkanal districts, respectively in Gujarat and Orissa. Using a quasi-experimental research design that controlled for village size, nine villages with high, medium and low levels of development were selected in each district. The survey team consisted of H. R. Chaturvedi and me, and two research assistants were specially recruited for the project on 'Participation in Rural Development' and were trained by us. I directed the Orissa phase of the survey which took about three months towards the end of 1978. The Gujarat phase, directed by H. R. Chaturvedi, took an equivalent period and was completed during early 1979.

For the purpose of village selection, we first identified three blocks in Surat and three police circles in Dhenkanal that were, in the opinion of district officials, at the highest, medium and lowest levels of development. In order to control for population size, the difference between the biggest and the smallest village in each unit was divided in three and a list of all villages that fell into the middle category of population was then made for each unit. The lists were further screened to identify those villages which had at least a primary school and a post office, and which were connected by at least a *kuchcha* (i.e. not black topped) road which gave the village all-year access, at least by jeep, the ubiquitous work horse of India's development bureaucracy. These villages were again divided into three categories in consultation with local officials and one was chosen from each category. In table A.1 is the list of eighteen villages that emerged out of this sampling process.

We conducted two surveys simultaneously in our study villages. The first was addressed to a sample of a cross-section of the rural population, chosen on the basis of a random probability sample of all adult males. The second concentrated on the local elites, identified with the help of the reputational technique (already discussed in chapter three). The results of the first survey were published in a coauthored work – Chaturvedi and Mitra (1982) – but the elite study was set aside until

243

Table A.1 List of study villages

States	Districts	Blocks/Police Circles	Villages
Gujarat	Surat	Bardoli	Sarbhon
			Varad
			Balda
		Vyara	Kapura
			Balpur
			Umarvavdur
		Valod	Shiker
			Andhatri
			Ambach
Orissa	Dhenkanal	Dhenkanal	Beltikadi
			Nadiali
			Mahulpada
		Angul	Khalari
			Rantalu
			Kumari Singha
		Athmallik	Lipbi
			Kukswar
			Bahadi

1985 when I joined the University of Hull and decided to start the analysis. A personal research grant from the Nuffield Foundation helped me to go back to the field to collect further social and historical data.

The questionnaire design reflects the impact of the survey research techniques developed at the Centre for the Study of Developing Societies, which pioneered large-scale sample surveys in India. The questionnaires were translated into Oriya and Gujarati. Mostly, only vernacular versions were used for field surveys. However, the English versions and the research design were made available to respondents who wished to consult them or who evinced curiosity about our 'employers' and the possible end products of the project. Those who have done survey research in rural India would appreciate the extreme importance of these apparently innocuous questions posed by respondents, for the credibility of an entire project can be compromised on the basis of an inadequate or unsatisfactory reply to queries with no obvious connection to the central issues being raised in the study. Some of these desires to ensure communicability and to earn credibility from our subjects are reflected in the syntax of the 'Indian English' in which the questions have been framed. It satisfied two needs: first, to cut down the scope for ambiguity within the research team itself; and, secondly, to retain the word order and the grammatical conventions of the respective vernacular languages.

The survey team used school buildings in Orissa and Ashramshalas in Gujarat for overnight stays. The strategy was to cover a village quickly and exhaustively before our presence could affect the developmental environment of the village to the point of creating attitudes where none might have existed. There were no outright refusals to be surveyed and the non-response rate was generally low. Some people however did express surprise and occasional discontentment at not having been included in our list of village netas. Happily, we were able to fend off such requests on 'scientific' grounds without giving offence.

THE QUESTIONNAIRE AND THE PRINCIPAL RESULTS OF THE SURVEY

In this section we set out all the questions we have asked in the survey. Though, where possible, they are identified by theme, they are presented in the order in which they were asked. To facilitate comprehension, Gujarati and Oriya translations of the questionnaire were used respectively in Gujarat and Orissa. The percentage distributions are given only for the structured questions. The responses to the open-ended questions include too many categories to warrant a detailed presentation. However, they have been included in the analysis in an aggregated form. Since one of the main purposes of the survey was to establish a basis of comparison between Surat and Dhenkanal (representing Gujarat and Orissa, selected for reasons explained in chapter two), the percentage distributions are presented separately for each district.

Problems

[Q 1]   What would you say are some of the most pressing problems of the people in your area (village/taluka)?
(Code only the first five problems)

Solutions

[Q 2]   In view of the above problems, which of the schemes/programmes would you suggest on a priority basis?
(Code only the first three solutions)

Organisations to carry out programmes

[Q 3]   Which of the three agencies in your opinion should carry out these programmes?
(Probe for each programme mentioned. Code for all three programmes suggested in Q 2.)

Agency for first programme	Gujarat %	Orissa %
1 Village panchayat	35.9	7.8
2 Taluka panchayat/panchayat samiti	21.4	18.6
3 Zilla panchayat	2.3	1.0
4 Government (State)	29.8	63.7
5 Government (central)	0.8	4.9
6 Voluntary organisation	6.1	—
9 No response	3.8	3.9

245

Information about past programmes

[Q 4] Since independence quite a few programmes have been undertaken for the development and welfare of the rural people. Thinking of your area (village/taluka) which are some of the major programmes that have been carried out during the last ten or fifteen years?

(Code only three programmes)

[Q 6] On the whole, how satisfied are you about what has been done so far for the development and welfare of people in your area (village/taluka)?

	Gujarat %	Orissa %
3 A great deal	18.3	14.7
2 Somewhat	71.0	63.7
1 Not at all	10.7	21.6
9 No response	—	—

[Q 7] Development programmes have been extended to all the districts, talukas and villages. But it is the general experience that some districts, talukas and villages have done better than others. Comparing your area (village/taluka) to others, would you say that it has done much better than others, somewhat better than others, not better than others, or worse than others?

	Gujarat %	Orissa %
3 Much better than others	28.2	13.7
2 Somewhat better than others	37.4	48.0
1 Worse than others	17.6	21.6
9 No response	—	1.0

[Q 7A] If says much better, ask what it is due to.

(Code two answers)

[Q 7B] If says worse than others, ask why it has performed so badly.

(Code two answers)

Sectional benefits from development

[Q 8] Considering all development work during the last ten to fifteen years, which of the following groups have benefited more from development than others?

	Gujarat %	Orissa %
Landless		
2 More benefited	12.2	20.6
1 Less benefited	64.1	79.4
9 No response	23.7	—
Farm servant		
2 More benefited	12.2	9.8
1 Less benefited	80.9	90.2
9 No response	6.9	—
Small and marginal farmers (below 5 acres)		
2 More benefited	39.7	44.1
1 Less benefited	56.5	55.9
9 No response	3.8	—
Sharecropper		
2 More benefited	14.5	5.9
1 Less benefited	41.2	80.4
9 No response	44.3	13.7
Big farmers/manager farmers		
2 More benefited	73.3	60.8
1 Less benefited	18.3	38.2
9 No response	8.4	13.7
Tenant cultivators		
2 More benefited	60.3	27.5
1 Less benefited	25.2	71.6
9 No response	14.5	1.0
Artisans		
2 More benefited	52.7	25.5
1 Less benefited	35.9	65.7
9 No response	11.5	8.8
Medium-sized cultivators		
2 More benefited	43.5	26.5
1 Less benefited	50.4	68.6
9 No response	6.1	4.9
Small businessmen		
2 More benefited	39.7	53.9
1 Less benefited	47.3	41.2
9 No response	13.0	4.9
Big businessmen		
2 More benefited	58.0	60.8
1 Less benefited	15.3	11.8
9 No response	26.8	27.5
Service castes (Barber, Dhobi, Teli, etc.)		
2 More benefited	26.0	19.6
1 Less benefited	51.9	73.5
9 No response	22.2	6.9
People in services		
2 More benefited	65.6	79.4
1 Less benefited	30.5	18.6
9 No response	3.9	2.0

Evaluation of development

[Q 9] A lot of difference of opinion prevails about the effect of development programmes in the country. Compared to the last ten or fifteen years, some people say that because of development programmes conditions in the village have improved and others say no. Conditions, they suggest, have in fact deteriorated. Considering your area (village/taluka), would you say that conditions have improved, remained the same or deteriorated because of development programmes?

	Gujarat %	Orissa %
4 Improved	78.6	62.7
3 Remained the same	14.5	16.7
2 Deteriorated	6.9	19.6
1 Any other	—	—
9 No response	—	1.0

Contacting by people of the area

[Q 11] There are occasions when people are unhappy and dissatisfied with the development works in their area (village/taluka). In such a situation, which of the following things do people of your area generally do?

	Gujarat %	Orissa %
Contact the officials		
2 Generally do	89.3	85.3
1 Generally do not do	10.7	13.7
9 No response	—	1.0
Contact panchayat leaders like Sarpanch, and Chairman, Zilla Panchayat		
2 Generally do	95.4	94.1
1 Generally do not do	3.8	5.9
9 No response	0.8	—
Contact upper-level leaders like M.L.A., M.P. and Ministers		
2 Generally do	72.5	56.9
1 Generally do not do	24.4	43.1
9 No response	3.1	—
Contact leaders of the ruling party		
2 Generally do	62.6	53.9
1 Generally do not	33.6	45.1
9 No response	3.8	1.0
Contact leaders of the opposition party		
2 Generally do	44.3	14.7
1 Generally do not do	51.5	83.3
9 No response	4.6	2.0

	Gujarat %	Orissa %
Resort to some kind of direct action like morcha, demonstration, dharna, etc.		
2 Generally do	15.3	13.7
1 Generally do not do	80.9	85.3
9 No response	3.8	1.0

Response when contacted

[Q 12]   There are occasions when people take their grievances and complaints to leaders like you. In such situations which of the following do you generally do and which do you not do generally?

	Gujarat %	Orissa %
Take up the matter with relevant officials		
2 Generally do	90.1	75.5
1 Generally do not do	7.6	22.5
9 No response	2.3	2.0
Refer it to panchayat officials like Sarpanch, Pramukh and Chairman of Zilla Panchayat		
2 Generally do	92.4	79.4
1 Generally do not do	6.1	19.6
9 No response	1.5	1.0
Represent before upper-level leaders like M.L.A., M.P. or Minister		
2 Generally do	67.9	60.8
1 Generally do not do	29.0	37.3
9 No response	3.1	2.0
Involve party leaders		
2 Generally do	52.7	55.9
1 Generally do not do	43.5	41.2
9 No response	3.8	2.9
Resort to some kind of direct actions like morcha, dharna or demonstration, etc.		
2 Generally do	9.2	5.9
1 Generally do not do	84.7	92.2
9 No response	6.1	2.0
Handle it personally		
2 Generally do	84.0	87.3
1 Generally do not do	13.7	10.8
9 No response	2.3	2.0

Popular interest in development programmes

[Q 13]   Many times it is observed that in some areas (village/taluka) there is more interest and involvement of people in development programmes than in other areas. What would you say about the people in your area (village/taluka)? Would you say that they have a great deal of interest and involvement in development works, they are not so much interested or do you think they are indifferent?

	Gujarat %	Orissa %
4 A great deal of interest	1.5	—
3 Not much of interest	51.1	81.4
2 Least interest/indifferent	32.1	16.7
1 Any other	15.3	2.0

[Q 15]   In the course of our studies we have come across broadly two types of communities, namely (i) communities in which different groups of people cooperate with each other in any programme of development, and (ii) communities in which there are two or three groups which generally oppose one another in any programme of development. Broadly speaking, which of the above two describe the situation in your village/taluka best?

	Gujarat %	Orissa %
3 Active cooperation	71.8	71.6
2 Active opposition	26.7	15.7
1 Any other: inaction, apathy, and some support	0.8	12.7
9 No response	8.0	—

Initiatives and contacts by respondents

[Q 17]   Leaders have to take the help of other leaders for getting things done. Thinking of yourself how often do you contact the following leaders?

	Gujarat %	Orissa %
Village leaders		
4 Often	64.9	77.5
3 Sometimes	22.1	20.6
2 Rarely	7.6	1.0
1 Never	3.1	1.0
9 No response	2.3	—

	Gujarat %	Orissa %
Taluka leaders		
4 Often	47.3	39.2
3 Sometimes	33.6	48.0
2 Rarely	7.6	7.8
1 Never	7.8	4.8
9 No response	3.8	—
District leaders		
4 Often	19.8	11.8
3 Sometimes	38.9	25.5
2 Rarely	19.8	37.3
1 Never	13.7	25.5
9 No response	7.6	—
State leaders		
4 Often	9.2	5.9
3 Sometimes	17.6	15.7
2 Rarely	26.0	28.4
1 Never	35.1	50.0
9 No response	12.2	—

[Q 18] Generally speaking which of the following leaders have been consistently most helpful and which consistently least helpful to you in getting things done?

	Gujarat %	Orissa %
Village leaders		
2 Most helpful	80.2	86.3
1 Least helpful	16.0	13.7
9 No response	3.8	—
Taluka/block leaders		
2 Most helpful	71.0	62.7
1 Least helpful	19.8	36.3
9 No response	9.2	1.0
District leaders		
2 Most helpful	30.5	10.8
1 Least helpful	56.5	87.3
9 No response	13.0	2.0
State leaders		
2 Most helpful	13.0	5.9
1 Least helpful	67.9	91.2
9 No response	19.1	2.9

[Q 19] Leaders have to take the help of officials for getting things done. Thinking of yourself how often do you contact the following officials?

251

	Gujarat %	Orissa %
Village officials		
4 Often	64.1	73.5
3 Sometimes	24.4	15.7
2 Rarely	6.9	1.0
1 Never	2.3	6.9
9 No response	2.3	2.0
Taluka/block officials		
4 Often	52.7	53.9
3 Sometimes	33.6	35.3
2 Rarely	5.3	2.9
1 Never	5.3	4.9
9 No response	3.1	3.0
District officials		
4 Often	19.8	7.8
3 Sometimes	35.1	34.3
2 Rarely	24.4	23.5
1 Never	12.2	31.4
9 No response	8.4	3.0
State officials		
4 Often	6.9	2.0
3 Sometimes	14.5	9.8
2 Rarely	31.3	28.4
1 Never	33.6	56.9
9 No response	13.7	3.0

[Q 20] Generally speaking, which of the following officials have been consistently most helpful to you in getting things done?

	Gujarat %	Orissa %
Village officials		
2 Most helpful	79.4	82.4
1 Least helpful	18.3	16.7
9 No response	2.3	1.0
Taluka/block officials		
2 Most helpful	83.2	77.5
1 Least helpful	10.7	19.6
9 No response	6.1	3.0
District officials		
2 Most helpful	29.8	14.7
1 Least helpful	58.0	82.4
9 No response	12.2	3.0
State officials		
2 Most helpful	10.7	4.9
1 Least helpful	69.5	92.2
9 No response	19.8	3.0

Attitudes towards participation

[Q 16]   There are some situations that leaders face in the course of their work. We have listed some statements that describe these situations. I will read the statements one by one. You kindly tell me how far do you agree or disagree with each, that is, do you strongly agree, agree, disagree or strongly disagree. Let us take the first statement.

	Gujarat %	Orissa %
A good leader should refrain from making proposals that divide the community even if these are important for development.		
4 Strongly agree	29.0	32.4
3 Agree	30.5	5.9
2 Disagree	38.2	56.9
1 Strongly disagree	2.3	3.9
9 No response	—	1.0
Participation of people is not necessary if decision-making is in the hands of a few trusted and competent leaders.		
4 Strongly agree	14.5	29.4
3 Agree	42.0	11.8
2 Disagree	35.1	53.9
1 Strongly disagree	8.4	3.9
9 No response	—	1.0
Any decision on an issue, even though important but is likely to alienate a section or group in the community should be avoided.		
4 Strongly agree	10.7	37.3
3 Agree	35.9	13.7
2 Disagree	43.5	48.0
1 Strongly disagree	9.2	—
9 No response	0.8	1.0
Only those who are adequately informed on an issue should be allowed to vote on it.		
4 Strongly agree	10.7	51.0
3 Agree	35.9	16.7
2 Disagree	45.8	28.7
1 Strongly disagree	6.9	2.9
9 No response	0.8	1.0
Involving many people in decision-making often leads to unnecessary conflicts.		
4 Strongly agree	9.9	40.2
3 Agree	59.5	7.8
2 Disagree	26.7	45.1
1 Strongly disagree	3.8	5.9
9 No response	—	1.0

		Gujarat %	Orissa %
	Leaders who are over-concerned about resolving conflicts can never carry out community programmes successfully.		
4	Strongly agree	13.7	24.5
3	Agree	42.7	8.8
2	Disagree	32.8	49.0
1	Strongly disagree	9.9	15.7
9	No response	0.8	2.0
	Participation of as many citizens as possible in decision-making is necessary even if it takes a lot of time and expenditure.		
4	Strongly agree	9.9	57.8
3	Agree	37.4	22.5
2	Disagree	37.4	17.6
1	Strongly disagree	15.3	1.0
9	No response	—	1.0
	If there is disagreement about a programme a leader should be willing to give it up.		
4	Strongly agree	16.8	33.3
3	Agree	44.3	16.7
2	Disagree	31.3	45.1
1	Strongly disagree	7.6	3.9
9	No response	—	1.0
	Allowing many people to have their say in matters pertaining to the village will only interfere with getting things done.		
4	Strongly agree	10.7	32.4
3	Agree	45.8	11.8
2	Disagree	32.8	41.2
1	Strongly disagree	9.9	12.7
9	No response	0.8	2.0

Source of political support

[Q 21] In all areas (village/taluka) there are several groups and communities. Thinking of your area (village/taluka) which groups and communities extend the maximum support to you?

[Q 22] Which groups and communities in your area extend you the least support?

Power of local bodies

[Q23] There is a lot of talk about decentralisation these days. Do you think that panchayat bodies should have the same powers as they have today or that they should be given more powers?

APPENDIX

	Gujarat %	Orissa %
3 Status quo	35.9	10.8
2 More power	60.3	88.2
1 Less power	2.3	—
9 No response	1.6	1.0

– Reasons for status quo
– Reasons for more powers
– Reasons for less powers

Record of achievements and disappointments

[Q 25]   As a leader of this area (village/taluka) for the last so many years what do you consider to be your major achievement?

– What do you attribute it to?

[Q 26]   What do you consider to be your major disappointments, that is something that you would have liked to do but could not do?

– Why were you not able to do them?

Future programmes

[Q 27]   Considering your plans for the future, to what programmes and activities would you like to devote most of your time and energy in coming year or two?

Distribution of benefits of development

[Q 28]   Some people say that whatever progress was made over the last few years through government planning has benefited only the well-to-do, others say no, the poor and the needy have also benefited from it. What would you say? Have the benefits of progress through planning gone only to the well-to-do, or have the poor and needy also benefited from such progress?

	Gujarat %	Orissa %
3 All have benefited	32.1	8.8
2 Poor and needy have benefited	27.5	58.8
1 Benefits have gone to the well-to-do	39.7	29.4
9 No response	0.8	3.0

Radicalism

[Q 29]   There has been a lot of concern about events in the countryside in which the poor and depressed have been making a lot of demands and they have also organised themselves and agitated to fulfil them. Thinking about your area (village/taluka) to what extent is this happening?

	Gujarat %	Orissa %
3 To a great extent	11.5	—
2 To some extent	37.4	10.8
1 Very little	48.1	86.3
9 No response	3.1	3.0

[Q 29a]   What would you attribute it to? Is it due to political influences from outside this area or is it due to the internal situation within the area?

	Gujarat %	Orissa %
3 Both are responsible	15.3	—
2 External factors	31.3	1.0
1 Internal factors	46.6	46.1
9 No response	6.9	53.0

[Q 30]   Some people say that it is through protests and agitations that the poor and depressed will improve their conditions. Others say that protests and agitations of this kind hinder development and will not benefit any one. What do you think?

	Gujarat %	Orissa %
2 Hinder development	59.5	69.6
1 Improve conditions	38.2	29.4
9 No response	2.3	1.0

[Q 31]   Some people say that the government should pass legislation so that people are not allowed to own and possess a large amount of land and property. Others say that people should be allowed to own as much land and property as they can acquire. What would you say?

	Gujarat %	Orissa %
3 Limit ownership	87.0	69.6
2 Should not limit ownership	12.2	28.4
1 Other	0.8	1.0
9 No response	—	1.0

[Q 32]   Some political leaders and parties have been advocating that poor people with no land and property should forcibly occupy a part of land and property of those who have large amounts of land and property. Do you approve of this or do you disapprove?

	Gujarat %	Orissa %
2 Approve	74.0	19.6
1 Disapprove	12.2	78.4
9 No response	13.7	2.0

Modes of political action

[Q 33]   It has been seen that people engage in different kinds of acts for drawing attention of concerned authorities to their demands and grievances. Please consider each and tell me how frequently people of your area engage in it.

	Gujarat %	Orissa %
Representations like signature campaigns or memoranda		
3 Frequently	46.6	55.9
2 Sometimes	37.4	26.5
1 Rarely	14.5	10.8
9 No response	1.5	6.9
Joining demonstrations		
3 Frequently	2.3	2.9
2 Sometimes	15.3	12.7
1 Rarely	59.5	74.5
9 No response	22.9	9.8
Attending meetings		
3 Frequently	41.2	28.4
2 Sometimes	44.3	55.9
1 Rarely	11.5	8.8
9 No response	3.1	6.9
Demonstrations, morchas, processions		
3 Frequently	5.3	1.1
2 Sometimes	26.7	7.8
1 Rarely	45.0	83.3
9 No response	22.2	7.8

		Gujarat %	Orissa %
	Gheraoes		
3	Frequently	—	—
2	Sometimes	7.6	2.0
1	Rarely	64.1	90.2
9	No response	28.2	7.8
	Strikes		
3	Frequently	3.1	—
2	Sometimes	7.6	2.0
1	Rarely	57.3	90.2
9	No response	21.4	8.8
	Non-payment of taxes		
3	Frequently	3.1	—
2	Sometimes	7.6	2.0
1	Rarely	58.8	90.2
9	No response	30.5	7.8
	Contacting important leaders		
3	Frequently	49.6	5.9
2	Sometimes	37.4	73.5
1	Rarely	9.2	13.7
9	No response	3.8	6.9
	Contacting important officials		
3	Frequently	48.9	11.8
2	Sometimes	33.6	67.7
1	Rarely	13.7	17.6
9	No response	3.8	6.9

Normative approval of modes of political action

[Q 34] Now I will read the same list again. Please tell me which of these acts you personally approve or disapprove of.

		Gujarat %	Orissa %
	Representations like signature campaign or memoranda		
2	Approve	93.1	94.1
1	Disapprove	5.3	5.9
9	No response	1.5	—
	Joining demonstrations		
2	Approve	19.8	39.2
1	Disapprove	76.3	59.8
9	No response	3.8	1.0
	Morcha, procession		
2	Approve	37.6	31.4
1	Disapprove	58.8	68.6
9	No response	3.8	—

	Gujarat %	Orissa %
Gherao		
2 Approve	6.9	11.8
1 Disapprove	88.5	88.2
9 No response	4.6	—
Strike		
2 Approve	12.2	15.7
1 Disapprove	84.0	84.3
9 No response	3.8	—
Non-payment of taxes		
2 Approve	9.9	7.8
1 Disapprove	84.7	89.2
9 No response	5.3	2.9
Contacting important leaders		
2 Approve	95.4	98.0
1 Disapprove	3.1	2.0
9 No response	1.5	—
Contacting important officials		
2 Approve	93.9	98.0
1 Disapprove	3.8	2.0
9 No response	2.3	—

Personal benefits of development: financial

[Q 8]   In this study we are interested in finding out how people are getting along financially these days. As far as you and your family are concerned, are you well satisfied with your present financial situation, more or less satisfied, or not satisfied?

	Gujarat %	Orissa %
3 Fully satisfied	49.6	12.7
2 Partly satisfied	40.5	57.8
1 Not satisfied	9.2	29.4
9 No response	0.8	—

[Q 8a]   During the last few years has your financial situation been getting better, getting worse, or has it stayed the same?

	Gujarat %	Orissa %
3 Improved	77.1	24.5
2 Remained the same	16.8	40.2
1 Deteriorated	6.1	33.3
9 No response	—	—

APPENDIX

Personal benefits: 'inputs of development'

[Q 9] During the past couple of years several special benefits have been given to rural people. A few of these are mentioned below. Please indicate from which of these you have benefited.

		Gujarat %	Orissa %
	Improved seeds		
2	Received	58.0	67.6
1	Not received	28.2	32.4
9	No response	13.8	—
	Chemical fertiliser		
2	Received	58.0	62.7
1	Not received	29.0	37.3
9	No response	13.0	—
	Irrigation		
2	Received	47.3	26.5
1	Not received	39.7	73.5
9	No response	13.0	—
	House sites		
2	Received	6.9	5.9
1	Not received	80.9	94.1
9	No response	12.2	—
	Land to landless		
2	Received	2.3	6.9
1	Not received	84.7	93.1
9	No response	13.0	—
	Bank loans		
2	Received	45.8	54.9
1	Not received	41.2	45.1
9	No response	13.0	—
	Subsidy		
2	Received	43.5	30.4
1	Not received	43.5	69.6
9	No response	13.0	—
	Improved implements		
2	Received	28.2	3.9
1	Not received	58.0	96.1
9	No response	13.7	—
	Promotion of small-scale industries		
2	Received	6.1	—
1	Not received	82.2	100.0
9	No response	13.7	—

Personal background

- age
- caste
- religion
- level of education
- proficiency in languages (Gujarati, Oriya, Hindi, English)
- occupation
- size of landholding

Political background

[Q 11]   What was your age when you first started taking interest in politics and public affairs?

[Q 12]   Was there any important event that attracted you to politics or was there no such event?

[Q 13]   Which political party are you currently affiliated to?

[Q 13a]   Have you held positions in the party?

[Q 13b]   Nature of position currently held by the respondent.

[Q 14]   Have you held any post in this or other parties?

NOTES

CHAPTER 1 LOCAL ELITES AND THE POLITICS OF RURAL DEVELOPMENT

1 I am grateful to Professor Bruce Graham for drawing my attention to the normative assumptions behind Indian development (Personal communication; 1988). The resilience of the Indian village in the face of rapid change is the burden of an impressive body of literature. See in particular, F. G. Bailey, 'For a Sociology of India?', *Contributions to Indian Sociology*, 3 (1959), p 94.

2 For the concept of the interface, see Long (1989).

3 Following Gurr, (1970), relative deprivation implies the differential between the legitimate expectations and actual situation of an individual. Poverty and unequal distribution of wealth are necessary but not sufficient conditions for the existence of relative deprivation.

4 For applications of methodological individualism to situations of collective decision-making, see Olson (1965), Popkin (1979) and Riker (1986).

5 Scott (1976) argues in terms of the complementarity of interests within a group where individuals place the sense of group-interest and solidarity before their own interest.

6 Catherine Gwin and Lawrence Veit, 'The Indian Miracle', *Foreign Policy*, 58 (Spring 1985), p 79. This article provides the image of sustained progress achieved by the Indian economy during recent years.

7 Economist Intelligence Unit *India to 1990: How Far Will Reform Go?* Special Report No 1054 (London: Economist Intelligence Unit; 1986), p 1. Also see Rubin (1985) and Kohli (1989).

8 Ahluwalia (1978).

9 Dhanagare sums up the findings of several authors.

> What accounts for the immiserisation of the rural poor and what precisely obstructs the trickle-down to agricultural labourers either of agricultural growth or of aid and relief? . . . Mechanisation displaces labour and new agricultural/rural

development policy and strengthens the rural elite (mainly the rich farmers): the administered prices of food-grains rise while labour wages lag, and immigration brings heavy supplies of agricultural labour, depressing the wages further . . .

(D. N. Dhanagare, 'Rural Development, Poverty and Protest', *Contributions to Indian Sociology*, NS, 19(2), 1985, p 356)

10 On the basis of the analysis of the fate of the peasant from a cross-section of countries which have experienced the social implications of change from the pre-industrial to the industrial, Moore, (1966) shows that the 'Poorest must pay the prices of progress'. The 'Indian Paradox', which is also the title of Weiner (1989), demonstrates how, in a post-colonial situation where the marginalised poor also have the right to participation, the politics of populism can lead to the slowing down of growth, instability and localised violence. This can also lead to a politics of stalemate in terms of the inability of the political system to generate the momentum for social and economic change. See Bardhan (1984) and Herring (1989).

11 This can be seen by comparing R. Kothari's *Politics in India* (Boston: Little, Brown; 1970) with his *State Against Democracy: In Search of Humane Governance* (Delhi: Ajanta; 1990). Morris-Jones, who in the first edition of his *The Government and Politics of India* (London: Hutchinson; 1964) spoke confidently of the successful interpenetration of the society and polity in India, appears less optimistic about the state of affairs in his later work. See Epilogue (pp 259–72) in the 1988 edition of the book.

12 The comparatively optimistic view of the Rudolphs (L. and S. Rudolph, *In Pursuit of Lakshmi: The Political Economy of the Indian State* (Chicago and London: University of Chicago Press; 1987), should be compared with Frankel (1978), Manor (1983), Kaviraj (1984) and Saberwal (1986).

13 The 'actor-oriented' approach needs to be distinguished from the conventional liberal-democratic approach and the radical-structural approach which, respectively, give primacy to such 'objective' and 'impersonal' factors as the rational operations of the market and the modes of production and class conflict.

14 See Tilly (1975a), Gurr (1970) and Marsh (1977).

15 Huntington (1968).

16 See Taylor and Herman (1971) and Hibbs (1973). While taking issue with the practice of establishing an operational equivalence between anti-system attitudes and extremist parties (because the same party might behave in different ways under different circumstances), Mitra (1979, 1980) nevertheless demonstrates a strong, positive relationship between the existence of an anti-system dimension and governmental instability.

17 G. B. Powell 'Extremist Parties and Political Turmoil: Two Puzzles', *American Journal of Political Science*, 30 (May, 1986), p 374.

18 F. G. Bailey *Politics and Social Change: Orissa in 1959* (Berkeley, CA: University of California Press; 1963), p 223.

19 For further discussion of power and agenda setting, see Bachrach and Baratz (1962, 1963); on the three dimensions of power see Lukes (1974); and for applications of rational choice methods for the calculation of power see Denardo (1985).

20 The steady incorporation of these new concepts into the lexicon of Indian English is yet another testimony to the conservative dynamism of the system. For endogenous terms of discourse as strategies of political conflict, see Mitra (1990c).

21 Most of these definitions are drawn from Robert L. Hardgrave Jr. and Stanley Kochanek, *India: Government and Politics in a Developing Nation* (San Diego: Harcourt Brace Jovanovich; 1986), pp 153–7. For further useful discussions see Robert L. Hardgrave, Jr., *India Under Pressure: Prospects for Political Stability* (Boulder, CO: Westview Press; 1984), pp 14–16. A glossary of these 'Indian' forms of protest is to be found in Kaufman (1981).

22 Berger (1972).

23 These metaphysical categories which provide the ideological rationale for the varna scheme and the exchange of status and services based on the *jajmani* system, would correspond to Scott's (1976) use of the concept of moral economy.

24 For a criticism of theories of perpetual peasant rebelliousness in India, see Sumit Sarkar, 'Keynote Address', National Seminar on Tribal Resistance Movements, Sambalpur University (1985), p 10, cited in Mohanty (1988), p 49.

25 Tarrow (1977).

26 See Reddy and Hargopal (1985) and Elwert and Bierschenk (1988).

27 Moore (1966) and Frankel (1978).

28 References to the repressive, parasitical and reactionary role of a self-perpetuating local elite are a constant refrain in the writings on rural development in India. The grass-roots movement approach, prominently identified with Lokayan, constitutes an exception in the sense that it emphasises the importance of a view of the development process from below while insisting that this initiative has to come from the civil society, presumably outside the structure of local elites. See Kothari (1984) and Sheth (1983, 1984).

29 M. Esman and N. Uphoff, *Local Organization and Rural Development: The State of the Art* (Ithaca, NY: Rural Development Committee, Cornell University; 1982), p ix.

30 ibid.

31 The 'moral economy' approach (Scott (1976)), based on an organic view of rural community, is presented in the contemporary debate on development as a contrasting category to the political economy approach, based on the perception of the village as an aggregation of rational, expected-utility maximising peasants (Popkin (1979)).

32 Alavi (1972). Alavi has extended the theme to a formulation on the politics of military–bureaucratic–authoritarian states in post-colonial societies in Alavi (1990).

33 Johnson (1982). For an application to East Asia, see Kirby (1990).

34 G. Rosen, *Democracy and Economic Change in India* (Berkeley, CA: University of California Press; 1967), pp 67–81.

35 The following articles of the Constitution of India, placed in the Directive Principles of State Policy (which are not legally binding) are of particular interest:

Article 39
The state shall, in particular, direct its policy toward securing (a) that the citizens, men and women equally, have the right to an adequate means of livelihood (b) that the ownership and control of the material resources of the community are so distributed as best to subserve the common good (c) that the operation of the economic system does not result in the concentration of wealth and means of production to the common detriment. . . .

Article 41
The state shall, within the limits of its economic capacity and development, make effective provision for securing the right to work.

Article 43
The state shall endeavour to secure, by suitable legislation or economic organisation or in any other way, to all workers, agricultural, industrial or otherwise, work, a living wage, conditions of work ensuring a decent standard of life and full enjoyment of leisure and social and cultural opportunities.

Article 46
The state shall promote with special care the educational and economic interests of the weaker sections of the people.

36 The strains between economic and religious nationalism within the Jan Sangh – a party self-consciously committed to the revival of the lost glory of the Hindus – can perhaps be attributed to the power of the developmental idiom which became an obligatory part of the political discourse of all competing political forces during the period after independence (see Graham (1987)). For the limited success of Hindu nationalism, see Graham (1990).

37 Government of India, Planning Commission, *Third Five Year Plan* (Delhi: Government of India; 1967), 'Objectives', pp 1–18.

38 See Barrington Moore, *The Social Origins of Dictatorship and Democracy: Lord and Peasant in the Making of the Modern World* (Boston: Beacon Press; 1966), p 392 for a scathing criticism of the official expectation of popular participation through 'felt needs', a jargon that seemed to have found favour with the Planning Commission.

39 Despite some differences on details, because of the general convergence of their premises, we can place Alavi (1965), Frankel (1978) and Bardhan (1984) among radical critics of Indian development and of the nature of state and economy in India.

40 The concept of 'bullock capitalists' provides a dynamic link between

the traditional and the modern sectors of Indian economy. The bullock capitalists are small-scale, self-employed farmers 'who rely more on family labour and their own capital than on wage workers or machines' (Rudolph and Rudolph (1987) op. cit., p 2). Used more in the figurative than in the literal sense, the bullock capitalists possess considerable social and economic heterogeneity, and on some occasions, present themselves as 'tractor capitalists'. Politically, the ubiquitous bullock capitalists present themselves as opponents of both industrial capital and the urban sector in the name of remunerative prices and better terms of trade between the country-side and the city. Their presence serves to articulate agrarian politics in sectoral rather than class terms and provides a dynamic link between legitimacy of the state and expansion of the rural economy.

41 As early as the beginning of the century, the Congress party was putting forward demands for the reform of Legislative Councils through the inclusion of representatives of local councils, set up in the 1880s. See Sumit Sarker, *Modern India, 1885–1947* (Delhi: Macmillan; 1983), p 89. As a result of nationalist agitation and the colonial policy of seeking to neutralise it through selective accommodation, local municipal councils had representation on provincial councils and ultimately at the centre from 1892. Though full independence came only in 1947, a significant move was made towards self-government in incremental degrees during the colonial period. See Chiriyankandath (1992).

42 The convergence of reciprocity in status and exchange of goods within the jajmani system provides a strong parallel to Scott's (1976, op. cit.) notion of the moral economy.

43 'Non-decisions' are an effective method for enforcing the power of those social groups who control political institutions. By virtue of their control over the means through which issues are brought into public focus, those in power may contrive to shift public attention away from contentious subjects. Not being on the agenda, they become a part of 'non-decisions', which shelter the interests of the powerful from potential challenges. Depending on the nature of the issue, local elites can use such 'negligence of local interests' as a means for mobilising support. See Bachrach and Baratz (1970).

44 I prefer gaon ka neta to *janata ka neta* – leader of the people – used by Singh to refer to the achieved status of local elites as distinguished from their earlier ascribed status, because of the specific reference it makes to the village seen as a social system and a political arena. See Singh (1988), p 42.

45 In the course of the electoral campaign in an Orissa village in 1977, a section of the members of the former untouchable communities, led by a young, college educated person of the Pana caste, challenged the established leadership of their own community and moved over to the Congress party. This reduced the bargaining power of the divided Panas for the time being, but the new, younger

and more aggressive Pana leader became a member of the local elite from then on. See Mitra (1982).

46 Reddy and Hargopal (1985) op. cit., pp 1148–62.
47 Frankel (1978) op. cit., p 548. She also writes:

> Institutional changes, in particular, would have to be implemented in the villages through the existing local authorities, that is, the very rural elites against whose power they were directed. At the villages, the loudest voices still belong to members of the dominant landowning classes.
>
> (Frankel (1978), p 17)

Frankel appears to have changed her earlier position on the local political system as a closed, oligarchic order. See Frankel and Rao (1989/1990).

48 See Wood and Church (1984) for detailed discussions of the state of mobilisation of the Backward Classes in various Indian States.
49 See George Rosen, *Democracy and Economic Change in India*, (Berkeley and Los Angeles, CA: University of California Press; 1967), pp 67–81.
50 See Mitra (1990a).
51 Moore (1966), op. cit.
52 Harrison (1960).
53 Bailey (1963).
54 Reddy and Hargopal (1985), op. cit., p 1148.
55 See Srinivas (1969) for social/class differentiation.
56 Jan Breman, *Of Peasants, Migrants and Paupers: Rural Labour Circulation and Capitalist Production in West India* (Delhi: Oxford University Press; 1985), p 400.
57 ibid.
58 Rudolph and Rudolph (1988), op. cit., p 257.
59 Hardgrave and Kochanek (1986). op. cit., p 155.
60 ibid.
61 ibid.
62 Charles Tilly, 'Food Supply and Public Order in Modern Europe', in Tilly (ed.) *The Formation of Nation States in Western Europe* (Princeton, NJ: Princeton University Press; 1975a), p 390.
63 For a discussion of the strategic use of these new forms of agitation and mass protest, see Hardgrave and Kochanek (1986), op. cit., pp 154–7.
64 See Oomen (1984).
65 Rudolph and Rudolph (1988), op. cit., p 2.
66 See Frankell and Rao (1989/1990).
67 See Brittan (1973).
68 Chaturvedi and Mitra (1982).
69 See Popkin (1979) and Bates (1981).
70 See Scott (1976).
71 See Greenough (1983) and Appadorai (1984).
72 Some of the recent changes in the theories of developments are best understood by comparing some of the earlier works of

major writers with their more recent findings. For example, see
Huntington (1968, 1981), Apter (1971, 1987), Kothari (1970, 1988)
and Long (1977, 1989).
73 See Mitra (1980a).

CHAPTER 2   THE REGIONAL CONTEXT: THE SOCIAL AND ECONOMIC BACKGROUND OF RURAL DEVELOPMENT

1 The *District Gazetteer*, testimony to the patient labours of generations
of British district Collectors and their successors in independent
India, is the most important source of background information
on India's administrative districts, which, along with the village,
constitute the most enduring units of economic, political and
cultural life in India (see Government of Orissa (1972) and
Government of Gujarat (1981)). In addition to the *Gazetteer*, the
District Statistical Handbook, indicative of the growing concern with
factual details of development, is another important source (see
Government of Orissa (1980) and Government of Gujarat (nd).
Secondary sources and interviews have been used to supplement
the information available from these primary sources. The *Techno-
economic Surveys* of Gujarat and Orissa on which we have also drawn
are further testimony to the growing need for social and economic
statistics and increasing sophistication in its collection and distribution (see Government of India (1962) and Government of Orissa
(1963)).
2 The causal sequence and hierarchy of relations that specify the
linkage between development at the village, regional, national and
international arenas have been specified in figure 1.2, p 20.
3 Dunsire (1978).
4 Clay and Schaffer (1984).
5 This follows closely similar assumptions by Popkin (1979, 1989) and
Riker (1986). It does not require the individual to be necessarily
'individualistic', 'selfish' or 'materialistic' – terms which have a
pejorative connotation in Orissa and even in Gujarat which has a
much longer experience of capitalism. The basic assumption of the
maximisation of expected utility merely requires the political actor
to be aware of alternative states of the world and attempt, through
rhetoric, strategic political action and coalition formation, to
manipulate events in a direction preferable to him.
6 The shared interests of a group of which the individual actor is a
member are not necessarily episodic, and can have considerable
social and historical continuity. The analytical mistake one can make
here is to reify them to the extent where they become superordinate
to the interests of the individual and assume an autonomous
character of their own. In this analysis, the social class is the basis
of shared value, perception of collective interest and source of
political support. But, as the field data show, social class is rarely

the exclusive or even the most important determinant of rhetoric and action. The attempts of individuals to reorder that political universe to make it more felicitous for 'people like themselves' can thus lead to the redefinition of the basis of community and group formation. Hence, one encounters the rise of neo-castes as units in which 'men associate for competition against others' (W. H. Morris-Jones, *The Government and Politics of India* (Wistow, Huntingdon: Eothen Press; 1987), p 260).

7 The most general statement associated with this position is Dumont (1970). For a discussion of the sociological approaches influenced by Dumont and a critique, see Mitra (1990c).

8 The competing assumptions of free will as against social determination are at the basis of philosophical disputes that go as far back in history as Plato and have continued through social theorists closer to our times including Marx, Weber and Mannheim. Sartre's position on this issue is of particular interest here: that men make history within conditions imposed by history.

9 Government of India, Planning Commission (1961).

10 One exception to the overall Congress hegemony of 1947–67 was a brief interval of communist rule in Kerala in 1957–9. See Nossiter (1988). The hegemonic position of the Congress did not imply the authoritarian rule of its leaders, for Congress power was based on the widest possible accommodation of divergent interests within the structure of a dominant one-party system. This provided ample opportunity for negotiation and bargaining with opposition parties and political forces with the intention of identifying a consensus, which in turn provided the political basis of policy making. See Subrata Mitra, *Governmental Instability in Indian States* (Delhi: Ajanta; 1978), pp 4–11.

11 Frankel and Rao (1989/1990).

12 The rich base of secondary material on Gujarat compared to the absence of such research on Orissa only indicates the cumulative nature of knowledge of the developed and lack of information on the backward regions. On Gujarat, see Wood (1984), Breman (1985) and Desai et al. (1985).

13 See Mitra (1987).

14 See Wood (1984b) and Sheth and Menon (1986).

15 Church (1984).

16 Pravin Sheth, *Patterns of Political Behaviour in Gujarat* (Ahmedabad: Sahitya Mudranalay; 1976), p 75. Also see P. Sheth (1965).

17 Mitra (1987), op. cit.

18 Shah (1984b) and P. Sheth (1983).

19 Mohanty (1990a).

20 M. Mohanty (1990b).

21 Hardiman (1980).

22 Mohapatra (1990).

23 Mitra (1982). The Khandayats 'rediscovered' ritual relations with the former King and supported his party in course of the electoral mobilisation, rather than making common cause with other cultivating castes.

24 For example, James Freeman's *Untouchable* (1979) records these suppressed feelings of bitterness and anger. Politics only skims the surface of the sea of unhappiness. The survey research reported here tries to combine the insights of imaginative literature and individual life history and tries to apply them on a wider scale with the possibility of comparison.

25 Mohanty (1989).

26 Breman (1985).

27 A few vignettes from life in the 'bustling, booming' city of Surat, taken from M. Rehman, 'Surat: City of Dreams', in *India Today*, March 15 (1991) provide an indication of the competitive and entrepreneurial culture of Gujarat.

> Sevanti Shah, 43, came to Surat in 1963 taking the long route via Bombay from his village near Pallanpur in north Gujarat. A matriculate without any resources, Shah found employment in this historic South Gujarat city. Today, he is one of Surat's most prominent businessmen – he employs some 500 people, has a total estimated turnover of Rs. 45 crore from his three diamond-cutting units this year, and is the state convenor of the Gem and Jewellery export Promotion Council (p 70)
>
> Nur Mohammaed, 40, arrived in Surat only three years ago. A villager from Gujarat's Mahesana district, he slogged for nearly 17 years in Bombay and Ahmedabad as a taxi-driver. Even so, he could never acquire his own vehicle. But two years after he moved to Surat, Mohammed bought a second-hand Premier Padmini for Rs. 70,000. He had just Rs. 10,000 – the rest came from newly-made friends. The happy taxi-driver now does brisk business at the busy railway station. He has already repaid Rs. 40,000 and dreams of bringing his family to live in Surat one day (ibid.)

This vibrant, enterprising culture has proved hospitable for the mingling of communities and mobility of backward classes. Ghanshyam Shah, cited in this report, suggests: 'Surat's culture has been shaped by Ka, Kha, Ga, Gha – Kanbi, Khatri, Gola and Ghanchi, all intermediate castes. As a result, there is much greater social interaction between communities' (p 70).

28 After an interview, a bystander, who confessed to 'not being interested in politics at all' invited me to visit his factory which was close by. The 'factory' consisted of one large room with twenty-two motorised lathes, used for polishing diamonds. My host, who hails from the Patidar caste, had started life as a worker in a diamond 'factory', saved up enough to buy two lathes and start up on his own and raised loans from his extended family to expand his enterprise. He spoke little Hindi and no English, and his workshop was part of a primitive putting-out system which linked the diamond mines of South Africa to a Patidar intermediary in Eindhoven in the Netherlands who imported these low grade stones and through a contact in Bombay had them distributed, polished and collected in a number of 'factories' in rural Gujarat (Interview, Surat, 1979).

29 On social differentiation of Tribals under the impact of economic change, see Shah (1985).

30 Hardiman (1985).

31 Breman (1985), op. cit.

32 H. R. Chaturvedi and S. Mitra, *Citizen Participation in Rural Development* (Delhi: IBH; 1982), p 40.

33 In addition to the *Gazetteer*, one of the earliest studies of Dhenkanal is Frieda Hauswirth, *A Marriage to India* (London: Hutchinson; 1931), the bitter sweet memories of a Swiss-American woman who met her husband, an agronomist from Dhenkanal, at Stanford University before the first world war and followed him to his home in India where he intended to set up a sugar plantation and factory. In agonising detail, she recounts the story of the eventual demise of an idealistic dream of industrialisation of the native princely state of Dhenkanal, sabotaged partly through the suspicion of the colonial bureaucracy afraid of yet another nationalist plot to overthrow the Raj and the complete lack of infrastructure.

34 See Panigrahi (1989) and Bhuyan (1987).

35 Interview with the Block Development Officer, Dhenkanal (6th June, 1979).

36 ibid.

37 For details, see Chaturvedi and Mitra (1987).

38 Interview with the Sarpanch, Govindpur village, Dhenkanal (July, 1979).

39 Government of Orissa, *Orissa District Gazetteers: Dhenkanal* (Cuttack: Orissa Government Press; 1972), p 69.

40 From a report of the incident in the *Amrit Bazar Patrika*, Independence number (1947), cited in Government of Orissa (1972), op. cit., p 69.

41 ibid., p 70.

42 ibid.

43 Interview with Mr Jena, aged sixty, a Freedom Fighter, in Dhenkanal (May, 1978).

44 Surat was adjudged as the best district panchayat in India in the mid 1980s. Its president Sahadev Chaudhury, a tribal leader, was one of the main supporters of Mr. Amar Singh Chaudhury, the Chief Minister of Gujarat. He was a keen supporter of the tribal Chief Minister in his rivalry for supremacy of the State Congress party against the faction led by Congress stalwarts Madhavsingh Solanki and Jinabhai Darji during 1986–9.

CHAPTER 3 THE ELEMENTS OF DESIGN

1 A distinction has to be made between the local elite (equivalent to Bailey's 'broker') and another ubiquitous presence, the 'touter'. Bailey (F. G. Bailey, *Politics and Social Change: Orissa in 1959* (Berkeley: University of California Press; 1963)) makes a useful distinction between three categories of public persons present in the

271

village, namely, the broker, the touter and the agitator: 'a broker
. . . is a man of substance, furthering his business interests by
making contacts and recruiting followers for politicians. The touter
is merely a man who lives on his wits' (p 149). The term 'touter' was
originally used to designate a man who acted as agent for a Pleader
or Advocate, persuading people to go to law. From this the term
has been extended into the political field to describe people who
have a nose for trouble, and the knack of making trouble worse
while pretending to restore order, and who profit from the trouble.
The 'agitator', evoking the fading aura of the national struggle for
independence, is 'a man seeking to redress a public grievance in the
only way possible' (Bailey (1963), op. cit., p 149).

2 See K. Seshadri and S. P. Jain, *Panchayati Raj and Political Perceptions
of Electorate: A Study of Electoral Behaviour in the Mid-Term Poll of
1971 in Hyderabad Constituency* (Hyderabad: National Institute of
Community Development; (1972), pp 54–5.

3 See Bailey (1963), op. cit., p 62.

4 See R. G. Reddy and G. Hargopal, 'The Pyraveekar: the "Fixer" in
Rural India', *Asian Survey*, 25 (11) (November, 1985), p 1148.

5 Kreuger (1974).

6 See Bailey (1969), op. cit., p 42.

7 See Government of India, Planning Commission (1961).

8 The contrasting characterisation of political action in terms of
principal actors rather than through the exclusive agency of the
impersonal forces of class or region has its own advocates in the
literature on development. The former understands social action in
terms of the sum of individual actions and transactions (Popkin
(1979), Riker (1986) whereas the latter conceptualises social outcomes as the clash or mutual accommodation of large, internally
undifferentiated groups (Scott (1963), op. cit.).

9 See Long (1977, 1984 and 1988).

10 The reputational approach consists in obtaining from a broad
group of 'nominators' ordered lists of people who are in a position
of leadership in the village. The lists are then compared and the
overlapping set is retained as the set of people who are reputed to
be the local elites in a village. It is important not to suggest the
criteria of selection (such as class, status, formal positions) for
identification or ranking but to infer them from the sample so
obtained. The method, first used by Hunter (1953), has had further
applications (see Agger (1956), Agger and Ostram (1956); Barth
and Abu-Laban (1958); Miller (1958a, 1958b); and Schulze and
Blumberg (1957)). Others have been more critical (see Dahl (1958);
and Polsby (1959a, 1959b). For a particularly critical note, see
Wolfinger (1960 and 1962). For applications in India, see Oomen
(1970) and Singh (1988).

11 It is assumed here that total variation in a phenomenon, or a
dependent variable, can be attributed to several factors. Thus, when
it comes to variables such as the responses and initiatives taken by
local elites in their dealings with the decision-makers at higher

levels, these depend upon their socio-demographic features and their attitudinal attributes as well as the features of the political arena within which they operate. Specific features of this macro-context such as the extent to which opportunities for participation are available and are institutionalised, the nature of the economy and the size of the market might also influence behaviour. If the relationship between socio-demographic features and attitudinal attributes on the one hand and the repertoire of elite response on the other is what we intend to study, we need to eliminate from the data the effect of the context. Once we have identified our experimental variables (in this case the repertoire of elite response), we control for other systemic factors that might cause variations in the data. For further thoughts on the method of semi-experimental research designs, see Przeworski and Teune (1970), p 37.

12 Unlike the local roots of Indian politics which have been dealt with at length in village studies and in the literature on India's struggle for independence, the local basis of development in India has received comparatively less attention. As an area of research, it has not quite found a constituency of its own. The development planner, with his faith in the 'trickle-down' approach, has tended to treat local knowledge and initiative as obstacles to rational planning and implementation. The neo-Gandhian dissenters, who can be expected to take the local level more seriously, do not provide much enlightenment on this either because of their anti-integrationist postures towards the state and the market. In this sense, Robinson (1988) provides a fresh departure. It is firmly anchored on an intimate understanding of social life and political and economic transactions at the local level. At the same time, it succeeds in articulating their meaning to macro-level development and to the competitive political arena by showing the interlocking aspects of local, regional and national politics.

13 For other examples of the use of the administrative district as the unit of analysis, see Kohli (1989) and Singh (1988).

14 See A. Przeworski and H. Teune, *The Logic of Comparative Social Inquiry* (New York: Wiley-Interscience; 1970), p 34 for the methodology of experimental models.

15 R. Singh, *Land, Power and People: Rural Elite in Transition, 1801–1970* (New Delhi: Sage; 1988), p 31, criticising Sirsikar (1970), Carter (1974) and Narain et al. (1976).

16 The maintenance of elite status involves overt conflict and a considerable degree of potential tension.

> Mobility striving, while intrinsic in caste systems, is a constant threat to the status quo. It is suppressed whenever possible, but the process of suppression is difficult and never completely effective. ... It takes much physical and psychic energy to maintain an inherently unstable, conflictive situation in a semblance of working order. The dominant high status groups must suppress mobility striving among others; rules restricting social interaction must be enforced; the purity and integrity of the

273

group must be maintained despite constant denigration; resentment must be suppressed or carefully channelled.
(E. R. A. Seligman, *Encyclopaedia of the Social Sciences* (New York: Macmillan; 1957), Vol 3, p 336).
The maintenance of local power structures requires consummate skills at normal times. Under the heat generated by elections, it is often impossible to fend off new aspirants to local elite status. See Mitra (1982) for the discussion of the electoral process in an Indian village in course of which an older local leader from the untouchable Pana caste was cut down to size by a young and aggressive member of the same caste who, thereafter, became part of the group of local elites of the village.

17 The Panas, who are the leading elements among Harijans in Dhenkanal, have aggressively promoted their material benefits through the instrumental use of politics. This is less true of Adivasis who have received material benefits more as the consequence of government policy (Mitra (1982), op. cit.).

18 This is equivalent to Bailey's use of the concept of political elites: 'The *political elite* are those within the community entitled to compete for honours and power. The boundary between members and elite is not always sharp, and the elite may contain within itself many grades' (F. G. Bailey, *Stratagems and Spoils: A Social Anthropology of Politics* (Oxford: Blackwell; 1969), p 23).

19 J. Scott, 'Political Clientelism: A Bibliographic Essay', in S. Schmidt, L. Guasi, C. Lande and J. Scott (eds), *Friends, Followers and Factions* (Berkeley: University of California Press; 1977), p 486.

20 See Parsons (1974) and Roth (1968).

21 The basic references to the theoretical literature on clientelism by Scott (1977), op. cit., and drawn from Latin America as well as India. Included are Wolf (1956) and Bailey (1963), op. cit. Patronage and related concepts are analysed in Boissevain (1974) and forms of clientelism, land tenure and labour organisation are analysed in Mayer (1967).

22 See Nicholas (1963).

23 See Graham (1968), Pocock (1957) and Nicholas (1963), op. cit.

24 Scott (1977a), op. cit., p 492.

25 M. S. Robinson, *Local Politics: The Law of the Fishes: Development through Political Change in Medak District, Andhra Pradesh (India)* (Delhi: OUP; 1988), p 13.

26 See Bailey (1968); Nicholas (1963) and Nicholson (1972).

27 Fox (1969) provides a general schema that links together localised jatis within a series of regional varna schemes which are themselves linked together through the framework of the pan-Indian varna scheme. It is thus possible to constitute a status ranking of jatis within a particular regional varna scheme and locate the functional equivalent of a particular jati from within one varna scheme with one or a cluster of jatis from a different region. For the status ranking of jatis in Gujarat, see Wood (1984b). For the status ranking

of jatis in Orissa, see Bailey (1963), op. cit.; Government of Orissa (1972); Mitra (1982), op. cit.

28 Breman (1985).

29 ibid.

30 The concept of social class closely follows Dahrendorf's definition of a social stratum as 'a category of persons who occupy a similar position on a hierarchical scale of certain situational characteristics such as income, prestige, style of life' (Ralf Dahrendorf, *Class and Class Conflict in Industrial Society* (Stanford, CT: Stanford University Press; 1971), p ix).

31 See Freeman (1979) for an example of the social rivalry and new group formation arising out of the organisation of jatras in an Orissa village.

32 Bjorkman and Chaturvedi (1991).

CHAPTER 4   SETTING THE LOCAL AGENDA: THE PROBLEMS, PROGRESS AND AGENCY OF RURAL DEVELOPMENT

1 See Lipton (1976), Chambers (1983) and Chambers et al. (1989).

2 The rural agenda, which is one of the main ideological planks of the *Janata Dal* and the various *Lok Dals* that gained prominence in the 1970s, was first given concrete political shape by Charan Singh in his *India's Poverty and its Solutions* (London: Asia Publications; 1964) and, by the same author, *India's Economic Policy: The Gandhian Blueprint* (New Delhi: Vikas; 1978).

3 In England, during the process of rapid transformation of the agrarian economy, as Moore reminds us, 'Sheep ate men' (Barrington Moore, *The Social Origins of Dictatorship and Democracy: Lord and Peasant in the Making of the Modern World* (Boston: Beacon Press; 1966), p 12).

4 See Gurr (1970), Oberschall (1973), and Olson (1965).

5 The Indian National Congress, by reorganising its provincial units on the linguistic principle in 1920, set in motion a process which achieved concrete constitutional shape in 1956 when the States Reorganisation Commission recommended the creation of regional units on the basis of linguistic homogeneity. See Brown (1985).

6 Riker describes the process as *heresthetic*, 'structuring the world so that you can win' (William Riker, *The Art of Political Manipulation* (New Haven: Yale University Press; 1986), p ix).

7 The main objective of the sixty-fourth Amendment Bill placed before the Parliament by the Rajiv Gandhi government in 1989 was to endow local-level government with statutory political and financial powers so as to transform India to a genuine three-tier federation. Though the bill failed to secure the support of an absolute majority in both houses of the Parliament, it has nevertheless put on the agenda the importance of the third level of governance in India, after the national and the regional.

8 An incident from fieldwork in Orissa is quite revealing. In the village in question, the Sarpanch, who was our main contact, gave us a tour to show us the main development projects. The *piece de resistance* was a connecting road, constructed on land 'voluntarily donated' by the village to make the construction of the road possible. The land in question was good paddy land which in the first place aroused my suspicion. With a little discreet investigation I found out that the 'voluntary gift' was in fact forced on the donor, a Scheduled Caste person, who later confirmed the incident. In 'return' for his gesture, the donor was 'given' a piece of land from the uncultivated waste belonging to the village. The transaction was profitable to the village but not to the 'donor' who got land of inferior value compared to what he had to forgo. One might want to know as to why the aggrieved party in this case did not go to court. The reasons are complex, for the fear of retribution and public sanction are further compounded by the fact that it is not unusual for people in the area to cultivate a piece of land without a formal title deed. When ownership is based essentially on custom, the collective voice of village influentials can acquire an added dimension of inevitability (fieldwork, Dhenkanal, 1978).

9 S. K. Dey, 'Some Issues', in M. V. Mathur and Iqbal Narain (eds) *Panchayati Raj, Planning and Democracy* (Bombay: Asia Publishing House; 1969), p 13.

10 'power may be, and often is, exercised by confining the scope of decision-making to relatively "safe" issues' (Peter Bachrach and Morton Baratz, 'Two Faces of Power', *American Political Science Review*, 56 (1962), pp 947–52).

11 Reddy and Seshadri (1972), Seshadri and Jain (1972) and Narain et al. (1976).

12 Peter Bachrach and Morton Baratz, 'Decisions and Nondecisions: An Analytical Framework', *American Political Science Review*, 57 (1963), p 632.

13 See Arce (1989).

14 See Apter (1987).

15 Norman Long, An Introduction to the Sociology of Rural Development (London: Tavistock; 1977), p 3.

16 Harold Brookfield, *Interdependent Development* (London: Methuen), p ix.

17 David E. Apter, *Choice and the Politics of Allocation: A Developmental Theory* (New Haven, CT and London: Yale University Press; 1971), p 16.

18 David E. Apter, *Rethinking Development: Modernization, Dependency and Post-Modern Politics* (Beverley Hills, CA: Sage; 1987), p 16.

19 the grass-roots initiatives in India today are in the nature of both a critique and protest against the prevailing model of development and the emergence of a new and alternative approach to rural development that is more holistic, transcends economism and managerial ethics, is self-consciously political and it is political on

276

behalf of those sections of society whom modern 'development' has rendered impoverished, destitute and starving.
(D. L. Sheth, 'Grassroots Initiatives in India', *Economic and Political Weekly*, 9(6) (February, 1984, p 261) Among the people who stand to benefit from these grass-roots initiatives are 'the vast populations of Tribals, artisans, small and marginal farmers and the landless labour' who are excluded from the potential benefits of state or market-induced development. On this theme, also see Kothari (1983a).

20 The classic developmental state confers the authority to make policy decisions to a restricted group of specialists, bureaucrats and financial and industrial managers rather than keeping it exclusively in the hands of the representatives of the people per se. See Johnson (1982).

21 See James Warner Bjorkman, *Politics of Administrative Alienation in India's Rural Development Programs* (Delhi: Ajanta; 1979), p 22.

22 A different opinion is expressed by V. A. Paipanandikar and S. S. Khirsagar who observe that 'the bureaucratic structure and its orientation to a developmental role are not mutually incompatible'. They have made a series of recommendations towards a proper synthesis of the administrative and developmental roles of the bureaucracy. They recommend that
(a) the higher levels of the bureaucracy should be politicised and integrated with the political system;
(b) people's institutions should be given more say in developmental functions and panchayats should be developed as a part of the administrative apparatus rather than as political institutions;
(c) voluntary organisations in fields like education, health, agriculture and small-scale industry should be developed as instruments of developmental efforts and cooperatives utilised as less expensive organs of efficient implementation and development; and
(d) people's committees could be set up functionally or in aggregate areas to ensure greater involvement of the people.
See V. A. Paipanandikar and S. S. Khirsagar, *Bureaucracy and Development Administration* (New Delhi: Centre for Policy Research; 1978).

23 Government of India Planning Commission, Committee on Planned Projects, *Report of Team for the Study of Community Projects and National Extension Service* (Delhi: Government of India; 1957), Vol 1, pp 1–9.

24 See David C. Potter, *Government in Rural India: An Introduction to Contemporary District Administration* (London: London School of Economics and Political Science/Bell; 1964), pp 45–7.

25 The institutional structure of panchayati raj was expected to undergo a major change as a result of the sixty-fourth Constitutional Amendment Bill, introduced in the Parliament in July 1989. Its main features were

the establishment of a three-tier system of rural self-government, periodical polls under the Election Commission supervision, and 30 per cent reservation of seats for women. ... The bill also provides for a finance commission to be set up in the States every five years to review panchayat finances and ensure their sound position through designated taxes, duties, tolls and fees.

(*Statesman Weekly* Saturday, 20th May, 1989), p 1)

26 Balwantrai Mehta, 'Some Recent Trends in Panchayati Raj in India', *Indian Journal of Public Administration*, 8(4) (October 1962), p 458.

27 See Baviskar and Attwood (1984) and Chaturvedi and Mitra (1987).

28 Voluntary bodies themselves have become embroiled in local politics and ceased to be strictly non-political (Sheth (1984), op. cit.).

29 See Government on Gujarat Legal Department (1987) for the legal infrastructure of panchayati raj in Gujarat. For Orissa, see Government of Orissa Community Development and Social Welfare (Gram Panchayat) Department (nd); and Government of Orissa Community Development and Rural Reconstruction Department (1987).

30 Generally speaking, the inability to communicate a problem can itself be a problem of the most serious kind. The investigator sets himself as a catalyst who has no power of intervention as such but can help in the articulation of problems by lending a sympathetic ear. See Appendix on field methodology.

31 Reddy and Seshadri (1972), op. cit., p 4.

32 P. Berger and T. Luckman, *The Social Construction of Reality: A Treatise in the Sociology of Knowledge* (New York: Viking Penguin; 1966), p 56.

33 ibid, p 59.

34 Epistemic communities are understood as 'social networks' or 'the chains of interactions and communications linking actors in a realm of human activity' (Louk Box 'Knowledge, Networks and Cultivators: Cassava in the Dominican Republic', in Norman Long (ed.) *Encounters at the Interface* (Wageningen: Agricultural University Wageningen; 1989), p 167. Social class, as an intermediate construct between the individual and larger structures such as society, state and the market, is assumed to have some of the properties of a network of knowledge interchange and collective action. Also see van der Ploeg (1989).

35 For exemplars of this ideal type, see Downs (1957), Bates (1981) and Popkin (1979).

36 Growing political consciousness, community formation and regional associations on the lines of caste are indicative of the formation of large epistemic communities.

37 See the list of questions and principal results in the Appendix.

38 See Breman (1985), Hardiman (1985) and Shah (1991).

39 See Bailey (1963).

40 Of course, it could be argued here that the respondents are conscious of the fact that they are being interviewed in their capacity as local leaders and, as such, their evaluation of what has

been done for the development and welfare of the people in the area cannot be totally devoid of a sense of personal responsibility. That could introduce an upward bias to their evaluation of what has been done for development. It is reassuring, therefore, to note that their opinions are not simply an artifact of their position. When asked the identical question, the cross-section of the population of the area comes up with comparable results, with, respectively, 70 per cent of the people in Gujarat and 58 per cent in Orissa expressing themselves a great deal or somewhat satisfied. See H. R. Chaturvedi and Subrata Mitra, *Citizen Participation in Rural Development* (Delhi and Oxford: IBH; 1982), p 72 for details of the survey of the cross-section.

41 For cultural solutions to the problem of collective goods, see Olson (1965) and Popkin (1979).

42 See Scott (1976) and Bailey (1963).

43 See Narain et al. (1976) and Seshadri and Jain (1972).

CHAPTER 5   THE SOCIAL CONSTRUCTION OF LOCAL CONFLICT: UNEQUAL BENEFITS, RADICAL PROTEST AND SOCIAL COHESION

1 Growing conflict is indicative of the loss of hegemony by the traditional wielders of power who are increasingly called upon to use force to uphold their position because the ideological modes of domination are no longer effective.

Adult franchise has become so widespread that local *satraps* can no longer assume that the poor, illiterate masses will vote 'as expected'. Politicians desperate to cling to office increasingly resort to sordid practices. Consequently, political mobilization at once expands democracy and poses a significant challenge to it.

(Sumit Ganguly, 'Troubled India: A Doomsayer's Paradise',
Dissent (Fall, 1991), p 466).

2 An arena defines the territorial limits of authority vested in a particular political institution. The internal political life of an arena is governed by a set of rules derived from custom, conventions and laws. While an arena has a distinct identity, its authority is not exclusive, except of course at the highest level where the state claims to be the ultimate arbiter of right and wrong. Seen from below, arenas like the village, tehsil, district, region and, ultimately, the state can be seen as a series of concentric circles. As an essential part of state formation, political integration entails multiple membership of arenas by individuals. A given arena thus becomes a group with respect to the arena above it. Bailey describes the process as 'fission' and 'fusion' in segmentary political systems (F. G. Bailey, *Politics and Social Change: Orissa in 1959* (Berkeley, CA: University of California Press; 1963), p 225.

3 These institutions together constituted an elite entrepreneur network which grew in depth and complexity in course of the struggle for independence. See Sisson (1988).

4 Arjun Appadurai, 'How Moral is South Asia's Economy? – A Review Article', *Journal of Asian Studies*, 43 (3) 1984, p 481.

5 Field research in an Orissa village during the campaign leading up to the parliamentary elections of 1977 revealed considerable animosity between the upper-caste *bhadralok* and the Adivasi/Harijan, the former regretting the past when the village operated as one large family under the leadership of the traditional village panchayat, consisting of some upper-caste, male heads of households. However, despite the pressure exerted by competitive elections and universal franchise, the cleavage on caste and status lines did not lead to a polarisation of the local political arena because of fluid cross-caste factions. The earlier 'village unity' was replaced with a fragmented political arena where no particular group was in a position to speak for the whole village or the entire membership of a particular community. See Mitra (1982).

6 The two-volume study of regional politics in India, edited by Francine Frankel and M. S .A. Rao, *Dominance and State Power in Modern India: Decline of a Social Order* (Delhi: Oxford University Press; 1989/1990) reports a significant increase in conflict at the local level in practically all States of India. For the 'criminalisation of politics', a euphemism for the resort to force and violence by all social strata for the settlement of local conflicts, see Francine Frankel, 'Caste, Land and Dominance in Bihar', ibid., pp 46–132. For a diachronic study of social polarisation and increasing conflict at the local level, see Robinsion (1988).

7 See Patel (1985).

8 The decay of the intermediate structure of parties, bureaucracy and judiciary, responsible for the largely peaceful bargaining characteristic of the early decades following independence, followed by growing conflict and overt use of force, has been described in various ways: as 'deinstitutionalisation' by James Manor (1983); as a social 'crisis' by Arun Bose (1989); as the creation of 'social blanks' by Satish Saberwal (1986). See also Kothari (1988b).

9 See Bailey (1969) for games on the rules of the game. Also Saberwal (1986), op. cit.

10 On the integrative functions of conflict as regards the creation and maintenance of boundaries, see Coser (1956) and Barth (1965).

11 Bailey's distinction between political and warlike situations is comparable to the distinction between ordinary conflict and meta-conflict being suggested here.

> The political is that aspect of any act which concerns the distribution of power, providing that there is competition for this power, and provided, secondly, that the competition takes place under a set of rules which the competitors observe and which ensure that the competition is orderly. . . . [However] If the competitors do not agree upon rules and institutions which

make for orderly competition and resort to violence, then their actions are warlike and not political.

(F. G. Bailey, *Stratagems and Spoils: A Social Anthropology of Politics* (Oxford: Blackwell; 1969), p 223)

12 On the basis of his fieldwork in Orissa, Bailey (1963) suggested that in Oriya politics, 'there is no homogeneity at all levels; the issues which are at stake in State politics have to be translated into something else at constituency level and have to be translated yet again at village level'. (F. G. Bailey, *Politics and Social Change: Orissa in 1959* (Berkeley, CA: University of California Press; 1963), p 232.) The incorporation of the specific within general rules becomes feasible through social interaction and political transaction. Mohanty suggests polarisation on the lines of class conflict (see Mohanty (1990a)).

13 See W. H. Morris-Jones, 'Epilogue' in his *Government and Politics in India* (Wistow, Huntingdon: Eothen Press; 1987); and Kothari (1988b), op. cit.

14 See Manor (1983) op. cit., Kohli (1990) and Brass (1990).

15 See Shah (1990), op. cit.

16 D. A. Washbrook, 'Caste, Class and Dominance in Modern Tamil Nadu', in Frankel and Rao (1989), op. cit., Vol. I, p 227. The contested character of social dominance derives from its fragile social base and the functioning of representative democracy in contemporary India. Washbrook draws attention to this in his study of Tamil Nadu: 'The anarchy arises from the extent to which the merest sight or smell of privilege in any area of society instantly provokes antipathetic response from among those who see or smell it. No privilege is inherently legitimate and no authority exists uncontested' (ibid.).

17 See Mitra (1987).

18 See Hardiman (1985).

19 See Shah (1984a).

20 See Scott (1976) and Greenough (1983).

21 See Breman (1985).

22 Mitra (1982), op. cit., provides a case study of the political linkages that Panas, a rather aggressive scheduled caste of Orissa, established with political parties from outside in course of an electoral campaign. James Freeman (1979) gives a graphic account of the nature of dominance and protest on the basis of the biography of an untouchable from Orissa.

23 Greenough (1983), op. cit.

24 Bailey (1963), op. cit.

25 Mitra (1982), op. cit. and Mohanty (1990), op. cit.

26 See Mitra (1990b).

27 Breman (1985), op. cit. Breman shows how capitalist transactions can very well coexist cheek-by-jowl with political repression of dissident minority groups and a wide section of the society might connive at such repression.

28 Scott (1976), op. cit., p 4.

NOTES

29 Scott (1976), op. cit., p 11.
30 ibid., p. 17.
31 Samuel Popkin, *The Rational Peasant: The Political Economy of Rural Society in Vietnam* (Berkeley, CA: University of California Press; 1979), p 18.
32 Thorner (1982).
33 Greenough (1983), op. cit.
34 This kind of anomic political environment is referred to as the 'Law of the Fishes' (*Matsyanyaya*) by Marguerite S. Robinson, *Local Politics: The Law of the Fishes: Development through Political Change in Medak District, Andhra Pradesh (South India)* (Delhi: Oxford University Press; 1988), p 1. Lack of order can be self-reinforcing because of the problem of collective goods.
35 See Mitra (1991a).

CHAPTER 6 INSTITUTIONAL PARTICIPATION AND RADICAL PROTEST: THE STATE, SOCIETY AND ROOM FOR MANOEUVRE IN THE MIDDLE

1 For the changing notion of entitlement, see Amartya Sen, 'Poverty and Entitlements', in A. Sen, *Poverty and Famines: An Essay on Entitlement and Deprivation* (Delhi: Oxford University Press; 1981), p 18.
2 For a discussion of the 'responsive state' see Hage, Hanneman and Gargan (1989).
3 See Popkin (1979).
4 For two different accounts of these cultural values, see James C. Scott, *The Moral Economy of the Peasant: Rebellion and Subsistence in Southeast Asia* (New Haven, CT: Yale University Press; 1976) and Ainslee Embree, *Utopias in Conflict: Religion and Nationalism in Modern India* (Berkeley, CA: University of California Press; 1990), p 30.
5 See Alavi (1972).
6 See Krueger (1974).
7 Paul R. Greenough, 'Indulgence and Abundance as Asian Peasant Values: A Bengali Case in Point', *Journal of Asian Studies*, 42(4), (August, 1983), p 846.
8 Abbé Guillaume Raynal, *A Philosophical and Political History of the Settlements and Trade of the Europeans in the East and West Indies*, (translated by J. Justamond), 2nd edition (London: Reprint Editions; New York: Negro Universities Press; 1969), pp 437–8. Cited in Greenough (1983), op. cit., p 847.
9 Sen (1981), op. cit., estimates the numbers at the higher figure of three million.
10 Nanavati Papers '1944–1945. Memoranda and oral proceedings before the Famine Commission' (mss). (New Delhi: National Archives of India). Cited in Greenough (1983), op. cit., p 847.
11 E. P. Thompson, 'The Moral Economy of the English Crowd

282

in the Eighteenth Century', *Past and Present*, 50 (1971), p 78.

12 Greenough (1983), op. cit.

13 The boundary condition for the room for manoeuvre for the neta is provided by the relatively fluid, factional structure of local politics compared to the picture of a rather rigid, semi-authoritarian presence of the UMNO in James C. Scott, *Weapons of the Weak: Everyday Forms of Peasant Resistance* (New Haven, CT and London: Yale University Press; 1988).

14 See Jain (1990) and Potter (1964) for bureaucratic corruption.

15 Scott (1988), op. cit., p xvi.

16 See Brittan (1975).

17 Robert Hardgrave and Stanley Kochanek, *India: Government and Politics in a Developing Nation* (New York: Harcourt Brace Jovanovich; 1986), p 156.

18 See Manor (1988).

19 A. Marsh, *Protest and Political Consciousness* (Beverley Hills, CA and London: Sage; 1977), p 57, explains the depiction of protest behaviour as the antithesis of the conventional political process in terms of the 'puzzled reaction to the outbursts of students and blacks in the 1960s', which 'encouraged a striving after cognitive simplicity among many commentators'. Among them he mentions Lipset who 'tended to ascribe the growth of protest movements to a breakdown of inflexible orthodox politics in the face of alternative methods arising directly from increasing popular contempt for establishment politics'. Marsh suggests that the alternatives 'need not be mutually exclusive'. As supportive evidence, he suggests, citing the study of Aberbach and Walker (1969) that 'unconventional and conventional political behaviour among blacks was contingent upon distrust of political authorities, and that remedy was sought through both kinds of activity'. Additional supportive evidence is provided by Muller (1972), which, from a study of German farmers, workers and intellectuals 'indicated a gamma correlation coefficient of 0.705 between his scale measures of protest potential and a conventional behaviour index'. (ibid.)

20 This is related to what will subsequently be presented as the 'two faces of development'. C. A. Bayly comments as follows on the two faces of the Indian National Congress, competing and cooperating with the British Raj through a complex political strategy of alternately mobilising and containing the masses.

> Congress had emerged as the only political group, besides the government itself, which could deploy and attempt to control representatives at all levels of political life. In the United Provinces, no alternative regional or sectional party emerged. Congress was reluctantly accepted by government as a channel of petition; it was capable of containing the most disaffected groups in the political constellation, and yet could at the same time work

for relatively circumscribed aims within the maturing organs of local and provincial self-government.

(C. A. Bayly, *The Local Roots of Indian Politics: Allahabad, 1880–1920* (Oxford: Clarendon Press; 1975), pp 1–2)

21 See E. J. Clay and B. B. Schaffer, 'Self-awareness and the Policy Process', in E. J. Clay and B. B. Schaffer (eds) *Room for Manoeuvre: An Exploration of Public Policy in Agriculture and Rural Development* (London: Heinemann; 1984), pp 191–2, Clay and Schaffer describe these change agents, awareness on whose part creates the room for manoeuvre, as 'anyone concerned with the potential changes implied by public policy, and particularly by anyone concerned with changing policy itself' (p 191).

22 Alavi (1972), op. cit.

23 See Hayward (1986) for the concept of the policy community.

24 See Rudolph and Rudolph (1987).

25 Breman recounts methods through which the cooperative sugar-cane farmers have learnt to combine different political techniques to manipulate the legal and bureaucratic processes to their own advantage (Breman (1985), op. cit., p 303).

26 An incident from Orissa, widely reported in the national press, indicates the collective anger that lurks just beneath the politics of this rather quiet State.

When Chief Minister Biju Patanaik announced two months ago that the people should beat up corrupt officials, little did he realise what he was in for. In his rhetorical enthusiasm he suggested that even he should not be spared. Patnaik paid for it with a bleeding nose when an angry crowd attacked him in Bhawanipatna soon after. Patnaik was however cautious to include the proviso that he be given prior intimation before the officials are assaulted. Now, the Chief Minister's office is flooded with requests to rough up errant officials.

(Ruben Banerjee, 'Orissa: Up in Arms', *India Today* (15th February, 1991), p 55)

In the absence of institutionalised channels, this potential anger can quickly erupt into acts of localised but extreme violence. In one such incident two years before the survey, Prime Minister Mrs. Gandhi was attacked and injured in a public meeting in Bhubaneswar.

27 See Raynal (1969) and Greenough (1983), op.cit.

28 See Breman (1985).

29 See Bailey (1963).

CHAPTER 7 CONCLUSION: THE TWO FACES OF DEVELOPMENT: PROTEST AND PARTICIPATION IN INDIA

1 Morris-Jones (1967).

2 Saberwal (1986).

3 Manor (1983).

4 Moore (1966).
5 Barrington Moore, *The Social Origins of Dictatorship and Democracy: Lord and Peasant in the Making of the Modern World* (Boston: Beacon Press; 1966), p. 410.
6 Popkin (1979).
7 Scott (1985).
8 White (1986).
9 John P. Lewis, *Quiet Crisis in India* (New York: Anchor; 1964), p. 8.
10 See Mitra (1991b) for the resilience of constitutional democracy in India. For the structural sources of challenge to stability and the crisis of governability, see Frankel and Rao (1989/1990); and Kohli (1985 and 1990).
11 For a discussion of the scale and intensity of gherao (literally, to surround a decision-maker) and its progeny – rasta roko (obstructing roads to disrupt traffic), morcha (militant procession), mass casual leave, dharna (refusal to clear an area when ordered to do so), etc. – see R. L. Hardgrave Jr and S. Kochanek, *India: Government and Politics in a Developing Nation* (San Diego: Harcourt Brace Jovanovich; 1986), p 156; James Manor, 'Collective Conflict in India', *Conflict Studies*, 212, (London: Centre for Security and Conflict Studies; 1988), p 4, Geoffrey Moorhouse's *Calcutta: The City Revealed* (Harmondsworth: Penguin; 1974), pp 213–14 captures the form and spirit of gherao and its other variations which are part of a new, authentically Indian genre of collective protest.
12 With reference to secessionist violence in Punjab, three points should be noted. The issue of legitimacy of the state in India continues to divide Sikh opinion giving the state a continuing social base; though contested by terrorism, political participation continues to be perceived as the basis of legitimacy; and the state still holds the upper hand in choosing its strategy in transactions with political actors. For the resilience of democracy in India, see Kohli (1988) and Myron Weiner, *The Indian Paradox: Essays in Indian Politics* (Delhi: Sage; 1989) which singles out the party as the 'key' factor (p 330).
13 The findings reported in Joel D. Barkan and Frank Holmquist, 'The Social Base of Self-help in Kenya', *World Politics*, 41 (3) (1989), 359–80, provide cross-cultural support to this conjecture. They present the 'marriage of the peasant and the state in self-help' as a dynamic factor which has 'imbued the system with a measure of legitimacy and forced the Kenyan state to be minimally accountable to the public' (p 361).
14 In a different context, Sidney Tarrow has drawn our attention to the political and social function of local elites who facilitate the political adaptation of their communities to social and economic change. See Tarrow (1977). Some studies of panchayati raj in India have raised this problem at the empirical level. See Narain et al. (1976).
15 Huntington (1968); Gurr (1970); Moore (1966), op. cit.
16 This is the argument that runs through Huntington (1968),

NOTES

op. cit.: anti-system party strength and cabinet instability (Taylor and Herman (1971)), communist party membership and political instability (Hibbs, (1973); and strength of extremist parties and reduced cabinet durability (Dodd (1976)). In his subsequent work Huntington has increasingly tended to see collective protest as a factor that can lead to reform and institutional realignment. See Samuel P. Huntington *American Politics: The Promise of Disharmony* (Cambridge, MA: Harvard University Press; 1981), especially pp 203–10.

17 Bert F. Hoselitz and Myron Weiner, 'Economic Development and Political Stability in India,' *Dissent*, 8 (Spring, 1961), p 173. Huntington specifies his model in terms of a series of causal statements which link social mobilisation, discontent and political instability (Huntington (1968), op. cit., p. 55 (fn. 6)).

18 Huntington (1968), op. cit.

19 See Gurr (1970), op. cit., for the empirical specification of this concept.

20 Some of these arguments have been presented in Mitra (1991a).

21 The polarisation model is very popular with India's indigenous left and their western sympathisers. See Byres (1981).

22 Lichbach (1989). Lichbach questions the assumption that under the pressure of righteous anger arising out of relative deprivation people give vent to their collective frustration in a spate of irrational violence.

23 For applications of the same approach, see Bates (1981) and Popkin (1979), op. cit.

24 For a discussion of state responsiveness and state activism, see Hage et al. (1989).

25 G. Bingham Powell, 'Extremist Parties and Political Turmoil: Two Puzzles', *American Journal of Political Science* (May, 1986), p 374.

26 See Scott (1985).

27 For a discussion of the induction of new social forces into the bureaucracy, see Jain (1989).

28 James C. Scott, *Weapons of the Weak: Everyday Forms of Peasant Resistance* (New Haven, CT and London: Yale University Press; 1985), p 350.

29 'not so much a prejudice as . . . a realistic assessment of the fate of workers and peasants in most revolutionary states – a fate that makes melancholy reading when set against the revolutionary promise' (ibid.).

30 ibid. and Moore (1966), op. cit.

31 Esman and Uphoff (1982). For a pioneering study, see also Narain et al. (1976).

32 Norman Uphoff and Milton Esman *Local Organizations for Rural Development: Analysis of Asian Experience* (Ithaca, NY: Rural Development Committee, Cornell University; 1974) p. ix.

33 The complementarity of conventional political participation, through voting, contacting and lobbying, and radical protest has been pointed out by Aberbach and Walker (1969) and Muller (1972).

34 Kaase (1972) and Muller (1972).

35 von Eschen et al. (1969).

36 Bondurant (1965); Carter (1973).

37 Cerny (1982). Also see Berger (1972).

38 Powell (1986), op. cit., p 357.

39 I am reminded here of a question by one of my British students: 'Why can't Indian peasants collect their agricultural loans at the bank counter as people in Britain collect their welfare cheques at the post office?' Indian democracy simultaneously requires intermediaries and decries them. This would be familiar to those who have followed the allegations about the payment of commissions to intermediaries connected with the purchase of Bofors guns from Sweden.

40 The powerful and numerous group of 'bullock capitalists' are small-scale, self-employed farmers who rely more on family labour and their own capital than on wage workers or machines. The political power of these social groups, connected to the Janata Dal and various Lok Dals, is indicative of both the vitality of the process of agrarian capital formation and the effectiveness of social limits to the growth of predatory capitalism. See Rudolph and Rudolph (1987).

41 C. A. Bayly, *The Local Roots of Indian Politics: Allahabad, 1880–1920* (Oxford: Clarendon Press; 1975), pp 1–2. Bayly comments as follows on the two faces of the Indian National Congress, competing and cooperating with the British Raj through a complex political strategy of alternately mobilising and containing the masses.

> Congress had emerged as the only political group, besides the government itself, which could deploy and attempt to control representatives at all levels of political life. In the United Provinces, no alternative regional or sectional party emerged. Congress was reluctantly accepted by government as a channel of petition; it was capable of containing the most disaffected groups in the political constellation, and yet could at the same time work for relatively circumscribed aims within the maturing organs of local and provincial self-government.
>
> (ibid.)

42 F. Barth, *Political Leadership among the Swat Pathans* (London: University of London and Athlone Press; 1959), p 132. Also see Gould (1991).

43 Local protest movements came into prominence in the early 1970s following the deinstitutionalisation of the Congress party and the decline of intermediate structures. The fieldwork was conducted during the aftermath of the lifting of the national Emergency (1975–7) which had imposed severe restrictions on the freedom of political activity. The full range of political activities had been restored for about two years when the survey was conducted. The combination of plebiscitary politics at the national level and protest movements at the regional and local level which characterised the spatio-temporal context of the survey has continued to be the

dominant theme of Indian politics during the 1980s. See Rudolph and Rudolph (1987), op. cit., pp 127–58 for the rise of plebiscitary politics and pp 247–58 for demand groups. For the results of the survey of the cross-section, see Chaturvedi and Mitra (1982). The elite data which continue to be interesting because of the enduring importance of local protest movements and the distinctive styles of Gujarati and Oriya politics, have so far not been published.

44 For the application of the reputational technique for elite studies in India, see Singh (1988).

45 See Government of India (1962) and Government of India (1963) for the socio-economic background of Orissa and Gujarat.

46 It can of course be argued here that the growth of labour markets should offset some of the hardship faced by those without any capital except their labour. However, the migration of poorer people can in effect send both the prevailing wage rate and the annual availability of work downwards. See Jan Breman, *Of Peasants, Migrants and Paupers: Labour Circulation and Capitalist Production in West India* (Delhi: Oxford University Press; (1985), p xx.

47 Scott (1985), op. cit.

48 Freeman (1979); Scott (1985), op. cit.; Breman (1985), op. cit.

49 *Times of India* (Ahmedabad) (3 April 1991), p 6.

50 Robinson (1988).

51 Marguerite Robinson, *Local Politics: The Law of the Fishes: Development through Political Change in Medak District, Andhra Pradesh (South India)* (Delhi: Oxford University Press; 1988), p 40.

52 An Oriya equivalent of the empowerment of the former Untouchables is reported in Mitra (1982). A single member of the Hadi caste, refusing to beat the drum, could stop the Dussera, the major festival of the landowning Kshatriyas of the area in an Orissa village. Though the drum is an essential ritual of the festival, the Hadi had a 'monopoly' over playing this instrument for its touch is considered polluting which gave this lowly Untouchable a 'control' over the local arena. This control remained potential as long as the function was considered natural and as such, a non-issue. Once however it was made an issue, its transactional value became clear to all actors.

53 Robinson (1988), op. cit., p. 246.

54 Supportive evidence of this form of mobility is provided by the literature on electoral mobilisation which informs us of the remarkable progress made by the Backward Classes in several Indian States, who, in the politically turbulent 1960s, were successful in dislodging the upper-caste leadership from their dominant position. Evidence of electoral mobilisation of agrarian interests through 'Backward Caste movements' is provided by Rudolph and Rudolph (1987), op. cit., pp 54–5. Also see the contributions of John Wood and Rhoderick Church in Wood (1984a) for detailed discussions of the state of mobilisation of the Backward Classes in various Indian States. On the mobilisation of the lower castes in

Gujarat, see Wood (1984b) and, for upper-caste backlash against the policy of reservation in favour of the former Untouchables, Tribals and Backward Classes, see Mitra (1987), op. cit.

55 Harrison (1960). The early writing of V. S. Naipaul on India, particularly *India: A Wounded Civilisation* (London: Deutsch, 1977), belongs to this genre.
56 Sisson and Wolpert (1988).
57 Alavi (1972) and Reddy and Hargopal (1985).
58 Huntingdon (1968), op. cit.; Gurr (1970), op. cit.
59 For a discussion of the role of political transaction in state formation in India, see Subrata Mitra, 'Between Transaction and Transcendence: The State and the Institutionalisation of Power in India', in Mitra (1990a).
60 *The Statesman Weekly* (Calcutta) (21st September, 1991).
61 Moore (1966), op. cit.
62 See Rudolph and Rudolph (1987), op. cit., part 3 for demand groups.
63 See Herring (1989).
64 See Bardhan (1984); and Rudolph and Rudolph (1987), op. cit.
65 Rudolph and Rudolph (1977), op. cit.
66 Kothari (1988); Sheth (1984).
67 See Bréchon and Mitra (forthcoming).
68 Weiner (1989), op. cit.
69 As prototype exemplars of this genre, Bailey (1970) indicates the gradual disappearance of multiplex relations leading to the growth of specialised interest groups which will use a common political idiom. Smith (1963) suggests a not-too-distant future when religion in India would become entirely a matter of personal faith and the public arena would be confined to issues of economic and social policies.
70 The point is discussed in Mitra (1991c).
71 Kothari (1988), op. cit.; Morris-Jones (1987), op. cit.
72 See Mitra (1990a), op. cit., for a discussion of the institutionalisation of power through the creation of new political arenas along the lines of language and ethnic identity.
73 Bjorkman and Chaturvedi (1991).
74 This is reminiscent of 1985–6 when a techno-managerial elite acquired considerable political influence under the leadership of Rajiv Gandhi, who at that time was a political novice himself.
75 Scott (1985), op. cit., p 317.
76 Breman (1985), op. cit., p 432
77 Scott (1985), op. cit., p 243.
78 See Kohli (1990), op. cit.
79 The *Economist*, which had strongly endorsed Indian economic policy in the mid-1980s, has been more critical recently. See *The Economist: A Survey of India* (4th May, 1991):

> The future of India looks more threatened than for many years. In recent months its government has been all but paralysed by political squabbling. The country is divided by violence over caste, religion and demands for regional autonomy. Economic growth is slowing and poverty on a scale that defies the imagination seems beyond all remedy. (op. cit., p 3)

BIBLIOGRAPHY

Aberbach, J. D. and J. L. Walker (1969) 'Political Trust and Racial Ideology', *American Political Science Review*, 63, 83–99.

Adams, R. (1970) 'Brokers and Career Mobility Systems in the Structure of Complex Societies', *Southwestern Journal of Anthropology*, 26(4), 315–27.

Agger, Robert E. (1956) 'Power Attribution in the Local Community', *Social Forces*, 34, 322–31.

Agger, Robert E. and V. Ostram (1956) 'Political Structure of a Small Community', *Public Opinion Quarterly*, 20, 81–9.

Ahluwalia, Montek (1978) 'Rural Poverty and Agricultural Performance in India', *Journal of Development Studies*, 14(3) (April), 298–324.

Alavi, Hamza (1965) 'Peasants and Revolution', in Jonathan Saville and Ralph Miliband (eds), *The Socialist Register* (London: Merlin Press).

Alavi, H. (1972) 'The State in Post-Colonial Societies: Pakistan and Bangladesh', *New Left Review*, 74, 59–81.

Alavi, H. (1990) 'Authoritarianism and Legitimation of State Power in Pakistan', in S. Mitra (ed.) *The Post-Colonial State in Asia: Dialectics of Politics and Culture* (London: Harvester Wheatsheaf), 19–71.

Alexander, K. C. (1980) *Rural Organisations in South Asia: The Dynamics of Laborer and Tenant Unions and Farmers' Associations in Kerala and Tamilnadu* (Ithaca, NY: Cornell University Press).

Almond, Gabriel (1973) *Crisis, Choice and Change: Historical Studies of Political Development* (Boston, MA: Little Brown).

Appadorai, Arjun (1984) 'How Moral is South Asia's Economy? – A Review Article', *Journal of Asian Studies* 43(3), 481–97.

Apter, David E. (ed.) (1964) *Ideology and Discontent* (New York: Free Press)

Apter, David E. (1971) *Choice and the Politics of Allocation: A Developmental Theory* (New Haven, CT and London: Yale University Press).

Apter, David E. (1987) *Rethinking Development: Modernization, Dependency and Post-Modern Politics* (Beverly Hills, CA: Sage).

Arce, A. (1989) 'The Social Construction of Agrarian Development: A Case Study of Producer–Bureaucrat Relations in an Irrigation Unit in Western Mexico' in Norman Long (ed.) *Encounters at the Interface* (Wageningen: Agricultural University Wageningen), 11–52.

BIBLIOGRAPHY

Bachrach, Peter and Morton Baratz (1962) 'Two Faces of Power', *American Political Science Review*, 56, 947–52.

Bachrach, Peter and Morton Baratz (1963) 'Decisions and Nondecisions: An Analytical Framework', *American Political Science Review*, 57, 632–42.

Bachrach, Peter and Morton Baratz (1970) *Power and Poverty: Theory and Practice* (Oxford: Oxford University Press).

Bailey, F. G. (1959) 'For a Sociology of India?', *Contributions to Indian Sociology*, 3.

Bailey, F. G. (1963) *Politics and Social Change: Orissa in 1959* (Berkeley, CA: University of California Press).

Bailey, F. G. (1965) 'Decisions by Consensus in Councils and Committees', in *Political Systems and the Distribution of Power*, ASA Monographs 2 (London: Tavistock).

Bailey, F. G. (1968) 'Para-Political Systems', in Marc Swartz (ed.) *Local Level Politics* (Chicago, IL: University of Chicago Press).

Bailey, F. G. (1969) *Stratagems and Spoils: A Social Anthropology of Politics* (Oxford: Blackwell).

Bailey, F. G. (1977) *Morality and Expediency* (Oxford: Blackwell).

Banerjee, Ruben (1991) 'Orissa: Up In Arms', *India Today* (15th February), 55.

Banfield, Edward C. (1968) *The Moral Basis of a Backward Society* (New York: Free Press).

Bardhan, Pranab (1984) *The Political Economy of Development in India* (Delhi: Oxford University Press).

Barkan, Joel D. and Frank Holmquist (1989) 'Peasant–State Relations and the Social Base of Self-Help in Kenya', *World Politics*, 41 (April), 359–80.

Barkan, Joel D. and Frank Holmquist (1989) 'The Social Base of Self-Help in Kenya', *World Politics*, 41(3), 359–80.

Barry, Brian (1970) *Sociologists, Economists and Democracy* (London: Macmillan).

Barth, F. (1959) *Political Leadership among the Swat Pathans* (London: University of London and Athlone Press).

Barth, T. A. E. and Abu-Laban (1958) 'Power Structure and Negro Subcommunituy', *Sociological Review*, 24, 69–76.

Bates, Robert (1981) *Markets and States in Tropical Africa: The Political Basis of Agricultural Policies* (Berkeley, CA: University of California Press).

Baviskar, B. S. and Attwood, D. W. (1984) 'Capital and the Transformation of Agrarian Class Systems: Sugar Production in Western and Northern India', in Meghnad Desai, Susanne Rudolph and Ashok Rudra (eds) *Agrarian Power and Agricultural Productivity in South Asia* (New Delhi: Oxford University Press and Berkeley, CA: University of California Press), 20–50.

Bayly, C. A. (1975) *The Local Roots of Indian Politics: Allahabad, 1880–1920* (Oxford: Clarendon Press).

Benewick, R. and T. A. Smith (eds) (1972) *Direct Action and Democratic Politics* (London: Allen and Unwin).

Berger, Peter (1977) *To Empower People: The Role of Mediating Structures in Public Policy* (Washington, DC: American Enterprises Institute).

Berger, Peter and Thomas Luckmann (1966) *The Social Construction of Reality: A Treatise in the Sociology of Knowledge* (Harmondsworth: Penguin and New York: Viking Penguin).

Berger, Suzanne (1972) *Peasants Against Politics: Rural Organization in Brittany, 1911–1967* (Cambridge, MA: Harvard University Press).

Bhuyan, B. (1987) 'Evaluation of IRD Programme of Dhenkanal District, 6th Plan' (Bhubaneswar: Economic Appraisal Cell, Orissa University of Agriculture and Technology).

Bjorkman, James (1979) *Politics of Administrative Alienation in India's Rural Development Programs* (Delhi: Ajanta).

Bjorkman, J. W. and H. R. Chaturvedi (1991) 'Panchayati Raj in Rajasthan: The Penalties of Success', in K. Schomer, J. L. Erdman, D. O. Lodrick and L. I. Rudolph (eds) *The Idea of Rajasthan: Exploration in Regional Identity*, 2 vols (Delhi: Manohar Publications).

Blair, Harry (1974) *The Elusiveness of Equity: Institutional Approaches to Rural Development in Bangladesh* (Ithaca, NY: Cornell University Press).

Blair, Harry (1982) *The Political Economy of Participation in Local Development Programmes: Short Term Impasse and Long Term Change in South Asia and the United States from the 1950s to the 1970s* (Ithaca, NY: Cornell University Press).

Blau, P. (1964) *Exchange and Power in Social Life* (New York: John Wiley and Sons).

Blumenthal, M. D., R. L. Kahn, F. M. Andrews and K. B. Head (1972) *Justifying Violence* (Ann Arbor, MI: Michigan University Press).

Boissevain, J. (1974) *Friends of Friends: Networks, Manipulator and Coalitions* (Oxford: Blackwell).

Bondurant, J. (1965) *The Conquest of Violence: The Gandhian Philosophy of Conflict* (Berkeley, CA: University of California Press).

Booth, David (1985) 'Marxism and Development Sociology: Interpreting the Impasse', *World Development* 10, 60–73.

Bose, Arun (1989) *India's Social Crisis* (Delhi: Oxford University Press).

Box, Louk (1989) 'Knowledge, Networks and Cultivators: Cassava in the Dominican Republic', in Norman Long (ed.) *Encounters at the Interface* (Wageningen; Agricultural University Wageningen), 165–82.

Brass, P. R. (1984) 'National Power and Local Politics in India: A Twenty Year Perspective', *Modern Asian Studies*, 18(1), 89–118.

Brass, P. R. (1990) *The Politics of India since Independence* (Cambridge: Cambridge University Press).

Bréchon, Pierre and Subrata Mitra (forthcoming) 'The National Front in France: The Emergence of an Extreme Right Movement', *Comparative Politics*.

Breman, Jan (1978) 'Seasonal Migration and Cooperative Capitalism: The Crushing of Cane and of Labour by Sugar Factories of Bardoli, South Gujarat', *Economic and Political Weekly of India*, 8, 1317–60 and *Journal of Peasant Studies* 6 (1978), 41–70 and (1979), 168–209.

Breman, Jan (1985) *Of Peasants, Migrants and Paupers: Rural Labour Circulation and Capitalist Production in West India* (Delhi: Oxford University Press).

Brittan, S. (1973) *Participation without Politics: An Analysis of the Role of Markets* (London: Institute of Economic Affairs).

Brookfield, Harold (1975) *Interdependent Development* (London: Methuen).

Brown, Judith (1985) *Modern India: The Origin of an Asian Democracy* (Delhi: Oxford University Press).

Byres, Terry (1981) 'The New Technology, Class Formation and Class Action in the Indian Countryside', *Journal of Peasant Studies*, 8.

Carter, A. (1973) *Direct Action and Liberal Democracy* (London: Routledge and Kegan Paul).

Carter, Anthony (1974) *Elite Politics in Rural India: Political Stratification of Alliances in Western Maharashtra* (Cambridge: Cambridge University Press).

Cavanna, H. (1970) 'Protest in France', in B. Crick and W. A. Robson (eds) *Protest and Discontent* (Middlesex: Penguin).

Cerny, Philip (ed.) (1982) *Social Movements and Protest in France* (London: Frances Pinter).

Chambers, Robert (1976) *Rural Development; Putting the Last First* (London: Longman).

Chambers, Robert, N. C. Saxena and Tushaar Shah (1989) *To the Hands of the Poor: Water and Trees* (London: Intermediate Technology Publishers).

Chaturvedi, H. R. and Subrata Mitra (1982) *Citizen Participation in Rural Development* (Delhi and Oxford; IBH).

Chaturvedi, H. R. and Subrata Mitra (1987) 'Rural Cooperatives: Hope or Despair? – A Comparative Study of Gujarat and Orissa', *Social Change*, 17(2), 16–25.

Chiriyankandath, J. (1992) 'Democracy under the Raj', in S. K. Mitra (ed.) *Democracy in South Asia*, a special number of the *Journal of Commonwealth and Comparative Politics* Vol. 30(2) (March), 39–63.

Church, R. (1984) 'Conclusion: The Pattern of State Politics in Indira Gandhi's India', in J. R. Wood (ed.) *State Politics in Contemporary India* (Boulder, CO and London: Westview Press), 229–50.

Clay, E. J. and B. B. Schaffer (eds) (1984) *Room for Manoeuvre; An Explanation of Public Policy in Agricultural and Rural Development* (London: Heinemann).

Cohen, John M. and Norman Uphoff (1977) *Rural Development Participation; Concepts and Measures for Project Design, Implementation and Evaluation* (Ithaca, NY: Rural Development Committee, Cornell University).

Coser, Lewis (1956) *The Function of Social Conflict* (New York: Free Press).

Dahl, Robert (1958) 'Critique of the Ruling Elite Model', *American Political Science Review*, 52, 463–9.

Dahrendorf, R. (1971) *Class and Conflict in Industrial Society* (Stanford, CT: Stanford University Press).

Dayal, Rajeshwar (1960) *Community Development Programme in India* (Delhi: Kitab Mahal).

De, Nitish (1979) 'Organising and Mobilising: Some Building Blocks of Rural Work Organisations', *Human Features*, Winter, 32–64.

DeNardo, J. (1985) *Power in Numbers* (Princeton, NJ: Princeton University Press).

Desai, I. P., Ghanshyam Shah and Dipankar Gupta (1985) *Caste, Class, Conflict and Reservation* (Delhi: Ajanta).

Dey, S. K. (1969) 'Some Issues', in M. V. Mathur and Iqbal Narain (eds) *Panchayati Raj, Planning and Democracy* (Bombay: Asia Publishing House).

Dhanagare, D. N. (1985) 'Rural Development, Poverty and Protest', *Contributions to Indian Sociology*, NS, 19(2).

Dodd, Lawrence (1976) *Coalitions in Parliamentary Government* (Princeton, NJ: Princeton University Press).

Downs, Anthony (1957) *An Economic Theory of Democracy* (New York: Harper and Row).

Dumont, L. (1970) 'The Individual as an Impediment to Sociological Comparison and Indian History' in L. Dumont, *Religion, Politics and History in India: Collected Papers in Indian Sociology* (Paris: Mouton).

Dunsire, A. (1978) *Implementation in a Bureaucracy: The Execution Process* (Oxford: Martin Robertson).

Dwivedi, O. P. and R. B. Jain (1985) *India's Administrative State* (Delhi: Gitanjali Publications).

Eckstein, Harry and Ted Robert Gurr (1975) *Patterns of Authority: A Structural Basis for Political Inquiry* (New York: Wiley).

Economist Intelligence Unit (1986) *India to 1990: How Far will Reform Go?* Special Report No. 1054.

Economist, The (1991) 'A Survey of India', *The Economist* (4 May), 3–18.

Eisenstadt, S. N. (1966) *Modernization: Protest and Change* (Englewood Cliffs, NJ: Prentice-Hall).

Elwert, G. and T. Bierschenk (1988) 'Development Aid as an Intervention in Dynamic Systems', *Sociologia Ruralis*, 28(2/3), 99–112.

Embree, Ainslee (1990) *Utopias in Conflict: Religion and Nationalism in Modern India* (Berkeley, CA: University of California Press).

Esman, Milton and Norman Uphoff (1982) *Local Organization and Rural Development: The State of the Art* (Ithaca, NY: Rural Development Committee, Cornell University).

Feierabend, I. K., R. L. Feierabend and T. R. Gurr (eds) (1972) *Anger, Violence and Politics* (Englewood Cliffs, NJ: Prentice-Hall).

Fox, R. G. (1969) '*Varna* Schemes and Ideological Integration in Indian Society', *Comparative Studies in Society and History*, 2, 27–44.

Franda, Marcus (1979) *India's Rural Development: An Assessment of Alternatives* (Bloomington, IN: Indiana University Press).

Frankel, Francine R. (1978) *India's Political Economy 1947–1977: The Gradual Revolution* (Delhi; Oxford University Press).

Frankel, Francine and M.S.A. Rao (eds) (1989–1990) *Dominance and State Power in Modern India: Decline of a Social Order*, Vol. 1 (1989) and Vol. 2 (1990) (Delhi: Oxford University Press).

Freeman, James M. (1979) *Untouchable: An Indian Life History* (London: Allen and Unwin).

Friedman, Milton and L. G. Savage (1948) 'The Utility Analysis of Choices Involving Risk', *Journal of Political Economy*, 56, 279–304.

Frohlich, Norman (1974) 'Self-Interest or Altruism, What Difference?', *Journal of Conflict Resolution*, 18 March, 55–73.

Frohlich, Norman (1971) 'I Get By with a Little Help from My Friends', *World Politics*, 23 (October), 104–20.

Frohlich, Norman (1974) 'The Carrot and the Stick: Optimal Program Mixes for Entrepreneurial Political Leaders', *Public Choice*, 19 (Fall), 43–61.

Gallanter, Marc (1984) *Competing Equalities: Law and the Backward Classes in India* (Delhi: Oxford University Press).

Gallanter, Marc (1989a) 'Pursuing Equality in the Land of Hierarchy: An Assessment of India's Policies of Compensatory Discrimination or Historically Disadvantaged Groups', in Rajeev Dhavan (ed.) *Law and Society in Modern India* (Delhi: Oxford University Press).

Gallanter, Marc (1989b) *Law and Society in Modern India* (Delhi: Oxford University Press).

Gamson, W. A. (1968) *Power and Discontent* (Homewood, IL: Dorsey).

Ganguli, Sumit (1991) 'Troubled India: A Doomsayer's Paradise', *Dissent* (Fall), 464–7.

Gluckman, M. (1968) 'The Utility of the Equilibrium Model in the Study of Social Change', *American Anthropologist*, 70, 219–37.

Geertz, Clifford (1962) 'The Rotating Credit Association: A "Middle Rung" in Development', *Economic Development and Cultural Change*, 10(3), 241–63.

Gould, Harold (1991) 'Natural Selection and Selective Cooptation: A Theoretical Note on Post-Independence Political Behaviour in India', Paper presented at the Annual Conference of the Political Studies Association, U.K.

Government of Gujarat (nd) *District Statistical Handbook: Gujarat* (Ahmadabad, Gujarat: Director, Government Printing).

Government of Gujarat (1981) *Surat District Gazetteer* (Ahmadabad: Gujarat Government Publications Depot).

Government of Gujarat Legal Department (1987) *The Gujarat Panchayat Act, 1961 (As Modified up to the 15th December 1986)* (Ahmadabad, Gujarat: Director, Government Printing).

Government of India (1960) *Seventh Evaluation Report on Community Development and Some Allied Fields* (Delhi: Government of India).

Government of India Planning Commission, Committee on Planned Projects (1957) *Report of Team for the Study of Community Projects and National Extension Service* 3 vols (Delhi: Government of India).

Government of India Planning Commission (1961) *The Third Five Year Plan* (Delhi): Government of India.

Government of India Central Statistics Organisation (1985) *Monthly Abstracts of Statistics* (January).

Government of Orissa (1972) *Orissa District Gazetteers: Dhenkanal* (Cuttack: Orissa Government Press).

Government of Orissa (1980) *District Statistical Handbook: Dhenkanal* (Cuttack: Orissa Government Press).

Government of Orissa Community Development and Rural Reconstruction Department (1987) *Orissa Panchayat Samiti Manual, 1988* (Cuttack: Orissa Government Press).

Government of Orissa Community Development and Social Welfare (Gram Panchayat) Department (nd) *The Orissa Grama Panchayat Manual, 1976 (Acts, Rules, Notifications, Instructions)* (Cuttack: Orissa Government Press).

Graham, Bruce D. (1968) 'The Succession of Factional Systems in the Uttar Pradesh Congress Party, 1937–66', in Marc Swartz (ed.) *Local Level Politics* (Chicago, IL: University of Chicago Press; 1968).

Graham, B. (1987) 'The Challenge of Hindu Nationalism: The Bharatiya Janata Party in Contemporary Indian Politics', *Hull Papers in Indian Politics*, October.

Graham, B. (1990) *Hindu Nationalism in Indian Politics* (Cambridge: Cambridge University Press).

Gran, Guy (1983) *Development by People: Citizen Construction of a Just World* (New York: Praeger).

Grant, James P. (1973) 'Development: An End to the Trickle Down?', *Foreign Policy*, 46 (Fall), 43–65.

Greenough, Paul (1983) 'Indulgence and Abundance in Asian Peasant Values: A Bengali Case in Point', *Journal of Asian Studies*, 42(4), 831–50.

Guessous, M. (1967) 'A General Critique of Equilibrium Theory', in W. E. Moore and R. M. Cook (eds) *Readings in Social Change* (Englewood Cliffs, NJ: Prentice-Hall).

Gurr, T. R. (1970) *Why Men Rebel* (Princeton, NJ: Princeton University Press).

Gwin, C. and L. Veit (1985) 'The Indian Miracle', *Foreign Policy*, 58, Spring.

Hage, G., R. Hanneman and E. Gargan (1989) *State Responsiveness and State Activism* (London: Unwin Hyman).

Hain, P. (1971) *Radical Regeneration: Protest, Direct Action and Community Politics* (London: Quartet).

Hardgrave, R. L. Jr (1984) *India Under Pressure: Prospects for Political Stability* (Boulder, CO: Westview Press).

Hardgrave, R. L. Jr and S. Kochanek (1986) *India: Government and Politics in a Developing Nation* (San Diego: Harcourt Brace Jovanovich).

Hardiman, David (1980) *Peasant Nationalists of Gujarat* (Delhi: Oxford University Press).

Hardiman, David (1985) *The Coming of the Devi: Adivasi Assertion in Western India* (Delhi: Oxford University Press).

Harrison, S. (1960) *India: The Most Dangerous Decades* (Princeton, NJ: Princeton University Press).

Harsanyi, John C. (1969) 'Rational Choice Models of Behavior v. Functionalist and Conformist theories', *World Politics*, 21 (July), 513–88.

Hauswith, F. (1931) *A Marriage to India* (London: Hutchinson).

Hayward, Jack (1986) *The State and the Market Economy: Industrial Patriotism and Economic Intervention in France* (Brighton: Wheatsheaf).

Herring, Ronald (1989) 'Dilemmas of Agrarian Communism: Peasant Differentiation, Sectoral and Village Politics in India', *Third World Quarterly*, 11(1) (January), 89–115.

Hibbs, Douglass (1973) *Mass Political Violence* (New York: Wiley).

Higgins, B. (1956) 'The Dualistic Theory of Underdeveloped Areas', *Economic Development and Cultural Change* 4, 99–115.

Hirshman, Albert (1981) *Essays in Trespassing: Economics to Politics and Beyond* (Cambridge: Cambridge University Press).

Hirshman, Albert (1970) *Exit, Voice and Loyalty* (Cambridge, MA: Harvard University Press).

Hobsbawm, E. J. (1959) *Primitive Rebels* (New York: Praeger).

Hoselitz, Bert F. and Myron Weiner (1961) 'Economic Development and Political Stability in India', *Dissent*, 8 (Spring).

Hunter, Floyd (1953) *Community Power Structure* (Chapel Hill, NC: University of North Carolina Press).

Huntington, Samuel P. (1968) *Political Order in Changing Societies* (New Haven, CT: Yale University Press).

Huntington, Samuel P. (1973) 'Postindustrial Politics: How Benign will it be?' *Comparative Politics*, 6(2), 163–92.

Huntington, Samuel P. (1981) *American Politics: The Promise of Disharmony* (Cambridge, MA: Harvard University Press).

Jain, R. B. (1990) 'The Role of Bureaucracy in Policy Development and Implementation in India', *International Social Science Journal*, 123, 32–46.

Johnson, Bruce and William F. Clark (1982) *Redesigning Rural Development: A Strategic Perspective* (Baltimore, MD: Johns Hopkins University Press).

Johnson, Chalmers (1982) *MITI and the Japanese Miracle: The Growth of Industrial Policy 1925–1975* (Stanford, CT: Stanford University Press).

Kaase, M. (1972) *Political Ideology, Dissatisfaction and Protest* (Mannheim: Institut für Sozialwissenschaften an der Universität Mannheim).

Kaufman, M. T. (1981) 'In India, There's a Protester to Suit Any Occasion', *New York Times*, 23 April.

Kaviraj, Sudipta (1984) 'On the Crisis of Political Institutions in India', *Contributions to Indian Sociology*, 18, 223–43.

Kirby, Steven (1990) 'South Korea: From Hermit Kingdom to Economic Polity', in S. Mitra (ed.) *The Post-colonial State in Asia: The Dialectics of Politics and Culture* (Milton Keynes: Harvester Wheatsheaf), 225–52.

Klein, A. (ed.) (1971) *Dissent, Power and Confrontation* (New York: McGraw-Hill).

Kohli, Atul (1985) *The State and Poverty in India* (Cambridge: Cambridge University Press).

Kohli, Atul (ed.) (1988) *India's Democracy: An Analysis of Changing State–Society Relations* (Princeton, NJ: Princeton University Press).

Kohli, Atul (1989) 'Politics of Liberalisation in India', *World Development*, March.

BIBLIOGRAPHY

Kohli, Atul (1990) *Democracy and Discontent: India's Growing Crisis of Governability* (Cambridge: Cambridge University Press).

Kothari, Rajni (1970) *Politics in India* (Boston, MA: Little Brown).

Kothari, Rajni (1983a) 'Party and State in our Times: The Rise of Non-party Political Formations', *Alternatives*, 595–618.

Kothari, Rajni (1983b) 'The Crisis in the Moderate State and the Decline of Democracy', in P. Lyon and J. Manor (eds) *Transfer and Transformation: Political Institutions in the New Commonwealth: Essays in Honour of W. H. Morris-Jones* (Leicester: Leicester University Press).

Kothari, Rajni (1984) 'The Non-party Political Process', *Economic and Political Weekly*, 5, February 4, 216–24.

Kothari, Rajni (1988a) *State Against Democracy: In Search of Humane Governance* (Delhi: Ajanta).

Kothari, Rajni (1988b) 'Decline of the Moderate State' in R. Kothari, *State Against Democracy: In Search of Humane Governance* (Delhi: Ajanta), 15–36.

Kothari, Rajni (1990) *Rethinking Development: In Search of Humane Alternatives* (Delhi: Ajanta).

Kreuger, A. (1974) 'The Political Economy of the Rent Seeking Society', *American Economic Review*, 64(5), 91–303.

Landsberger, Henry (1973) *Rural Protest: Peasant Movements and Social Change* (New York: Barnes and Noble).

Lele, Uma (1981) 'Cooperatives and the Poor: A Comparative Perspective', *World Development*, 9(1), 55–72.

Lemarchand, Rene (1972) 'Political Clientelism and Ethnicity in Tropical Africa', *American Political Science Review* 66(1), 68–90.

Lewis, John P. (1964) *Quiet Crisis in India* (New York: Anchor).

Lichbach, Mark Irving (1989) 'An Evaluation of "Does Economic Inequality Breed Political Conflict?" Studies', *World Politics*, 41(4), 431–70.

Lipsky, M. (1968) 'Protest as a Political Resource', *American Political Science Review*, 62, 1144–58.

Lipton, Michael (1968) 'The Theory of the Optimising Peasant', *Journal of Development Studies*, 4 (April), 327–51.

Lipton, Michael (1976) *Why Poor People Stay Poor: A Study of Urban Bias in World Development* (London: Temple Smith).

Lipton, Michael (1981) *Why Poor People Stay Poor?* (Delhi: Heritage).

Long, Norman (1977) *An Introduction to the Sociology of Rural Development* (London: Tavistock).

Long, Norman (1984) 'Creating Space for Change: A Perspective on the Sociology of Development', *Sociologia Ruralis*, 24)3/4), 168–84.

Long, Norman (1988) 'Sociological Perspectives on Agrarian Development and State Intervention' in A. Hall and J. Midgley (eds) *Development Policies: Sociological Perspectives* (Manchester: Manchester University Press).

Long, Norman (ed.) (1989) *Encounters at the Interface: A Perspective on Social Discontinuities in Rural Development*, Wageningen Studies in Sociology 27 (Wageningen: Agricultural University Wageningen).

Lukes, Steven (1974) *Power* (London: Macmillan).

Lyon, P. and J. Manor (eds) (1983) *Transfer and Transformation: Political Institutions in the New Commonwealth: Essays in Honour of W. H. Morris-Jones* (Leicester: Leicester University Press).

McPhail, C. (1971) 'Civil Disorder Participation: A Critical Examination of Recent Research', *American Sociological Review*, 36, 1058–73.

Manor, James (1983) 'Anomie in Indian Politics: Origins and Potential Wider Impact', *Economic and Political Weekly of India*, 18, 725–34.

Manor, James (1988) *Collective Conflict in India*, Conflict Studies, 212 (London: Centre for Security and Conflict Studies).

Marsh, A. (1974) 'Explorations in Unorthodox Political Behaviour: A Scale to Measure Potential', *European Journal of Political Research*, 2, 107–29.

Marsh, A. (1977) *Protest and Political Consciousness* (Beverly Hills, CA and London: Sage).

Mayer, Adrian C. (1967) 'Patrons and Brokers: Rural Leadership in Four Overseas Indian Communities', in Maurice Freedman (ed.) *Social Organization: Essays Presented to Raymond Firth* (London: Frank Cass).

Meehan, Eugene (1978) *In Partnership with People: An Alternative Development Strategy* (Washington, DC: Inter American Foundation).

Mehta, Balwantrai (1962) 'Some recent trends in Panchayati Raj in India', *Indian Journal of Public Administration*, 8(4), 450–72.

Mellor, J. W. (1976) *The New Economics of Growth: A Strategy for India* (Ithaca, NY: Cornell University Press).

Migdal, Joel (1974) *Peasants, Politics and Revolution* (Princeton, NJ: Princeton University Press).

Migdal, Joel (1974) 'Why Change? Toward a New Theory of Change among Individuals in the Process of Modernization', *World Politics*, 26 (January), 189–206.

Miller, D. C. (1958a) 'Industry and Community Power Structure', *American Sociological Review*, 23, 9–15.

Miller, D. C. (1958b) 'Decision-making Clique in a Community Power Structure', *American Journal of Sociology*, 64, 299–310.

Miller, Barbara (1980) *Local Social Organisations and Local Project Capacity* (Syracuse, NY: Maxwell School, Syracuse University).

Mitchel, Robert (1965) 'Survey Materials Collected in Developing Countries: Sampling, Measurement and Interview Obstacles to Intra and International Comparisons', *International Social Science Journal*, 17, 665–85.

Mitra, Subrata K. (1978) *Governmental Instability in Indian States* (Delhi: Ajanta).

Mitra, Subrata K. (1979) 'Ballot Box and Local Power: Electoral Politics in an Indian Village', *Journal of Commonwealth and Comparative Politics* 17(3), 282–99.

Mitra, Subrata K. (1980a) 'Norms and Modalities of Political Choice: Case Study of an Orissa Village', *Contributions to Indian Sociology*, NS, 14(1), 51–75.

Mitra, Subrata K. (1980b) 'A Theory of Governmental Stability in Parliamentary Systems', *Comparative Political Studies*, 13(2), 235–63.

Mitra, Subrata K. (1982) 'Caste, Class and Conflict: Organisation and Ideological Change in an Orissa Village', in Jacques Pouchepadass (ed.) *Caste et Classes en Asie du Sud*, Collection Purusartha No. 6 (Paris: École des Hautes Études en sciences sociales), 97–134.

Mitra, Subrata K. (1987) 'The Perils of Promoting Equality: The Latent Significance of the Anti-reservation Movement in India', *Journal of Commonwealth and Comparative Politics*, 25(3), 292–312.

Mitra, Subrata K. (ed.) (1990a) *The Post-colonial State in Asia: The Dialectics of Politics and Culture* (Milton Keynes: Harvester Wheatsheaf).

Mitra, Subrata K. (ed.) (1990b) *The Politics of Positive Discrimination: A Cross-National Perspective* (Bombay: Popular).

Mitra, Subrata K. (1990c) 'Flawed Paradigms: Western Representations of Indian Politics', Paper presented at the Terms of Political Discourse in India Conference, Bhubaneswar (Orissa).

Mitra, Subrata K. (1991a) 'Room to Manoeuver in the Middle: Local Elites, Political Action and the State in India', *World Politics*, 43(3), (April), 390–413.

Mitra, Subrata K. (1991b) 'Crisis and Resilience in Indian Democracy', *International Social Science Journal*, 129 (August), 550–70.

Mitra, Subrata K. (1991c) 'Desecularising the State: Religion and Politics in India after Independence', *Comparative Studies in Society and History*, 33(4) (October), 755–77.

Mitra, Subrata K. (ed.) (1992) *Democracy in South Asia*, a special number of the *Journal of Commonwealth and Comparative Politics*, 30(1) (March).

Mitra, Subrata K. and V. B. Singh (1979) 'Social Class and Belief Systems in the Indian elite', *Indian Journal of Political Science*, 40(1), 40–58.

Mohanty, Bikram Keshari (1988) 'Protest and Dissent Movements in Orissa: A Study of Nilgiri Uprisings', Ph.D. Thesis, Sambalpur University (Orissa).

Mohanty, G. (1990b) 'Class, Caste and Dominance in a Backward State', in F. Frankel and M. S. A. Rao (eds) *Dominance and State Power in Modern India: Decline of a Social Order*, Vol. 2 (Delhi: Oxford University Press).

Mohanty, Manoranjan (1990a) 'Class, Caste and Dominance in a Backward State: Orissa', in F. Frankel and M. S. A. Rao (eds) *Dominance and State Power in Modern India: Decline of a Social Order*, Vol. 2 (Delhi: Oxford University Press), 321–66.

Mohanty, M. and L. N. Mishra (1976) 'Orissa: Patterns of Political Stagnation', in I. Narain (ed.) *State Politics in India* (Meerut: Meenakshi Prakashan).

Mohapatra, B. N. (1990) 'The Politics of Oriya Nationalism', D.Phil. thesis, St Anthony's College, Oxford.

Montgomery, John and Milton Esman (1971) 'Popular Participation in Development Administration', *Journal of Comparative Administration*, 3(3), 358–82.

Moore, Barrington (1966) *The Social Origins of Dictatorship and Democracy: Lord and Peasant in the Making of the Modern World* (Boston, MA: Beacon Press).

BIBLIOGRAPHY

Moorhouse, Geoffrey (1974) *Calcutta: The City Revealed* (Harmondsworth: Penguin).
Morris-Jones, W. H. (1987) *Government and Politics of India* (Vistow, Huntingdon: Eothen Press).
Mukhia, H. (1989) 'Dynamics of Rural Power', *Economic and Political Weekly of India*, June 17, 1338.
Muller, E. N. (1972) 'A Test of a Partial Theory of Potential for Political Violence', *American Political Science Review*, 66, 928–59.
Naipaul, V. S. (1977) *India: A Wounded Civilization* (London: Deutsch).
Naipaul, V. S. (1990) *India: A Million Mutinies Now* (London: Heinemann).
Nanavati Papers (mss.) '1944–1945: Memoranda and Oral Proceedings before the Famine Commission' (New Delhi: National Archives of India).
Narain, I., K. C. Pande and M. L. Sharma (1976) *The Rural Elite in an Indian State: A Case Study of Rajasthan* (New Delhi: Manohar Book Service).
National Council of Applied Economic Research (1962) *Techno-Economic Survey of Orissa* (New Delhi: National Council of Applied Economic Research).
National Council of Applied Economic Research (1963) *Techno-Economic Survey of Gujarat* (New Delhi: National Council of Applied Economic Research).
Nelson, Joan (1979) *Access to Power: Politics and Urban Poor in Developing Nations* (Princeton, NJ: Princeton University Press).
Newby, Howard (1975) 'The Deferential Dialectic', *Comparative Studies in Society and History*, 17, 139–64.
Nicholas, Ralph W. (1963) 'Village Factions and Political Parties in Rural West Bengal', *Journal of Commonwealth Studies*, 2(1) (November), 17–32.
Nicholson, Norman K. (1972) 'The Factional Model and the Study of Politics', *Comparative Political Studies*, 5 (Fall), 291–314.
Nicholson, Norman K. (1973) *Panchayati Raj, Rural Development and the Political Economy of Village India* (Ithaca, NY: Rural Development Committee, Cornell University).
Nossiter, T. (1988) *Marxist State Governments in India: Politics, Economics and Society* (London: Pinter Publishers).
Nurkse, Ragnar (1953) *Problems of Capital Formation in Underdeveloped Countries* (Oxford: Blackwell).
Oberschall, Anthony (1973) *Social Conflict and Social Movements* (Englewood Cliffs, NJ: Prentice-Hall).
Olson, Mancur (1965) *The Logic of Collective Action* (Cambridge, MA: Harvard University Press).
Oommen, T. K. (1970) 'Rural Community Power Structure in India', *Social Forces*, 49(2), 226–39.
Oommen, T. K. (1984) 'Green Revolution and Agrarian Conflict: The Debate', in T. K. Oommen, *Social Structure and Politics: Studies in Independent India* (Delhi: Hindustan Publishing Corporation).
Paipanandikar, V. A. and S. S. Khirsagar (1978) *Bureaucracy and*

Development Administration (New Delhi: Centre for Policy Research).

Panigrahi, D. D. (ed.) (1989) *Studies in Regional Economy: Readings on the Economy of Dhenkanal District* (Dhenkanal: Monasa Press).

Parsons, Talcott (ed.) (1947) *Max Weber, The Theory of Social and Economic Organization* (New York: Macmillan).

Patel, Priyavadan (1985) 'Recent History and Politics of Communalism and Communal Riots in Gujarat', in Asghar Ali Engineer and Moin Shakir (eds) *Communalism in India* (Delhi: Ajanta).

Patel, Priyavadan (1989) 'Communal Violence and Politics', in Moin Shakir (ed.) *Religion, State and Politics in India* (Delhi: Ajanta), 91–102.

Pocock, D. (1957) 'The Basis of Factions in Gujarat', *British Journal of Sociology*, 7, 295–317.

Polsby, Nelson W. (1959a) 'The Sociology of Community Power', *Social Forces*, 37, 232–6.

Polsby, Nelson W. (1959b) 'The Problem in the Analysis of Community Power', *American Sociological Review*, 24, 796–803.

Popkin, Samuel (1979) *The Rational Peasant: The Political Economy of Rural Society in Vietnam* (Berkeley, CA: University of California Press).

Popkin, Samuel (1989) 'The Political Economy of Peasant Society', in Jon Elster (ed.) *Rational Choice* (Oxford: Basil Blackwell).

Potter, David C. (1964) *Government in Rural India: An Introduction to Contemporary District Administration* (London: London School of Economics and Political Science/Bell).

Powell, G. B. (1986) 'Extremist Parties and Political Turmoil: Two Puzzles', *American Journal of Political Science*, 30 (May), 357–78.

Prasad, Pradhan (1980) 'Rising Middle Peasantry in North India', *Economic and Political Weekly of India* Annual No., (February), 215–19.

Pressman, J. and A. Wildavsky (1973) *Implementation* (Berkeley, CA: University of California Press).

Priestly, H. (1968) *Voice of Protest* (London: Leslie Frewin).

Przeworski, A. and Teune, H. (1970) *The Logic of Comparative Social Inquiry* (New York: Wiley-Interscience).

Rahman, Anisur (1981) *Some Dimensions of People's Participation in the Bhoomi Sena Movement*, Report No. 81–2 (Geneva: United Nations Research Institute for Social Development).

Raynal, Abbé Guillaume (1969) *A Philosophical and Political History of the Settlements and Trade of the Europeans in the East and West Indies* (translated by J. Justamond), 2nd edition (London: Reprint Editions; New York: Negro Universities Press).

Reddy, G. R. and K. Seshadri (1972) *The Voter and Panchayati Raj: A Study of the Electoral Behaviour during Panchayat Elections in Warangal District, Andhra Pradesh* (Hyderabad: National Institute of Community Development).

Reddy, Ram G. and G. Hargopal (1985) 'The Pyraveekar: The "Fixer" in Rural India', *Asian Survey* 25(11) (November) 1148–62.

Redford, Robert (1967) *The Little Community and Peasant Society Culture* (Chicago, IL: University of Chicago Press).

Rehman, M. (1991) 'Surat: City of Dreams', *India Today* (March 15).

BIBLIOGRAPHY

Riker, William (1986) *The Art of Political Manipulation* (New Haven, CT: Yale University Press).

Robinson, Marguerite S. (1988) *Local Politics: The Law of the Fishes: Development through Political Change in Medak District, Andhra Pradesh (South India)* (Delhi: Oxford University Press).

Rogowski, Ronald (1978) 'Rationalist Theories of Politics; A Mid-term Report', *World Politics*, 30 (January), 296–323.

Rondinelli, Dennis (1982) 'The Dilemma of Development Administration: Complexity and Uncertainty in Control-Oriented Bureaucracies', *World Politics*, 35(1), 43–72.

Rosen, George (1967) *Democracy and Economic Change in India* (Berkeley, CA: University of California Press).

Rubin, B. (1985) 'Economic Liberalisation and the Indian State', *Third World Quarterly*, (October), 942–57.

Rudolph, Lloyd and Susanne Rudolph (1987) *In Pursuit of Lakshmi: The Political Economy of the Indian State* (Chicago, IL and London: University of Chicago Press).

Russell, Clifford and Norman Uphoff (eds) (1981) *Public Choice and Rural Development* (Baltimore, MD: Johns Hopkins University Press).

Saberwal, Satish (1986) *India: The Roots of Crisis* (Delhi: Oxford University Press).

Santhanam, K. (1958) *Planning and Plan Thinking* (London: Higginbothams).

Sarkar, S. (1983) *Modern India, 1885–1947* (Delhi: Macmillan).

Sarkar, S. (1988) 'Keynote Address', National Seminar on Tribal Resistance Movements, Sambalpur University.

Schulze, Robert O. and L. V. Blumberg (1957) 'Determinants of a Local Power Elite', *American Journal of Sociology*, 63, 290–6.

Scott, James C. (1972a) 'Patron–Client Politics and Political Change', *American Political Science Review*, 66(1), 91–113.

Scott, James C. (1972b) 'The Erosion of Patron–Client Bonds and Social Change in Rural South-east Asia', *Journal of Asian Studies*, 23 (November), 5–37.

Scott, James C. (1975) 'Exploitation in Rural Class Relations: A Victim's Perspective', *Comparative Politics* 7 (July), 489–532.

Scott, James C. (1976) *The Moral Economy of the Peasant: Rebellion and Subsistence in Southeast Asia* (New Haven, CT: Yale University Press).

Scott, James C. (1977a) 'Political Clientelism: A Bibliographic Essay', in Stepfen Schmidt, Laura Guasi, Carl Lande and James Scott (eds) *Friends, Followers and Factions* (Berkeley, CA: University of California Press).

Scott, James C. (1977b) 'Peasant Revolution: A Dismal Science', *Comparative Politics*, 9 (January), 232–48.

Scott, James C. (1985) *Weapons of the Weak: Everyday Forms of Peasant Resistance* (New Haven, CT and London: Yale University Press).

Scott, James C. and Benedict, J. Trai kerkvliet (eds) (1986) *Everyday Forms of Peasant Resistance in South-East Asia* (London: Frank Cass).

de Silva, G. V. S. et al. (1981) 'Bhoomi Sena: A Struggle for People's Power', *Development Dialogue* (Upsaala), Vol 2, 3–70.

Seligman, E. R. A. (1957) *Encyclopedia of the Social Sciences* (New York: Macmillan).

Sen, Amartya (1981) *Poverty and Famines: An Essay on Entitlement and Deprivation* (Delhi: Oxford University Press).

Seshadri, K. and S. P. Jain (1972) *Panchayati Raj and Political Perceptions of Electorate: A Study of Electoral Behaviour in the Mid-Term Poll of 1971 in Hyderabad Constituency* (Hyderabad: National Institute of Community Development).

Shah, Ghanshyam (1984a) *Protest Movements in Two Indian States* (Delhi: Ajanta).

Shah, G. (1984b) 'Caste Sentiment, Class Formation and Dominance in Gujarat' (Surat: Centre for Social Studies).

Shah, G. (1985) 'Tribal Identity and Class Differentiation: A Case Study of the Chaudhuri Tribe', in I. P. Desai et al., *Caste, Class, Conflict and Reservation* (Delhi: Ajanta).

Shah, G. (1991) 'Caste Sentiments, Class Formation and Dominance in Gujarat' in F. Frankel and M. S. A. Rao (eds) *Dominance and State Power in Modern India: Decline of a Social Order*, vol. 2 (Delhi: Oxford University Press), 59–114.

Sheth, D. L. (1983) 'Grassroots Stirrings and the Future of Politics', *Alternatives*, 1 (March), 1–24.

Sheth, D. L. (1984) 'Grassroots Initiatives in India', *Economic and Political Weekly*, 9(6) (February), 259–62.

Sheth, P. (1965) 'Political Awakening in Surat', *Journal of Gujarat Research Society* (April).

Sheth, P. (1976) *Patterns of Political Behaviour in Gujarat* (Ahmedabad: Sahitya Mudranalay).

Sheth, P. (1983) 'Caste, Class and Development', in D. T. Lakdawala (ed.) *Development in Gujarat: Problems and Prospects* (Delhi: Allied).

Sheth, P. and R. Menon (1986) *Caste and the Communal Time Bomb* (Delhi: IBH).

Singer, M. and B. S. Cohn (eds) (1968) *Structure and Change in Indian Society* (Chicago, IL: Aldine).

Singh, Charan (1964) *India's Poverty and its Solutions* (London: Asia Publications).

Singh, Charan (1978) *India's Economic Policy: The Gandhian Blueprint* (New Delhi: Vika).

Singh, Rajendra (1988) *Land, Power and People: Rural Elite in Transition, 1801–1970* (New Delhi: Sage).

Sirsikar, V. M. (1970) *The Rural Elite in a Developing Society* (New Delhi: Orient Longman).

Sisson, Richard (1988) 'Congress and Indian Nationalism: Political Ambiguity and the Problems of Social Conflict and Party Control', in Richard Sisson and Stanley Wolpert (eds) *Congress and Indian Nationalism: The Pre-independence Phase* (Berkeley: University of California Press), 1–19.

Sisson, Richard and Stanley Wolpert (eds) (1988) *Congress and Indian*

BIBLIOGRAPHY

Nationalism: The Pre-independence Phase (Berkeley, CA: University of California Press).

Skolnick, J. H. (1969) *The Politics of Protest* (New York: Ballantine).

Smith, D. E. (1963) *India as a Secular State* (Princeton, NJ: Princeton University Press).

Somjee, A. H. and Geeta Somjee (1978) 'Cooperative Dairying and Profiles of Social Change in India', *Economic Development and Social Change*, 26(3), 577–90.

Srinivas, M. N. (1966) *Social Change in Modern India* (Berkeley, CA: University of California Press).

Tarrow, Sidney (1977) *Between Center and Periphery: Grass Roots Politicians in Italy and France* (New Haven, CT: Yale University Press).

Taub, Richard P. (1960) *Bureaucrats under Stress* (Berkeley, CA: University of California Press).

Taylor, Michael and V. M. Herman (1971) 'Party Systems and Party Government', *American Political Science Review*, 65 (March), 28–37.

Thompson, E. P. (1971) 'The Moral Economy of the English Crowd in the Eighteenth Century', *Past and Present*, 50, 76–136.

Thorner, Alice (1982) 'Semi-feudalism or Capitalism: The Contemporary Debate on Classes and Modes of Production in India', in Jacques Pouchepadass (ed.) *Caste et Classe en Asie du Sud* (Paris: École des Hautes Études en Sciences Sociales), 19–72.

Tilly, Charles (1975a) *The Formation of Nation States in Western Europe* (Princeton, NJ: Princeton University Press).

Tilly, Charles (1975b), 'Food Supply and Public Order in Modern Europe', in Charles Tilly (ed.) *The Formation of Nation States in Western Europe* (Princeton, NJ: Princeton University Press), 380–455.

Tufte, Edward (1969) 'Improving Data Analysis in Political Analysis', *World Politics*, 641–54.

Uphoff, Norman and Milton Esman (1974) *Local Organizations for Rural Development: Analysis of Asian Experience* (Ithaca, NY: Rural Development Committee, Cornell University).

Uphoff, Norman, John M. Cohen and Arthur Goldsmith (1979) *Feasibility and Application of Rural Development Participation: A State of the Art Paper* (Ithaca, NY: Rural Development Committee, Cornell University).

Uphoff, Norman (ed.) (1982–83) *Rural Development and Local Organisation in Asia*, 3 vols (New Delhi: Macmillan).

van der Ploeg, Jan Douwe (1989) 'Knowledge Systems, Metaphor and Interface: The Case of Potatoes in the Peruvian Highlands', in Norman Long (ed.) *Encounters at the Interface* (Wageningen: Agricultural University Wageningen), 145–64.

von Eschen, D., J. Kirk and M. Pinard (1969) 'The Conditions of Direct Action in Democratic Society', *Western Political Quarterly* (June), 309–25.

Washbrook, D. A. (1989) 'Caste, Class and Dominance in Modern Tamil Nadu', in Francine Frankel and M. S. A. Rao (eds) *Dominance and State Power in Modern India: Decline of a Social Order*, Vol. 1 (Delhi: Oxford University Press), 204–64.

Weiner, Myron (1989) *The Indian Paradox: Essays in Indian Politics* (Delhi: Sage).

White, Christine Pelzer (1986) 'Everyday Resistance, Socialist Revolution and Rural Development: The Vietnamese Case', in James Scott and Benedict J. Tria Kerkvliet (eds).

White, Louise G. (1976) 'Rational Theories of Participation: An Exercise in Definitions', *Journal of Conflict Resolution*, 20 (June), 255–79.

Wilson, J. Q. (1961) 'The Strategy of Protest: Problems of Negro Civic Action', *Journal of Conflict Resolution* 5(3), 291–303.

Wolf, E. (1956) 'Aspects of Group Relations in a Complex Society: Mexico', *American Anthropologist*, 58(6), 1065–78.

Wolf, Eric (1977) 'Review Essay: Why Cultivators Rebel', *American Journal of Sociology*, 83 (November), 742–50.

Wolfinger, R. E. (1960) 'Reputation and Reality in the Study of Community Power', *American Sociological Review*, 25, 636–40.

Wolfinger, R. E. (1962) 'A Plea for a Decent Burial', *American Sociological Review*, 25, 841–7.

Wood, G. (1980) 'Bureaucracy and the Post-Colonial State in South Asia: A Reply [to Moore]', *Development and Change*, 11(1), 149–55.

Wood, J. R. (ed.) (1984a) *State Politics in Contemporary India: Crisis or Continuity?* (Boulder, CO and London: Westview Press).

Wood, J. R. (1984b) 'Congress Restored? The "KHAM" Strategy and Congress (I) Recruitment in Gujarat', in J. Wood (ed.) *State Politics in Contemporary India: Crisis or Continuity* (Boulder, CO and London: Westview Press), 197–228.

Wood, J. R. (1984c) 'Introduction: Continuity and Crisis in Indian State Politics', in J. Wood (ed.) *State Politics in Contemporary India* (Boulder, CO and London: Westview Press).

AUTHOR INDEX

SUBJECT INDEX